Mastering

World Religions

Ray Colledge

MACMILLAN

T | IPC

First published 1999 by
MACMILLAN PRESS LTD
Houndmills, Basingstoke, Hampshire RG21 6XS
and London
Companies and representatives throughout the world

ISBN 0–333–68107–X

A catalogue record for this book is available from the British Library.

This book is printed on paper suitable for recycling and made from fully managed and sustained forest sources.

10   9   8   7   6   5   4   3   2   1
08   07   06   05   04   03   02   01   00   99

Typeset by EXPO Holdings Malaysia

Printed in Hong Kong

Contents

List of Maps and Figures

◯ **Acknowledgements**

The author and publishers wish to acknowledge with thanks permission from the following to reproduce illustrative material: Carlos Reyes-Manzo Andes Press Agency, for Figures 4.1, 5.1, 5.2, 12.1, 12.3, 13.1, 15.1, 21.1, 23.2, 25.1, 27.1, 28.1, 29.1, 32.1, 35.1, 36.1; ICOREC Circa Photo Library, for Figure 12.2; Hulton Library, for Figure 17.1; Allen & Unwin for Figure 33.1, from K. Singh, *The Sikhs* (1995).

The author and publishers wish to thank the following for permission to use copyright material: Edexcel Foundation, London Examinations, Midland Examining Group, Northern Examinations and Assessment Board, and the Southern Examining Group, for specimen and past examination questions.

Every effort has been made to trace all the copyright-holders, but if any have been inadvertently overlooked the publishers will be pleased to make the necessary arrangement at the first opportunity.

The Southern Examining Group wish it to be known that any answers or hints on answers are the sole responsibility of the author and have not been provided or apporved by SEG.

Introduction

This book provides a comprehensive treatment to the subject of major World Religions. It is aimed primarily at those studying for the GCSE examination, but will also provide an excellent introduction for A Level, higher education and for the general reader who is fascinated by this subject. It will also be suitable for general and liberal studies courses and for those whose studies require them to understand the beliefs of the newer communities in out multicultural society.

The text covers the six religions currently precribed by the examination boards – Judaism, Christianity, Islam, Hinduism, Buddhism and Sikhism. It conveys clear information about every significant aspect of these religions.

At the time of writing, the number of students on religious studies courses is rising. Added to this, increasing numbers of people are looking for inpiration and guidance in today's secular and materialistic world. This book will help those engaged in such a quest.

Ray Colledge

PART I

Judaism

Origins and definitions

1.1 Introduction

The history of the Jewish people goes back some 4000 years. At that time a number of tribes called the Israelites lived in Israel; the 'Children of Israel'. They were also known as the **Hebrews** and spoke a language of the same name, in which their scriptures came to be written. Today's Jews are their direct descendants. 30 per cent of the 15 million Jews today live in the USA. 25 per cent live in Israel. The Jewish population of Britain numbers around 385 000. Jews believe that they are the chosen people of God, with a special role to play in His purpose. Anyone with a Jewish mother is automatically a part of their faith. Secular Jews do not practise the faith but they remain Jewish. An important aspect of Jewishness is sharing: festivals, food laws and rituals and so on. Most Jews are born so; few people convert to Judaism.

1.2 The patriarchs or founding fathers

Judaism originates with Abraham, his son Isaac, Isaac's son Jacob, and Jacob's son Joseph. These are the patriarchs or founding fathers of the Jews.

Abraham

Abram (as he was called at this time) was the son of Terah, and lived in his native land of Chaldea. Then, in response to a call from God, he left the city of Ur with his father, family and household to travel 300 miles north to Haran, where he lived for 15 years. Terah died there, and Abram now received a second call from God. He migrated to the land of Canaan where he received the great promise from God that 'I will make of thee a great nation' (Genesis 12:2, 3, 7). It was during this trek south that Abram's followers became known as Hebrews or 'they who crossed the river'. Then they journeyed to the Negev, a semi-desert between Hebron and the wider desert. Famine then drove them into Egypt, but when disease broke out, the pharaoh blamed Abram and his followers and forced them to leave the country. Then Abram's followers quarrelled with Lot's followers over water supplies, so they parted company. This was because the flocks had become too large for them all to stay together, the land being unable to sustain such numbers.

Isaac

Abram's wife Sarai had borne him no children but she had an Egyptian maid-servant named Hagar. She wanted Hagar to have a child by Abram; she bore him a son called Ishmael, whose descendants today are the Bedouin desert-dwellers. God now made a **covenant** with Abram, whose name was changed to Abraham (which means 'father of a multitude' – Abram meant 'exalted father'). Sarai's name was changed to Sarah (princess). The physical sign of the covenant was to be **circumcision**. They were also promised a son of their own. This son was Isaac (which means 'laughter').

Sarah, fearing for her son's inheritance, persuaded Abraham to send Hagar and Ishmael away. It is from Isaac that the Jews are descended. God told Abraham to sacrifice Isaac so he prepared to do it. However when God saw that he was obedient, he sent an angel to tell him that he did not have to. God now promised to make his descendants 'as numerous as the stars in the sky and as the sand on the seashore'.

Jacob

Isaac married Rebekah and their twin sons were called Esau and Jacob. Esau was the first-born and so would succeed Isaac as the head of the family, and inherit a double share of the estate. Esau became a hunter, Jacob stayed among the tents. Esau was the favourite of Isaac; but Rebeka loved Jacob. One day Esau came into the camp so hungry that Jacob was able to persuade him to sell his birthright for a meal of stew. When Isaac was old, Jacob deceived him into giving him Esau's rightful blessing as the eldest son. Esau wanted to kill Jacob, so Rebeka told him to stay with her brother Laban in Haran for safety. This episode spoilt the relationship between Isaac and Rebeka, and the latter never again saw her favourite son.

While on the way to Haran, Jacob had a dream in which he saw a stairway from earth to heaven on which angels were ascending and descending. God stood at the top and repeated the promise made to Abraham and Isaac. In the morning Jacob took the stone he had placed under his head and set it up as a pillar and poured oil on it. He named the place Bethel, meaning 'house of God'.

Jacob's communion with God went a step further. One night there was a strange episode in which he wrestled with a man during the night. The man told him that his name would no longer be Jacob, but Israel, which means 'wrestler with God'. Jacob called the place Peniel, which means 'the face of God'. He said it was because he had seen God face-to-face and was spared. It was after this that there was reconciliation between Esau and Jacob.

Joseph

Joseph was the elder of the two sons of Jacob by Rachel. He was his father's favourite son, and this made the others jealous, especially because of the gift of the special robe, now often called the coat of many colours, from his father. They were also angry about his dreams. They sold him to the Ishmaelites, who took him to Egypt (Map 1.1). In Egypt he became the pharaoh's vizier because he was able to interpret pharaoh's dreams. He predicted seven years of plenty, followed by seven years of famine. This famine caused Joseph's family to enter Egypt to find food and led to a reconciliation between Joseph and his brothers.

Map 1.1 The Bible lands

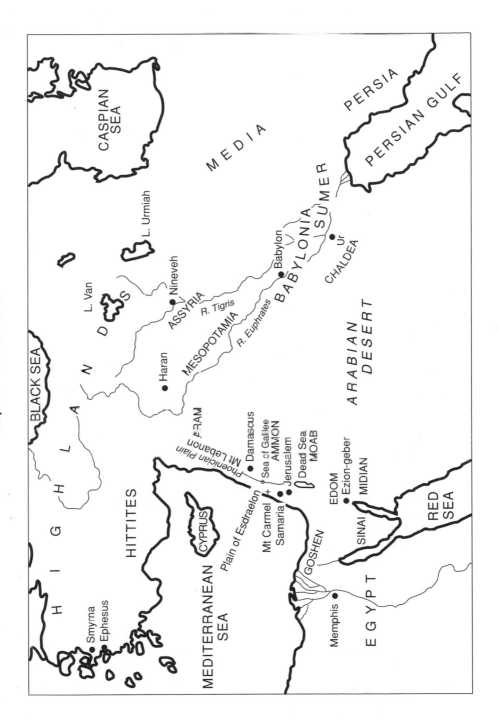

Summary

The patriarchal narratives in Genesis divide into four blocks:
- Abraham (12–25:18)
- Isaac (26)
- Jacob (25:19–33; 27–35)
- Joseph (37; 39–50)

1.3 Moses and the Mount Sinai covenant

Moses

Moses was born in Egypt during a time when the Jews had become slaves of the pharaohs. When the pharaoh ordered the death of all young Hebrew boys, Moses' mother hid him in the reeds on the banks of the Nile. Moses was found and brought up in the court as the son of the pharaoh's daughter. He killed an Egyptian he found whipping a slave and was made an outlaw, having to flee into the Sinai Desert. He lived with the nomads, who taught him how to survive in the desert. It was here that he experienced the presence of God, who told him to return to Egypt to free the Hebrews. Although pharaoh gave in and let them go, he changed his mind a few days later and sent an army after them. The army perished when it tried to follow the Hebrews through the parting of the Red Sea.

This period is important because during it the Jews became a nation and their faith and religion were formed. The festivals associated with the Exodus are:

- Passover
- Pentecost
- Tabernacles (Booths) and
- the Day of Atonement.

So by 'the Exodus' we mean the Hebrews' passage to freedom from slavery in Egypt.

The Mount Sinai Covenant

The Hebrews became the people of the Covenant at Mt Sinai. A priesthood was set up to sustain it by worship. The giving of the **Torah** is associated with this time. It was here that God gave the *Ten Commandments* (the **decalogue**) to Moses. The Israelites doubted God and so were made to wander through the desert for 40 years (Map 1.2). The doubting generation died during this time and the new generation was led by Joshua into Canaan.

During the 40 years God gave the Israelites many laws. The Torah gives 613 **mitzvot** known as *'Taryag'*. *Taryag* is a word formed from the initials of the words 'six hundred and thirteen'. There are 248 positive commandments and 365 things Jews are not allowed to do. As there are 365 days in a year, the Jews can remember God with the whole self every day.

Moses saw the Promised Land but was not allowed to enter it. His death before he could enter puts his life in place in Jewish tradition. He was nothing more than a man who was a great servant of God; The Hebrew nation was greater than any man or woman including Moses. The same applies to the Torah, in which the details of the Covenant are recorded.

Map 1.2 The Exodus from Egypt

1.4 Israel

God renewed the covenant with Joshua, Moses' successor, to lead the Jews into the Promised Land (Maps 1.3 and 1.4). It took almost 200 years to bring the land under their control. King David brought the whole area under his rule (Map 1.5). He made Jerusalem the capital and religious centre. His son Solomon built the first **temple** and it was to become the hub of the nation's religion (Map 1.6).

It was during Solomon's time that the empire built by David began to break up; in fact it became two kingdoms on his death in 930 BCE. The northern of the two kingdoms, Samaria was internally divided and under attack from outside, finally being conquered by Assyria in 721 BCE. Judah to the south remained independent for another 200 years.

Map 1.3   The routes of the Israelites entering the Promised Land

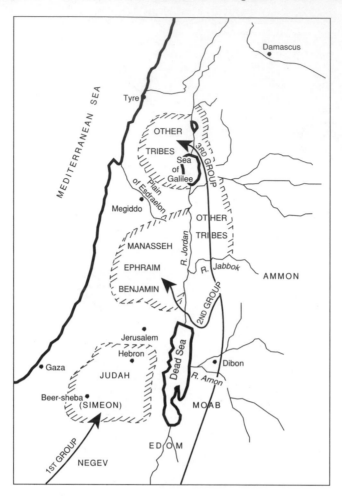

1.5 The Exile and Return

In 586 BCE the Babylonians captured Jerusalem and destroyed it completely. They looted and destroyed the temple and deported the whole population to slavery in Susa.

This period covered 50 years, but the Jewish religion survived. Cyrus's Persia became the dominant power in the area and allowed exiles to go home. The Jews were freed in 539 BCE and the first group reached home in 536 BCE. By 516 BCE the Temple had been rebuilt and was followed by the rest of Jerusalem.

1.6 The Greeks

The expansion of Alexander the Great's empire brought the Jews under the control of the Ptolemies and then the Seleucids, rulers of Egypt and Syria. They attempted to

Map 1.4   The Twelve Tribes of Israel

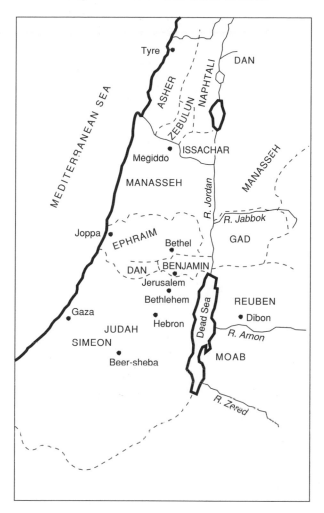

force Greek laws and customs on to the Jews. The last straw was the move to introduce Greek religion with an altar to the Greek gods in the Temple. A struggle began which was to last three years. In the end the Temple was restored to God's worship. Jews still celebrate this episode in the **Hanukkah** festival.

It was at this time that the **Diaspora** or dispersion of the Jews began, with many of them leaving to settle elsewhere.

1.7 The Romans

Roman rule of Israel began in 63 BCE. In 66 CE the Zealots led a major revolt against Rome. This led, in 68 CE, to the destruction of the Temple. Total defeat for the Jews meant that they lost their land and were destined to wander the Earth until the state of Israel was founded in 1948.

Map 1.5 The Kingdom of David

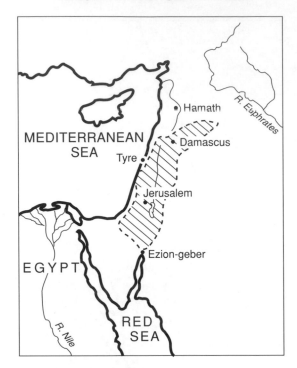

1.8   From the Fall of the Temple to the twentieth century

Two things ensured the survival of the Jews:

- the Torah
- the **synagogue**.

The **rabbis** played a crucial role in that they taught the Law and the practices of the faith. Schools of rabbis came into being and it was through them that the **Talmud**, the major source to Jewish law, came to be composed in its two forms:

- Babylonian
- Palestinian.

Judaism was revised in the Middle Ages to produce a reasoned religion that was compatible with knowledge and understanding.

- Maimonides (1135–1204) wrote the 13 Principles of Judaism and the 'Guide For The Perplexed'.
- Jewish medieval mysticism took shape in the **Kabbalah**; a spiritual movement interested in the promise of a messiah.
- It was followed by a number of messianic movements, some of which are still thriving.

The nineteenth century saw the rise of the liberal and reform movements. It was felt by some Jews that their religion should be reformed to give it an up-to-date appeal.

Map 1.6 The Kingdom of Solomon

Traditional practices were modified and the language of the people was used in worship. David Friedlander (1756–1834) led the movement. The first Jewish reform 'temple' was set up by Israel Jacobson. The first reform synagogue was set up in England in 1840. During the nineteenth century the movement spread to America. It was at this time that science began to challenge many of the old beliefs, and many Jews decided to face this challenge. Changes were made to:

- views in the Tenakh and Talmud
- the **halakhah** or legal system of Judaism
- traditional ceremonial rituals
- the language of services
- regulations governing the synagogue
- dress and dietary laws.

1.9 The twentieth century

Without a doubt, the outstanding events of the twentieth century for the Jews have been the **Holocaust** of the Second World War and the founding of the state of Israel in 1948. During the war nearly six million Jews were slaughtered by the Nazis. This was roughly half the Jewish population of Europe. This gave impetus to the demand for the return to the Jewish homeland in Palestine.

1.10   The State of Israel

The foundation of the modern state of Israel (14 May 1948) was seen as the fulfilment of the promise of God in the Torah. Many have connected it with the promise of a messiah. Extremists said that the state should only have been set up by the messiah. The **Zionists**, for example, oppose it. Others think that the Diaspora is God's Will. Yet another group think that it should not have become an independent state. Most Jews, though, regard it as their historical, cultural, spiritual and geographical home. Most Jews are pleased to have a country where they are safe from anti-Semitism.

1.11   The Jews in Britain

Edward I expelled the Jews from England in 1290 but Cromwell allowed them to come back in 1656.

Jews number about half a million today. Many fled to Britain from the **pogroms** (official persecution) of the Russian Tsars in the late nineteenth and early twentieth centuries, and from the Nazis in the 1930s.

The first synagogue was set up in the city of London in 1701. The best-known synagogue is the London United Synagogue.

British Jews are led by the Chief Rabbi of the United congregation. The Board of Deputies was founded in 1760 as the representative body of British Jews.

There are special colleges for training rabbis plus many Jewish schools. The Jews co-operate with other religious groups; for example, in 1942 the Council of Christians and Jews was formed. They are also very active in public life in fields such as politics, medicine, science and the arts.

Jewish beliefs and scriptures

2.1   God

The existence of God requires no proof as far as the Jews are concerned. Genesis 1.1 says: 'In the beginning God created the heavens and the earth'. The created universe and the history of the Jews as God's chosen people are enough to show that God exists.

The **Shema** prayer is said morning and evening by Jews. It is important because it contains the most basic belief about God: there is only one God.
Other beliefs include the following:

- There is no limit to His power
- He created the whole of nature, which is controlled by Him; He can be seen and experienced in the whole of nature
- He has no rivals
- All human activity is controlled by God
- To submit to this gives the whole of life unity
- He is not remote from us, for all His power
- God is SHEHINAH, meaning He is present everywhere.

2.2   The Covenant

Abraham's family was 'chosen' by God. God entered into a sort of contract or agreement which is called a covenant, with the descendants of this family. A covenant has two sides and in this case it said that:

- Israel must always remember God, keeping His laws and serving Him always and
- God will be faithful to Israel, continuing to be their God and treating its people as His own.

2.3   The Commandments

The commandments or law (*mitzvot*) were received by Moses from God on Mount Sinai (or Mount Horeb) during the journey from Egypt to the Promised Land. There are 613 commandments: 248 are positive beginning with 'Thou shalt ... ', the other 365 are negative *mitzvot* beginning 'Thou shalt not ...'.

The Ten Commandments are the guidelines for moral living.

The Ten Commandments

(1)   You shall have no other God but me.
(2)   Do not make graven (carved) images (for worship).
(3)   Do not misuse my name.
(4)   Keep the Sabbath day holy.
(5)   Respect your father and mother.
(6)   Do not murder.
(7)   Do not commit adultery.
(8)   Do not steal.
(9)   Do not give false evidence.
(10) Do not covet your neighbour's house, his wife or anything else of his.

2.4   The Messiah

The Messiah is the anticipated deliverer and king of the Jews. 'Messiah' means the 'anointed one'. Biblical psalms depict the Messiah as follows:

(1)   He will be called God's son.
(2)   He will bring the blessings that God wants for His people.
(3)   He will set up God's kingdom on earth.
(4)   The kingdom will be based on the principles of law and justice.
(5)   He will scatter Israel's enemies.
(6)   He will rule the world for all time.

In the eighth century BCE the Prophets, beginning with Isaiah, predicted the birth of a Messiah. There were actually two prophets called Isaiah. The first said that the sins of the fathers would be visited on the next generation, but a Messiah would deliver them. The second said that God is forgiving and introduced the idea that someone could suffer to atone for the sins of others. A servant of God would spread His Covenant to all peoples.

Later it was believed that a Messiah would rule the people just before the end. Some Jews hoped he would be a military leader, though they were not clear whether he would be human or more than human: there is no Jewish tradition that says the Messiah will be divine.

The rabbis have always discouraged speculation on when the Messiah will appear. Orthodox Jews are still waiting for the Messiah, God's anointed one. Reform Jews see it a different way, in that they look to a time when the people of the world will pull together to establish God's kingdom on earth, when there is peace, love and righteousness for all.

2.5   Preconditions for establishing the Kingdom

- the return of all Jews to the Holy Land
- the ending of war, injustice and immorality
- a world society underpinned by truth and justice
- a universal religion worshipping the one true God.

Jews agree on these criteria irrespective of whether they think the Messiah is one person or the whole of humankind.

2.6 Life after death

It is believed that a person survives death and has an after-life. In Biblical times it was believed that the soul entered **sheol** (hell), where the good and the bad lived as shadows. Later it was believed that there were two places called heaven and hell; the dead entered one of these for reward or punishment. A body is needed for the survival of the soul and so the soul is thought to survive in union with the body. This led to the belief that the good and the bad take part in a general resurrection.

Belief in an after-life is logical because the eternal God created each person as a living soul, so it is reasonable to assume it will spend eternity with Him. Faith and godliness will bring reward from God in the next life.

2.7 Ethics

There are three requirements set out in the 'Ethics of the Fathers' (*Pirke Aboth*): law, worship and kindness.

Laws

- The Law (*Torah*) is the foundation of right living.
- It teaches religion and morals.
- Torah means 'instruction' as well as 'Law'; it instructs the Jews on the question of what the Lord requires of them.

Worship

- This is the response of the whole person, both body and spirit to God.
- It comes from the question: 'What does the Lord require?'
- It is more than spiritual, in that it includes moral action.
- It sanctifies God's name not just in worship but in work and other aspect of day-to-day life.

Kindness

- Kindness stems from the Law and includes respecting the elderly, helping the weak, being hospitable, caring for servants.
- The *shema* requires that a Jew should 'love thy neighbour as thyself'.
- This sort of love is to be acted on, not just felt.
- It is a social duty, not a private one.

2.8 The importance of scriptures to Judaism

Judaism is a religion of revelation. Jews believe that God revealed himself to them at Mt Sinai where he gave them the Ten Commandments and the whole of the Pentateuch (Torah in Hebrew) through Moses. So the Torah is Divine and is God's only and final revelation, containing all that he wants his people to know. It is believed that there was an oral Torah as well as the written one, providing explanations of the latter. Historical events were to create a need for more scriptural development.

In 586 BCE the Kingdom of Judah was conquered by Nebuchadnezzar, and the Temple destroyed. The Jewish people were taken to Babylon in captivity. Until then, life in Judah had been based on Jerusalem and revolved around the Temple. In exile, the Jews started to meet in small rooms to study, pray and socialise. Such rooms became the model for the synagogue that later replaced the Temple. Prayer and study took the place of sacrifices.

Until this time there was no need for a written record of Jewish traditions, but the exile meant there was a danger of loss of identity, so scribes began to write down stories and traditions.

Cyrus of Persia conquered Babylon in 539 BCE and allowed the Jews to go home. The Temple was rebuilt but there was a change of emphasis in Jewish life. Scribes now concentrated on understanding and applying the texts to life.

In 66CE the Romans, who had been ruling Judah since 63 BCE, put down a Jewish revolt against them. The Temple and much of Jerusalem were destroyed. A further revolt in 135 CE failed and this time the Romans banned the Jews from returning to Jerusalem, so they had to settle elsewhere. The scriptures they took with them were to provide a focus for the survival of the Jewish race and religion.

2.9 The Tenakh

The Tenakh is the Hebrew name for the Jewish Bible. The Greek name is **Septuagint**, from the Greek word for 70, because it was translated by 70 people in 270 BCE. It is the same as the Old Testament of the Christian Bible but the books are in a different order. It is divided into three sections:

(1) Torah (the Law)
(2) *Nevi'im* (the Prophets)
(3) *Ketuvim* (the Writings).

The letters TNK which start each of these words form the basis of the word 'Tenakh'. The Torah is the most sacred.

There are 39 books altogether. For centuries these scriptures were spoken, but eventually they were written down and in 90 CE they were put together as the Jewish Bible. Jews regard their Bible as a dialogue between God and His chosen people.

2.10 The Torah

This is the first five books: Genesis, Exodus, Leviticus, Numbers and Deuteronomy. These five books are sometimes known as the *Pentateuch* (from the Greek for 'five books'). They are traditionally known as the Five Books of Moses.

Torah means 'law', and it is this law that the Jews try to live their lives by. The literal meaning is 'teaching'. It is written by hand, a task that takes a scribe a year to complete.

The Torah is divided into 54 weekly parts (*sidrot*, plural of *sidra*). This is because 54 is the maximum number of shabatot (plural of **shabbat**) in a year. Orthodox synagogues read all of the *sidra* each week, and so read all the *sidrot* in a year.

Progressive synagogues take three years to do this. Public readings in the synagogue are given from the **Sefer Torah** on:

* *shabbat* mornings and afternoons
* festival mornings
* Monday and Thursday mornings.

The person reading follows the words with a silver pointer called a **yad**. Reading from it is the most important part of Jewish worship because it is the revelation of God.

2.11   The Prophets (Nevi'im)

This comprises eight volumes, divided into the Former Prophets and The Latter Prophets.

* The Former Prophets contain the historical books: Joshua, Judges, Samuel and Kings.
* The Latter Prophets contain Isaiah, Jeremiah and Ezekiel.

God spoke to mankind through the Prophets. Readings from the Prophets accompany those from the Torah. The Prophets are the moral and spiritual conscience of Judaism; they inspire and interpret religion for the people.

2.12   The Writings (Ketuvim)

These are seen as having less value than the Torah and the Prophets. However, they contain the psalms, which are used in regular synagogue worship. The psalms deal with all aspects of human behaviour. Some of the books, especially Ecclesiastes, are very important to Jewish understanding, in that it teaches that wealth is not important because it cannot last, and that life is finite and beyond human understanding. Also, Job teaches that human suffering is a mystery without answer.

Ketuvim readings are used on festival days. There are 11 books: Psalms, Proverbs, Job, Song of Songs, Ruth, Lamentations, Ecclesiastes, Esther, Daniel, Ezra and Nehemiah (in one book), and Chronicles. Five of these are known as 'the five scrolls' and are read at special times:

* *Pesach* (Passover) – The Song of Songs
* *Shavuot* (Pentecost) – Ruth
* The fast day of the month of *Ab*, when the fall of the Temple is remembered – Lamentations
* *Sukkot* – Ecclesiastes
* *Purim* – Esther.

2.13   The Talmud

This is the most important book after the Bible. **Talmud** means 'teaching', and it can be used for reference on social and religious laws. It is made up of the **Mishnah**, the oral law as it was written down, and the **Gemara**, a collection of commentaries on these laws. There are 6000 pages and three million words.

The Mishnah was completed around 200 CE. It advises on many subjects such as holy days, temple service, hygiene and farming. There are six orders covering six topics in the Mishnah. The orders are the *Shisha Sedarim (Shas)*; each having several divisions called *masekhtot*.

The Talmud also contains the *Halakhah*, which gives instruction on legal matters, and the *Hagadah*, which deals with moral issues.

2.14   The Siddur

This is the Jewish prayer book. It is an order for prayer for use in the synagogue. The **Siddur** was compiled in the eighth century CE by Rabbi Amran of Susa. It brings together spiritual experiences from the time of Abraham onwards.

Although many prayer books have appeared since, they all have the same format:

- morning, afternoon and evening prayer
- the *hallel* psalms (nos 113–118)
- prayers for the new moon
- the **Kaddish**
- the **Amidah**
- prayers for holy days.

2.15   Midrash

'Midrash' means 'to search out, expound'. It is the teaching and commentaries of the rabbis on scripture. It has parables, myths and puns, plus stories to explain stories. It examines the inner meaning of the Tenakh.

Halakhic Midrash deals with the Law, *Aggadic Midrash* with the narrative of the scriptures.

2.16   The Haftarah

This selection was compiled by the rabbis. A passage from it is chosen to match that from the Torah. Unlike the Torah, which must be read from a scroll, the Haftarah can be read from a printed book. The reading is chanted using a different intonation from that used for the sidrah or *parchah* (portion) of the Torah that has been appointed.

2.17   Maimonides

Maimonides was a twelfth-century Talmudist (expert on the Talmud). He is chiefly remembered for compiling the 13 principles of faith.

The Thirteen Principles

(1) All creation past, present and future is the work of God.
(2) God is one.
(3) God does not have a physical body.
(4) God is first and last.
(5) Only God should be prayed to.
(6) The words of the prophets are true.
(7) Moses is the greatest prophet.
(8) God gave Moses the Torah.
(9) The Torah is unchangeable.
(10) God knows all things.
(11) God will reward those who keep the Commandments; He will punish those who do not.
(12) The Messiah will come one day.
(13) The dead will be resurrected.

2.18 The Noahide Code

These are the seven commandments or *sheva mitzvot* given to Noah after the Flood.

(1) Worship no god but God.
(2) Do not blaspheme.
(3) Do not murder.
(4) Do not steal.
(5) Do not commit sexual sin.
(6) Do not be cruel to animals.
(7) Man must live in harmony by the rule of law.

Every synagogue has an *Ark* to house the Biblical scrolls. Tradition demands that every Torah scroll is handwritten and perfect in every detail. It cannot be used if there is a mistake in copying. It is still sacred, though, and cannot be destroyed; instead it must be put in a genizah or burial place to rot naturally.

Worship and the synagogue

3.1 The Sabbath

Sabbath services begin on Friday evening. The Sabbath runs from sunset on Friday to sunset on Saturday. Jews like to go to a service at the synagogue and then welcome the sabbath with a ceremony at home.

At sunset the mother lights the candles and says a prayer. The father blesses bread (challah) which represents manna. He also says the **kiddush** or blessing over a cup of wine as well as saying verses about the Sabbath and creation.

The main act of worship for Orthodox and Reform Jews starts at 10 a.m. on Saturday; Liberal Jews have a service on Friday. Services last about two hours.

When the family arrive at an Orthodox synagogue the father sits in the main body of the synagogue downstairs. The wife sits upstairs in the balcony and children under 13 decide which parent to sit with. Men without a hat put on a skull cap (**yamulkah**). Those with a hat can choose whether to replace it with a yamulkah. Men take their prayer shawl (**tallit** or **tallith**) and daily prayer book from the little cupboard in the pew. A prayer is said before and after putting on the *tallit*. In Reformed and Liberal synagogues men and women sit together.

3.2 The service

This has a number of sections:

The Psalms

- Psalms are read (19, 33, 34, 90, 91, 92, 135, 136).
- Psalm 92 is known as a song for the Sabbath Day.
- 1 Chronicles 16: 8–36 is read.

Any man can lead the reading in this part of the service. The congregation reads the passage aloud from the prayer book.

The Shema

The **cantor** or chazan sings a section which tells of God's acts of redemption, the escape from Egypt in particular. God is thanked for being loving, faithful and merciful.

The Amidah

Amidah means 'standing'. It has 19 benedictions which form the central core of Jewish worship. It is a prayer which the congregation offers silently while standing facing the Ark (the same direction as Jerusalem). Note that no rabbi or priest says it for them, Judaism says they are responsible themselves.

The Scrolls

Next the scrolls, the Sefer Torah, are taken out of the Ark for reading. This happens on Monday, Thursday and Saturday mornings. The elders organise these readings. Two members of the congregation are invited to take the scrolls out of the Ark and put them on the reading desk. The rest of the congregation touch the scrolls with their *tallits*, which they then kiss. The scrolls are held up on the **bimah** (reading dais) in their covers for all to see while blessings are offered.

The Readings

- The crown and cover of the Torah scroll is taken off. A number of men read it one at a time. Then the scroll is covered again.
- There is a reading from the Haftarah scroll. The cantor or chazan usually does the reading because he is trained to read unpunctuated Hebrew (he may also intone it).
- Readers hold the Torah pointer to follow the words.
- In Britain, the cantor prays for the Queen, in English, when the readings are finished (all other prayers and readings are in Hebrew). Then he prays in Hebrew for the Queen, the nation and Israel.
- The scrolls are returned to the Ark while blessings and praises are offered.
- At this point the rabbi may preach a sermon.
- The cantor now says the Amidah, the Kaddish and the **Aleinu** (the Adoration).
- Lastly, either the cantor or a child will chant the Hymn of Glory, with the congregation speaking the alternate lines.

The Kaddish

This act of santification comes near the end, and is to praise God and secure His blessing. This prayer was written in Aramaic (Aramaic, the language Jesus spoke was the everyday language of his time) long before the fall of the Temple.

3.3 Private worship

Laying the Tefillin

The **tefillin** are a pair of black leather boxes (**phylacteries**) containing the words of the Shema. A Jewish man fastens them by leather thongs to the forehead (to remind him to think of his faith) and the biceps of the right arm, left arm if left-handed (to remind him to act on his faith). The boxes are fixed to the body to obey the command in Deuteronomy 6.

Every morning before he puts on the Tefillin he must cover his head with the small skull cap (*yamulkah*), and cover his shoulders with the tassled, blue and white prayer shawl (*tallit*) made of silk or wool.

Prayers are said morning, noon and evening.

Prayers

Prayers can be spontaneous or taken from the prayer book. There are no rules about women's prayer; Jewish women say this is because God can trust women, but men are lazy and need rules!!

The **Mezuzah** is a container holding verses of the Shema and which is attached to the door post. People touch it as they pass through the door to remind themselves that Jewish values can be shared, and to symbolise God's presence and love which is with those inside and which gives them guidance.

3.4   The synagogue

Origins and definitions

The original meaning of synagogue was 'gathering' (from Greek). Most towns with a Jewish population had one by the time the Romans destroyed Jerusalem (70 CE). It is a *kehilla* (community of people). It is called three things in Hebrew:

- *Bet t'filah* (house of prayer)
- *Bet hamidrash* (house of study)
- *Bet ha Knesset* (house of assembly) as a casual meeting place for the Jewish community.

There was a rule that said if there were ten adult males there could be a synagogue.

Inside the synagogue

- There are no statues or pictures, because the commandments do not allow 'graven images'.
- Modern buildings are rectangular. There are seats on three sides facing inwards. The remaining side is the most important and the focal point.
- The fourth side has a double door, hidden by a curtain and recessed into the wall, behind which is a cupboard containing the Torah scrolls in Hebrew. This cupboard is the Ark (**aron hakodesh**) and is always in the wall nearest Jerusalem. The cupboard doors may be decorated with the **Magen David** (Star of David).
- Two plaques with the 10 Commandments written in Hebrew can be found either side of the Ark, or above it. They represent the two tablets of stone mentioned in the Book of Exodus (31:18).
- To one side of the Ark is a candelabrum with seven branches. This candelabrum or menorah is one of the symbols of Judaism, reminding Jews of the one that stood in the Temple in Jerusalem.
- Similarly, the lamp of the perpetual flame (**ner tamid**) hangs from the roof in front of the Ark to remember the light that continually burned in the Temple and is a mark of respect for the holiness of the scrolls.
- The *bimah* (a raised platform with railings) stands almost in the centre of the building. Worship is conducted by the cantor from the *bimah* and Torah readings are performed from here.

- Between the *bimah* and the Ark are seats for the elders, who are elected to organise worship and govern the affairs of the synagogue.
- The pulpit stands between the Ark and the congregation. However, the space in front of the Ark is open so that the congregation can see clearly when the scrolls are taken out.

3.5 The functions of the synagogue

It has always been a community centre, as its names show. It is a place of education so that the scriptures, which are a concise guide for correct living, can be read, for the teaching of Hebrew and Jewish culture. There are also women's groups, youth clubs and so forth. They can be used as bakeries for unleavened bread at Passover time.

Older synagogues have a **mikreh** which is a large bath or pool from the time when Jews who had no such amenity could take a ritual bath. The **bet din** is a house of law or court to license butchers to sell **kosher** meat.

4 Festivals and pilgrimage

Festivals are central to Judaism because they fulfil the *mitzvot* or regulations of that faith. In fact the Jewish year is regulated by a cycle of festivals which are celebrated as an integral part of the Jewish religion.

4.1 Four reasons for the importance of festivals in Judaism

- **They link the past with the present**
  Festivals are an act of remembrance of some important event in the history of the Jews. They link past and present and look to the future.
- **They emphasise the central beliefs of the faith**
  Because all festivals are religious occasions, they deepen the experience of the faith, especially with their focus on the Torah and other religious teachings.
- **They are communal acts**
  They strengthen the unity and identity of the Jewish community by the practice of families and communities celebrating the festivals together in the home or synagogue.
- **They are a pattern of celebrations**
  There is a sense of coherence in Judaism because each festival links with every other in intention and purpose.

4.2 The Jewish year

Judaism uses a lunar calendar for religious purposes. This has 12 months totalling 354 days. The year begins with the seventh month, known as *Tishri*.

Hebrew Months

Nisan	Mar./Apr.
Iyar	Apr./May
Sivan	May/Jun.
Tammuz	Jun./Jul.

Av	Jul./Aug.
Eunl	Aug./Sept.
Tishri	Sept./Oct.
Cheshvan	Oct./Nov.
Kislev	Nov./Dec.
Tevet	Dec./Jan.
Shevat	Jan./Feb.
Adar	Feb./Mar.

In leap years there are 2 months of Adar (1 and 2).

The First month is Nisan but the New Year falls on the first day of 7th month or Tishri. The Jewish era begins in 300 BCE, so 2000 CE will be 5700. It's not known why this is the starting point, but it's possible that it's the minimum amount of human history recorded by the Jews.

4.3 The Jewish New Year: Rosh Hashanah

This festival has three themes:
- *Creation* – the anniversary of the world's creation
- *Judgement* – casting off sins for the start of a new year
- *Renewal* – the renewal of the bond between God and Israel.

This is a time of reflection on God's mercy and judgement, when Jews examine their lives and achievements. The traditional greeting is 'May you be inscribed in the Book of Life for a good year' or more simply 'Good Year!'

There is a special morning service based on the *Rosh Hashanah* prayer book. This will include reading Genesis 21 and 22 about Isaac. This is to emphasise the importance of faith and the acceptance of God's power when it comes to human endeavours. The additional service is divided into three parts, corresponding to the three themes and the three other names for *Rosh Hashanah*:

- *Malkhuyot* – the exaltation of God as King
- *Zikhronot* – Remembrance
- *Shfarot* – Blowing the Horn

Home rituals

These include:

- eating apples dipped in honey (for a sweet year)
- baking bread of the special *shabbat* dough in the shape of a crown (to recall divine sovereignty), or in the shape of a ladder (to link heaven and earth)
- eating pomegranates, which have many seeds (in the hope of fertility and that God may multiply the credit of goodness).

The afternoon ritual is the *tashlikh* ceremony, which involves saying prayers at a source of water, which should be running water if possible. Pockets are emptied into the water to shed sins symbolically. An instrument called a *shofar* (usually a ram's horn) is blown.

4.4 The Day of Atonement: Yom Kippur

Atonement means reconciliation between God and humanity (At-one-ment). This day of repentance takes place 10 days into the New Year. On the eve of Yom Kippur Jews ask forgiveness of each other for any wrongs or pain they may be guilty of, and it is gracious to forgive. Also, sins are confessed directly to God because Jews cannot have a mediator or intercessor, as no one can come between a person and God, and no person can take the part of God. There is a collective formal confession, though, because it saves personal embarrassment, and because everyone accepts responsibility for everyone else's sins. In fact there are six major conditions of sinning; they are in three pairs:

(1) compulsion and free will
(2) secretly and publicly
(3) unwittingly and knowingly.

Above all, this is a day of fasting and general abstention.
There are four reasons for fasting on Yom Kippur:

(1) to show sincerity in seeking forgiveness
(2) it requires a self-discipline which will help to improve the person
(3) the person can concentrate on improving the spirit by ignoring the body for a day
(4) to make a person more compassionate towards the needy.

There is a festive meal before the fast and special candles are lit. Food is sent to the poor, and the High Holy Day Appeal collects money for charity.

At the synagogue the Ark is covered in white and some people wear a long white smock called a *kittel*. A prayer (*Kol Nidrei*) is sung in memory of those Jews who have suffered persecution. The evening service is called *Kol Nidrei* because it is so closely bound up with this prayer. The account of the ritual of the temple in Jerusalem is read, telling how the high priest sacrificed on the Day of Atonement.

Yom Kippur is the only day of the year with five services. The closing service called *Neilah* summarises the day, being the time when the Temple gates were literally closed for the night. It closes the gates of mercy; a shutting, but not a shutting out, so that the mercy of God cannot now be lost. The service ends with the first line of the *Shema*:

'Hear, O Israel, the Lord is our God. The Lord is One'.

Then comes the triumphant shout of Elijah:

'The Lord – he is God!'

Then the blowing of the *shofar* after sunset brings the fast to an end.

4.5 The Festival of Lots: Purim

This festival commemorates the victory of Esther over the wicked Haman. It takes place on the fourteenth day of Adar (February/March). This has led to the expression 'When Adar approaches, joy increases'. There is also a popular greeting 'Be happy; it's Adar'.

Jews fast the day before Purim to commemorate Esther's three-day abstention at the palace. After this, eating and drinking become characteristic of Purim because the word *mishteh* (a feast) occurs 20 times in the book of Esther; note that this is as many times as it appears in the rest of the Bible put together. There is a festive meal which starts at midday, and candles are lit and gifts exchanged.

The main celebration is the reading of the Book of Esther at the service, morning and evening, which is held at the synagogue. When the name of Haman is mentioned, the people try to drown it out with rattles, cap pistols and alarm clocks, or by just booing and hissing. Some even write his name on the soles of their shoes and stamp up and down! There is also a *Shpeel*, which is a satirical or farcical play, in which students can mock their teachers and elect a '*Purim rabbi*' for the day.

4.6 *Passover:* Pesach

The Feast of the Passover is held from the fifteenth or sixteenth to the twenty-first or twenty-second days of the month of *Nisan* (March/April). The first and last days are for rest, and no work may be done. A number of points should be noted as vital to understanding this festival:

- God's connection with the Exodus and the importance of freedom in Judaism.
- Enslavement in Egypt and the act of redemption are not seen as isolated incidents, or just the birth of Israel; the theme of God's liberation in humanity is one that occurs again and again in Jewish life and thought.
- Tyrants and oppressors of any age are seen as 'pharaoh', and Godless regimes as 'Egypt'.
- When it is recalled how the angel of death passed over (*pesach*) the Jewish first-born, there is an awareness not just of God's saving work but of the violation of human rights today.

All ordinary food (*harmetz*) is eaten or removed so that the special passover ritual and meal (*seder*) can be prepared. Dishes and cutlery must be ritually prepared too; there may even be special sets of cutlery, crockery and cooking utensils kept only for this occasion. The family gathers and guests are invited. The fare offered includes three vital components in the seder:

- The *pesah* (bone)
- *Maror* (bitter herbs)
- *Matzah* (unleavened bread)

The seder plate has the following items:

- *Zeroa* – which is a piece of lamb shankbone to commemorate the ancient Temple sacrifice, and the use of lamb's blood in saving the Israelites in Egypt (the lamb is not eaten).
- *Beytza* – a roasted egg (again not eaten) to symbolise other sacrifices.
- *Karpas* – a spring vegetable, usually parsley, dipped in salt water representing the Israelites tears and sweat.
- *Maror* – bitter herbs and plants, such as radish, chives and chicory. Many regard lettuce as the best because it is sweet at first, and bitter later; just like the experience of the Israelites in Egypt.

On the first night of Pesach, every man and woman must drink at least four glasses of wine, each one representing a phrase of redemption:

(1) 'I shall liberate you from bondage'.
(2) 'I shall bring you to the land'.
(3) 'I shall deliver you from Egypt'.
(4) 'I shall take you to me as a people'.

There is a fifth term: 'I shall redeem you from servitude', so there arose the custom of the fifth glass of wine filled between the third and fourth glasses but never drunk. This is the 'cup of Elijah', and at this point the door is opened to welcome the prophet who is expected before the arrival of the Messiah. Between drinking the four glasses the youngest person present asks four traditional questions:

(1)   Why is this night different from other nights?
(2)   Why do we eat unleavened bread?
(3)   Why must we eat bitter herbs?
(4)   Why must we dip vegetables into salt water and bitter herbs into sauce?

There are two possible answers:

(1)   'We were slaves'.
(2)   'Our ancestors worshipped idols'.

Alternatively, an ancient text may be quoted. Essentially the Passover is a celebration of freedom and deliverance from slavery.

- Bitter herbs remind the Jews of slavery.
- Unleavened bread reminds them of the flight from Egypt.
- The egg and salt remind them of the new life after suffering.

The four glasses of wine stand for the four stages on the journey, which are:

(1)   the release from slavery
(2)   the entry into the promised land
(3)   becoming God's people
(4)   being redeemed.

Moses is not mentioned. This is to stress that God intervened directly in the history of Israel. The credit must not go to a human being, even if he is the greatest Jewish prophet. Today also, there are prayers for universal peace and brotherhood, such as this one on the Holocaust.

> . . . We remember with reverence and love the six millions of our people who perished at the hands of a tyrant more wicked than the Pharaoh who enslaved our fathers in Egypt . . . they slew the blameless and pure, men and women and little ones, with vapours of poison and burned them with fire. But we abstain from dwelling on the deeds of the evil ones lest we defame the image of God in which man was created . . .

4.7 Tabernacles: Sukkot

This seven-day festival known as the 'Season of Our Rejoicing' is celebrated from the fifteenth to the twenty-second day of the month of *Tishri*. Joy on Sukkot is mentioned three times in the Torah. The first and last days are set aside for rest, so no work may be done, and there are compulsory religious services. The festival falls five days after Yom Kippur and stresses the union of the body and soul intended by Torah and the Jewish tradition for the worship of God and community life.

On the first day, there is a service in the synagogue which includes a procession of waving *lulav* branches to the four points of the compass to symbolise God's universal blessing. *Lulav* branches are the four plants, citron, palm, myrtle and willow. They symbolize the final harvest. A *sukkah* (booth, hut, tabernacle) is built to recall the *sukkot* (plural) lived in by the Jews on their journey from Egypt to the Promised Land. These should be lived in for seven days. These booths symbolise God's provision and care, because the outside of each person's life is weak and fleeting, like the sukkah, but inside one is strong and everlasting. This is an autumn festival and the sukkah can be shaken by the wind, symbolising the vulnerability of human nature and the precariousness of human existence.

Another command for Sukkot is picking four plants: citron, palm, myrtle and willow, representing the heart, the spine, the eye and the lip respectively. All of these should be united in the worship of God: a sincere heart, dignified posture, inspiration of the eye and honest words.

On the last day of the festival, known as the Great Hosanna or *Hoshana Raba*, a willow branch is struck on a hard surface until the leaves fall off. This is because willows grow near water and the prayers at this time are for rain. The secret of understanding Sukkot is revealed in the prayer offered on the first day of the festival.

> May it be Your will, O my God and God of my fathers, that You cause Your divine presence to live among us, and may you spread a covering of peace over us.

4.8 The rejoicing in the Torah: Simhat Torah

This falls immediately after Sukkot, and there is a special service during which the Torah scrolls are taken out of the Ark by the cantor and paraded seven times around the synagogue in a procession led by the cantor. This is the custom of circuits and has been known since ancient times, for example by Joshua at Jericho.

This is a popular event which is well attended, especially by children. When a circuit is complete, the scrolls are handed on so that someone else can take a turn. Psalms and songs are sung, especially the refrain in Hebrew meaning 'Please Lord, save us. Please Lord, make us succeed'. The procession passes under the wedding canopy, which this may well be formed by holding up a prayer shawl (*tallit*). It may also be held over the 'bridegrooms' as they read the Torah passages.

Since 1967 this festival has been celebrated by huge crowds at the Wailing Wall in Jerusalem because it is the last remains of the Temple. It is also the festival with most meaning for the Jews of what used to be the USSR where they celebrated it as an act of defiance and solidarity.

4.9 Weeks: Shavuot

The Festival of Weeks is a harvest festival, and is held on the sixth day of the month *Sivan* (May/June), seven weeks after the Passover. This has more names than any other festival; these are:

- The Festival of the Harvest
- Day of the First Ripe Fruits

- The Season of the Giving of Our Torah
- Conclusion
- Conclusion of Passover
- The Festival of Weeks.

The home and the synagogue are decorated and summer fruits are eaten. The readings from the Torah are:

(1) Exodus 19 and 20 (ten commandments)
(2) Ezekiel 1 (about visions of God)
(3) Habakkuk 3 (God's power in revelation)
(4) Ruth (the most well known of Shavuot readings)
(5) Leviticus 23 (about leaving grain for the gleaners).

There is also a link with David, the great-grandson of Ruth, who was born and died on Shavuot. Thus psalms are read on the second night. There is great emphasis on the education of children. At one time, young children would be first taken to Hebrew classes with sweets on their writing slate, or literally with 'honey on the tongue'. Today, Jewish teenagers who have finished formal lessons as children are honoured collectively by:

- leading the services in the synagogue
- processing with the Torah
- reading the passages for the day
- initiating a discussion session
- hosting a special celebratory meal for family and friends.

At one time an offering was made of the first fruits to God, and each night between Passover and the Feast of Weeks, a measure (*omar*) of barley was brought into the Temple in Jerusalem. In Israel this festival is closely connected to the land and future prosperity and production.

4.10   The Festival of Lights: Hanukkah

Hanukkah lasts eight days from the twenty-fifth day of *Kislev* (December) to the second day of *Tevet*. Immediately after sunset a *Hanukkah* lamp is lit in the presence of the whole family, and placed in the window or open door. This is an eight-branched lamp, usually called a **menorah**. One lamp is lit each night of the festival while these words are said:

> 'These lights are holy and we are not permitted to make use of them, but only to see them in order to thank your name for the wonders, the victories and the marvellous deeds.'

Hanukkah celebrates the victory of the Jews over the Seleucid tyrant, Antiochus Epiphanes (Antiochus IV), who occupied Jerusalem in about 170 BCE. He wanted all his subjects to conform and obey him without question. In the case of the Jews, he tried to stop Judaism and wanted them to worship Greek idols and eat pork. The last straw for the Jews was when he set up a statue of the Greek god Zeus in the Temple.

In 168 BCE the Jews began a struggle for freedom, led by Mattathias, who formed a guerrilla force with his sons and a number of other Jews. When Mattathias died after a year, his son Judas took over as leader. From Judah's nickname Maccabeus (which means 'hammerer') his family came to be known as the **Maccabees**.

When Judas and his followers occupied the Temple in 164 BCE, he ordered the rededication of the Temple to God. This began on the twenty-fifth day of Kislev in 164 BCE and lasted for eight days. A jar of oil, untouched by their enemies and with the seal unbroken, contained enough oil for the perpetual lamp in the Temple for only one day; but it burned for eight days until more was obtained. This symbolised the light of Jewish faith, which seemed doomed, but which survived.

Judas decreed that the rededication should be celebrated by future generations.

Celebrating Hanukkah

In the synagogue the service has a reading from the Book of Zechariah (4:6) about God's Holy Spirit.

This is a special time for children and some of them will receive a present on each of the eight days. We can read in Anne Frank's diary how she managed to find gifts even while in hiding from the Nazis.

There are family gatherings and typical foods are those fried in oil; doughnuts in Israel, *latkes* (potato pancakes) elsewhere. The celebrations include card games and other forms of gambling.

The bottom line in this festival is that people have a right to be unique, individually and collectively; God will work with anyone who takes a positive stand to uphold those values which oppression tries to crush.

4.11 *The Sabbath:* Shabbat

- The Hebrew name '*shabbat*' means 'day of rest'. It is the most important day in the Jewish calendar.
- It starts on Friday, the eve of the seventh day, at sunset, and celebrates God's completion of creation and His rest afterwards.
- It begins in the home by the lighting of Sabbath candles. At the same time there is the recital of **kiddush** (sanctification), the benedictions over wine and bread, and over the Sabbath day.
- Parents bless their children, husbands praise their wives. There must be no work done. The Torah should be studied.
- The sabbath ends with the ceremony of *havdalah* (division) in which a candle is doused with wine, and with the smelling of sweet spices as a symbol of the beauty of the Sabbath as it ends for another week.

This is a day of joy and is prepared for with gladness. There is an evening service called the *Kabbalet Shabbat*, which celebrates the climax of creation when God had completed His work. When the mother has prepared the sabbath meal the father will say: 'A woman of worth is more precious than rubies. For her children rise up and call her happy'. There is the ritual washing of hands and special loaves (*hallot*) are broken and handed round. These are plait-shaped to symbolise the unity of God, His people and the Torah. Salt is sprinkled over these loaves to symbolise the dignity of human labour. Between courses, songs (*zemirot*) are sung and thanks given for the joys of the Sabbath.

After attending the morning service in the synagogue the family will eat a midday meal which has been prepared in advance. A cup of wine is drunk at the end of the day to carry the joys of the Sabbath into the other days. There is also the singing of a song about the coming of the messiah, when the joy of the Sabbath will be enjoyed universally.

Work on the Sabbath

Jews must

- 'Observe the Sabbath day and keep it holy' (Deuteronomy 5:8)
- 'Remember to keep the Sabbath day holy' (Exodus 20:8)

There are only two specific prohibitions in the Bible. They are:

- Exodus 16:29 – about not travelling outside the town where you live or are staying
- Exodus 35:3 – about lighting fires.

Both of these are hard work in terms of effort and are activities which are concerned with the material world and the attempt to control it.

The rabbis have classified 39 types of activities from which Jews should refrain on Shabbat. These are grouped under five headings.

---

(1) producing food (includes not just cooking, but ploughing too)
(2) making cloth (sewing, weaving and even sheep-shearing)
(3) writing (producing writing materials as well as writing)
(4) building (includes demolishing; lighting and putting out fires)
(5) carrying in a public place.

4.12   Pilgrimage

This is not an obligation as in some religions but it is only natural that Jerusalem, especially the Wailing Wall, should attract Jews from all over the world.

The Wailing Wall

This is also known as the Western Wall and is the remains of the temple built by Herod the Great on the site of Solomon's temple. The Jews grieve for the destruction of the Temple by the Romans in 70 CE. They pray in front of the Wall and kiss the stones, and they also put written prayers into the cracks between the stones (Figure 4.1). The hope is that the Temple will be built again one day. Many will remember the days before the capture of the old city in 1967 when Jews could not visit this holy place.

Yad Vashem

The Holocaust of the Second World War has given rise to the pilgrimage to *Yad Vashem* ('eternal memorial'), which is a bare room lit by a candle with the names of the concentration camps on the floor. This is in memory of those slaughtered in Hitler's 'Final Solution'. Also remembered are the 'righteous Gentiles' who helped Jews to escape.

Figure 4.1 Praying at the Western Wall in Jerusalem
(Carlos Reyes-Manzo Andes Press Agency)

Masada

This was a fortress defended by the Zealots against the Romans who finally captured it in 73 CE after a three-year siege. The Zealots were a Jewish sect that resisted Roman rule in Palestine. Pilgrims commit themselves to maintaining the faith and heritage of those who died there. This may take the form of support for Zionism, the protection of Israel. It is summed up in the slogan to be found on the stamps and medals issued in 1973 to mark the two-thousandth anniversary of Masada: 'Masada shall not fall again'.

Rites of passage

5.1 Birth, childhood and education

- Biblical Law states that the first-born male child is to be devoted to God (Numbers 3:11–13).
- The child was symbolically redeemed from the priest (*kohen*) in the *pidyan haben* ceremony (redemption of the first-born son).
- Every new life is God's gift and receives a joyous welcome into the family.
- Baby boys are circumcised on the eighth day after birth.
- Education starts at the age of five years, when children are sent to the *cheder* ('room'), a special class to learn Hebrew and Jewish religious history and principles.

5.2 Brit Milah: *The covenant of circumcision*

The Book of Genesis says that the decision to circumcise all Hebrew males was taken after God spoke to Abraham telling him that it was a sign of the covenant between God and the Jews. Tradition holds that the father is responsible for circumcision. Special circumcisers (*mohels*) are trained to do it.

- It takes place in the home.
- The baby is carried into the gathering by his grandmother because tradition says that his mother cannot attend.
- The child is handed to his godfather (*sandek*).
- He then passes him to his father who sits him in 'Elijah's chair'. It is called Elijah's chair because the prophet is believed to be present during the ceremony.
- The godfather now holds the baby on his knees while the *mohel* carries out the operation using a knife.
- The skin is secured to stop it growing again.
- During the operation, the *mohel* blesses the baby; then the father offers a blessing.
- Those present say a special response.
- The child is named and a drop of wine is put on his lips.
- His father drinks the rest of the glass and a celebration follows.

The baby is now religiously pure and is welcomed as a member of God's chosen people; his circumcision is the sign that will always remind him of it. It is the 'sign' in his flesh.

- **It must be emphasised that he is a Jew because he has a Jewish mother, not because he is circumcised.**

5.3 Bar Mitzvah

'Bar mitzvah' means 'son of the commandment'. Jewish boys are considered to be adults at the age of 13 years and one day, and so they become *bar mitzvah*. Education begins at an early age to make them aware of the commandments (*mitzvot*), which set out responsibilities.

Three reasons for Bar mitzvah

(1) The boy receives full privileges and takes on the responsibilities of an adult. He can wear:

  - the *tallit* (prayer shawl)
  - the *tefillin* (leather boxes containing biblical texts).

(2) He can read from the Torah in the synagogue.
(3) It is a chance to renew his Jewish commitment, because unless he had a serious dedication to God and Jewry, he would not undertake the rite.

The ceremony

This takes place on the first *shabbat* after a boy's thirteenth birthday. The main steps are as follows.

(1) For the first time, the boy is called to read from the Sefer Torah in Hebrew. He follows the words with a silver finger pointer (*yad*). This means that he has come of age, for only adult males are allowed this privilege in the Orthodox community.
(2) He receives his father's blessing.
(3) The father thanks God that his son is old enough to be responsible for his own sins and that he no longer has any responsibility for them.
(4) The *sendah* meal is eaten after the ceremony to show the value of the commandment that he has embraced.
(5) The boy gives a sermon (*derasha*) during the meal. He thanks everyone for the gifts they have brought, and his parents for everything they have done for him. Then he sets out his religious hopes for the years to come.

5.4 Bat Mitzvah

- This means 'daughter of the commandment'.
- This ceremony has been developed by the Reformed synagogues to acknowledge the importance of women in Jewish life. Orthodox Judaism does not have such a ceremony.
- The ceremony is held on the *shabbat*.
- Girls taking part have reached the age of 12.
- They read from the Talmud during the ceremony (Figure 5.1).

5.5 Bat Chayil

This means 'daughter of valour' (or 'excellence'). It is a status introduced by some Orthodox synagogues in recent years. Girls are not allowed to read from the Torah but they can read from the Prophets or the Writings.

Figure 5.1 Bat Mitzvah: girls reading the scrolls
(Carlos Reyes-Manzo Andes Press Agency)

5.6 Confirmation

This dates from the early nineteenth century when some Progressive synagogues in Germany, France and Italy brought in a confirmation service to replace *bar mitzvah*. It involved the following changes:

- before the service, boys and girls learned Judaism together (traditional synagogues taught them separately);
- boys and girls were confirmed together;
- the ceremony took place at the age of 16;
- technically, this ceremony could be held at any time of the year, but gradually it came to be part of the celebrations of Shavuot.

5.7 Marriage

Before the ceremony

The groom reads from the Torah or the prophets in the synagogue on the *shabbat* before the wedding. When his reading is finished, there are cries of '*Mazel tov*' ('good luck') from those present.

Tradition demands that the bride and groom fast in the hours before the wedding. The purpose of the fast is to secure the forgiveness of God for any sins so that they can start their married life with a clean slate.

Before the wedding ceremony, the *ketubah*, or marriage contract is signed in the presence of two male witnesses. The contract spells out what will happen to the bride if her husband divorces her, or in case he dies before she does.

The ceremony

This traditionally has two parts.

- The betrothal (*erusin*) is a pre-wedding commitment binding a man and a woman together before they can live together.
- The canopy (**huppah** or **chuppah**) is a symbol of the groom's reception of his bride into his home.

Modern Jewish weddings combine these two parts.

During the ceremony the groom stands under the *chuppah* facing Jerusalem (Figure 5.2). The rabbi and the cantor stand opposite him. The bride is taken to join the groom by her mother and future mother-in-law.

The five steps of the ritual

(1) The cantor sings for the couple, calling God's blessing on them.
(2) Two glasses of wine are poured to symbolise the common future of the couple.
(3) The groom offers his bride a plain gold ring with the words:

'Behold you are sanctified to me with this ring, according to the law of Moses and Israel.'

She takes the ring to show that she is willingly entering into marriage.

Figure 5.2   A Jewish wedding: a couple under the Chuppah, St John's Wood, London
(Carlos Reyes-Manzo Andes Press Agency)

(4) The *ketubah* is read to the bride before it is given to her. Then the cantor sings the seven benedictions of wedlock.
(5) Lastly, the bridegroom breaks a wine glass under his feet as the guests shout '*Mazel tov*'; this being the traditional way to lament the destruction of the Temple nearly 2000 years ago.

5.8 Death

After death the eyes and mouth of the corpse are closed by a near relative. Then the body is washed and wrapped in a shroud. Men can be wrapped in their *tallit* (prayer shawl). Burial normally takes place within 24 hours. At the brief funeral service, mourners accompany the body to the graveside where psalms are sung and the *Kaddish* prayer is said. Then the mourners fill the grave with earth.

5.9 Mourning

There are four main stages to mourning.

(1) Between the time of death and the funeral the mourner (called an '*onan*') is freed of all other obligations.
(2) There is a week of mourning (**shiva**) following the funeral during which the mourners stay home, sitting on the floor or small stools to receive visitors.
(3) Then there is a further period of 23 days during which mourners gradually take up their responsibilities again.
(4) Lastly, there is a less intense period of mourning which lasts for 11 months after the death. Once the earth has settled on the grave a headstone or some other form of memorial can be set up at a special ceremony.

Questions

1. (a) What is meant by:

    (i) *Yahrzeit*   [2]
    (ii) *Kaddish*?   [2]

    (b) Give a brief description of a Jewish funeral.   [4]

    (c) Explain the Jewish beliefs about death and dying.   [7]

    (d) 'People should live their lives well and not worry about what
         happens when they die.'

         Do you agree? Give reasons to support your answer and show
         that you have thought about different points of view. You must refer to
         Judaism in your answer.   [5]

2. (a) What are the origins of:
         (i) Orthodox Jews,
         (ii) Progressive Jews?   [8]

    (b) How might being **either** an Orthodox **or** a Progressive Jew affect
         the life of a believer?   [7]

    (c) 'It is a good idea to have different groups within a religion.'   [5]

3. Questions (a)–(d) can be answered in a single word, phrase or
    sentence. Question (e) requires a longer answer.

    (a) What is *Kashrut*?   (*1 mark*)

    (b) What is a covenant?   (*1 mark*)

    (c) Who received the Ten Commandments from God on Mount Sinai?   (*1 mark*)

    (d) Write out the first sentence of the *Shema*.   (*2 marks*)

    (e) Explain the meaning and importance of Shabbat for Jews.   (*5 marks*)

                                                              (*Total 10 marks*)

    (*SEG Paper 1480/1, Section A, 1998 Short Course Specimen Questions*)

4. (a) (i) When does the Sabbath begin and end?   (*2 marks*)
         (ii) How may Jews 'keep the Sabbath'?   (*6 marks*)

(b)   Explain the importance of *Bar Mitzvah* and *Bat Mitvah* (or *Bat Chayil*) for
      the Jewish community.   (*8 marks*)

(c)   'Religions should treat both sexes equally.' Do you agree? Give reasons
      for your answer showing you have considered another point of view.   (*4 marks*)

                                                                    (*Total 20 marks*)

(London (1479) Specimen Papers for 1st examination May/June 1999)

5. (a)   Name the **three** parts of the Tenakh.   [3]

    (b)   What do Jews believe about the Messiah?   [5]

    (c)   Explain why Jews believe that the Torah is so important.   [7]

    (d)   'It is important for religions to have a statement of belief like the *Shema*.'
          Do you agree? Give reasons to support your answer and show that you have
          thought about different points of view.   [5]

(MEG, Summer 1998, Sample Paper)

Judaism: A glossary

Afikomen
'Dessert': half a *matzah* hidden for children to find during the *Seder*
Aggadah
Part of the Jewish oral law; it deals with Biblical interpretations, theology and ethics
Aleynu (Aleinu)
The closing prayer at each service
Amidah
'Standing': a prayer said standing at all services; a series of 18 Benedictions, forming the core of Jewish worship
Aron hakodesh
'Holy ark' containing Torah scrolls
Ashkenazim
Jews from central and Eastern Europe
Atonement
The purpose of the ritual of *Yom Kippur* – the Day of Atonement (Leviticus 16): it refers to reconciliation between God and humanity (at-one-ment), the relationship, broken by sin, being restored
Bar Mitzvah
'Son of Commandment': initiation for 13-year-old boys marking the attainment of religious maturity
Bat Mitzvah
'Daughter of Commandment': initiation ceremony for 12-year-old girls
Bet Din
A Jewish court of three rabbis ruling on Jewish law
Bet t'filah
House of prayer
Bet hamidrash
House of study
Beytza
Roasted egg which is part of the seder plate and symbolises sacrifice
Bet ha Knesset
'House of Assembly': synagogue
Bimah
A desk or platform for reading the *Torah* and leading services
Brit(also **berit**)
Covenant
Brit milah
The 'Covenant of Cutting' (circumcision)
Challah
Yeast-leavened white bread made with egg, eaten on the Sabbath and ceremonial occasions

Hanukkah
The Feast of Dedication; also the Feast of Lights
Chazan
The leader of reading, singing and chanting in services. Also *Hazan* or *Cantor*
Cheder
A class in which Jewish children are taught Hebrew and Jewish religious history and principles
Circumcision
The rite of *Brit Milah*, involving the cutting off of the foreskin of boys on the eighth day after birth by a qualified *mohel*
Covenant
An agreement between God and men; for example, with Abraham
Day of Atonement
See *Yom Kippur*
Decalogue
The Ten Commandments given by God to Moses on Mt Sinai
Derasha
Sermon during Bar Mitzvah ceremony
Deuteronomy
Fifth book in the Bible, and part of the *Torah*
Diaspora
The dispersion of the Jews throughout the world, particularly after the fall of Jerusalem in 70 CE, it is often referred to by the Hebrew word *Galut*
Election
The belief that the Jews were selected by God for a special divine purpose
Erusin
Betrothal for marriage
Essenes
Jewish mystics and devotees of the *Torah* from the second century BCE to the second century CE. They often separated themselves in communities as at Qumran near the Dead Sea
Exodus
Second book in the Bible telling the story of the Hebrew's passage to freedom from slavery in Egypt
Gehenna
In Jewish apocryphal literature the equivalent of hell
Gemara (also **Gemarah**)
Commentary on *Mishnah*, included in the *Talmud*
Genesis
First book in the Bible, part of the *Torah*
Genizah
Storage place for disused scrolls
Haftarah
'Completion': a passage from the prophets read in the synagogue on the Sabbath
Hagadah
'Telling': the book used at the *Seder* ritual on the eve of the Passover to recount the liberation of the Jews from slavery. Also *Haggadah*
Hallot
Plait-shaped loaves shared on Sabbath
Halakhah
The legal system of Judaism
Harmetz
Ordinary food
Hallel
Chant of praise used in the Passover and some other holidays. Psalms 113–18
Hanukiah (also **Chanukiah**)
Eight-branched candelabrum used at the festival of *Hanukkah*
Hasidism (**Chasidism**)
A mystic pious movement dating from the eighteenth century

Hasidim
A movement of the second century BCE which opposed the Hellenizing of Jewish life; the *Essenes* and *Pharisees* were offshoots of this movement. Also: an eighteenth-century movement which favoured the power of simple, joyful piety rather than the intellectual requirements of talmudic learning

Haskalah
From a Jewish word meaning 'Enlightenment'; applied to an eighteenth-century movement which resulted in a new emphasis on education and a resurgence of the study of Hebrew and the Jewish scriptures in a modern context

Havdalah
'Distinction': a service held in the home at the end of the Sabbath; it can also be held in the synagogue

Hebrew
A Semitic language in which the Jewish scriptures are written, also used by Jews for prayer and study

Holocaust
The extermination by the Nazis of millions of Jews during the Second World War

Hoshanah Raba
The Great Hosanna. It's the last day of the festival of Sukkot

Huppah (or Chuppah)
Four-posted canopy used for wedding ceremony

Israel
'One who struggles with God'; this was the new name for Jacob. It refers to the world-wide community of Jews, and the land and state of Israel

Kabbalet Shabbat
Evening service celebrating climax of creation when God had completed his work

Kabbalah (or Cabala)
(Lit: 'that which is handed down') Jewish mysticism

Kaddish
'To make "holy"': a prayer of sanctification used in mourning ceremonies and in the synagogue service

Karpas
Spring vegetable usually parsley eaten at the Passover. It's dipped in salt and water to represent the sweat and tears of the Israelites

Kosher (Kasher)
Those categories of food that Jews are allowed to eat, it includes the preparation of such food according to the dietary laws

Kashrut
Jewish dietary laws

Kehilla
A community of people (referring to the synagogue)

Ketubah
The marriage document received by a Jewish bride from her husband, and signed by both, it sets out the duties which the bridegroom is to perform for her

Ketuvim
'Writings': the third section of the scriptures

Kibbutz
A voluntary, collective community   These are found in Israel, and are mainly agricultural; there is no private wealth, the community being responsible for the needs of the members and their families. It began in 1909 in Deganyah, and there are now over 200 such communities with around 100 000 members

Kiddush
'Holy': a prayer of sanctification at the start of the Sabbath

Kittel
Long white smock worn in the synagogue

Kohen
Priests in the temple; the word survives in the surname Cohen

Kol nidrei
Prayer said for persecuted Jews
Leviticus
Third book in the Bible, part of the *Torah*
Maccabees
A Jewish noble family which led the revolt against the attempt by Antiochus IV Epiphanes to crush the Jewish faith in 168 BCE; under Judah Maccabaeus the Jews restored the Temple in 164 BCE
Machzor
The prayer book for festivals
Magen David
'Shield of David' (usually called the Star of David): a hexagram made up of two interwoven equilateral triangles
Masekhtot
Divisions of the Shisha Sedarim
Maror
Bitter herbs; one of 3 components of the seder
Matzah
Unleavened bread (plural **matzot**) used in the Passover Festival to commemorate the Exodus from Egypt
Memra
Aramaic term for 'word', it is used in the Jewish *Targums* to avoid any possibility of suggesting that God acted directly or in human form
Menorah
Seven-branched candelabrum, originally there was a golden one in the Temple in Jerusalem; it now refers to the candelabrum used in the Feast of *chanukkah*
Mezuzah
A small metal container holding sections of the *Torah*; these are fastened to the right doorpost of the house and of rooms in Jewish homes
Midrash
('to search out, expound'): the teaching and commentaries of the rabbis on scripture; *Halakhic Midrash* deals with the Law and *Aggadic Midrash* deals with the narrative of scripture
Mikveh
A ritual bath for spiritual cleansing
Minyan
Quorum of ten men needed for a service; progressive communities include women but do not always need a *minyan*
Mishnah
The authoritative collection of oral law in Hebrew. It is the basis of the Palestinian and Babylonian Talmuds and dates from around 200 CE
Mishteh
A feast
Mitzvah (Plural: **Mitzvot**)
Literally means 'commandment'; also means obligation or duty required by God of the Jews
Mohel
Someone who performs circumcision
Moses
The leader and lawgiver at the time of Exodus
Nephesh
Hebrew 'soul', but also indicating emotions or physical appetites, this word occurs over 700 times in the Bible
Ner tamid
Eternal light above the Ark
Nevi'im (Nebi'im)
'Prophets', the second section of the scriptures
Numbers
The fourth book of the Bible, and part of the *Torah*

Omar
Ameasure, e.g. of grain
Onan
Mourner
Parev (Also **Pareve**)
'Neutral': food which is neither milk nor meat – for example, plants, eggs, fish
Pentateuch
First books of the Bible. Also called the *Torah*
Pesah
Bone; one of the 3 components of the seder
Pesach
Passover: festival commemorating the Exodus from Egypt
Pharisees
Aramaic: 'separated ones', the successors of the Hasidim, they were the founders of Rabbinic Judaism. They stressed the oral tradition and strictly observed the *Torah*
Phylacteries
see Tephilin
Pidyan naben
Redemption of the First-born son ceremony. The first rite of passage
Pirke Aboth 'Ethics of the Fathers': Law worship and kindness
Pogrom
Organised massacre, or exile, particularly in Russia and Romania in the nineteenth and twentieth centuries
Priest
A person called by God for the delivery of a special message, particularly those who have given their names to books of the Bible
Purim
The festival celebrated on *Adar* 14 with the reading of the book of Esther to commemorate her success in preventing the massacre of Jews by Haman
Rabbi (Also **Rebbe** – Hasidic)
Lit: 'My master', an authorised Jewish teacher
Rosh Hashanah
Literally 'Head of the Year': Jewish New Year autumn festival
Sadducees
Conservative Jewish priests, important in the first centuries BCE and CE, they recognized only the written Law, and denied resurrection and the after life. They died out after the destruction of Jerusalem in 70 CE
Sanctification
In the Jewish Bible this means purity and separateness. The Israelites were told to sanctify the Lord of Hosts (Isaiah 8:13), to recognize his sovereign claims, and to sanctify themselves (Leviticus 11:44)
Sanhedrin
The highest Jewish tribunal, it had 71 members which met in Jerusalem. The term derives from the 70 elders who advised Moses. It ceased to exist around 425 CE
Satan
Hebrew: 'the accuser'
Seder
Lit: 'order': the ritual followed at the Passover supper
Sefer Torah
Torah scroll kept in the synagogue Ark
Sefiroth
In Jewish mysticism (*Kabbalah*), these are the ten attributes of God which link the celestial to the earthly world.
Sendah
Meal eaten after Bar Mitzvah ceremony
Sephardim
Jews from the western Mediterranean, especially Spain, Portugal and North Africa

Septuagint
The Greek version of the Jewish Bible
Shabbat (Plural: **Shabatot**)
Day of rest, the seventh day when God rested after the six days of creation (Exodus 20:11), it also celebrates Israel's delivery from slavery in Egypt (Deuteronomy 5:15)
Shavuot
The Feast of Weeks, celebrated 50 days after the Passover. This marks the start of the wheat harvest, and remembers the giving of the Law to Moses on Mt Sinai
Shechita
Ritual killing of animals according to the rules for *Kosher* food by an authorized slaughterer
Shekhina
A term used in the *Targums* to signify God. It stands for the radiance, glory or presence of God
Shema
(Lit: 'Hear!') (Deuteronomy 6:4) 'Hear O Israel, the Lord is our God, the Lord is One'. This is said twice a day as an affirmation of belief in the doctrines of *Election* and Monotheism
Sheol
Old Testament place of the dead, equivalent to the Greek Hades; later it became the place where the wicked are punished after death
Shishah Sedarim
The 6 orders in the Mishnah (part of the Talmud or 'teaching')
Shiva/Shivah
Seven days 'sitting' by the bereaved in their homes
Shofar
Ram's horn blown in the synagogue at the festival of *Rosh Hashanah*, and at the end of *Yom Kippur*; it remembers Abraham's sacrifice of the ram instead of Isaac
Shulchan Aruch
Lit: 'The set table', refers to the book compiled by Joseph Caro (1488–1575 CE), an authoritative code of Jewish law
Siddur
'Order' or 'arrangement': the prayer book for daily use, and for the Sabbath and occasional use
Simhat Torah
Lit: 'Rejoicing in the *Torah*', it is a day at the end of the festival of *Sukkoth* that marks the start of the annual cycle of readings from the *Torah*
Soul
Hebrew thought saw human beings as bodies vitalized by the soul
Spirit
The Spirit of God is seen as the agent of Creation (Genesis 1), of Prophecy (Ezekiel 37), and of special powers in humankind (Numbers 11)
Sukkah (Plural: *Sukkot*)
'Tabernacle' or 'Booth': temporary shelter used for meals and sleeping during the Feast of Tabernacles
Sukkot(h)
Feast of Tabernacles celebrated in the Autumn, *Tishri* 15–21
Synagogue
Meeting place for worship
Tallit(h)
Prayer shawl, white and blue in colour, worn by males at morning services and at all services on the day of Atonement
Talmud
The major source of Jewish Law, it contains the *Mishnah* (oral law), and the *Gemara* (rabbinic commentaries on the *Mishnah*)
Targum
Aramaic interpretative translation of parts of the Hebrew Bible
Tashlikh ceremony
Afternoon ritual in which prayers are said at a source of water (running if possible)

Taryag
A word formed from the initials of the words six hundred and thirteen. It refers to the 613 mitzvot (laws) given by the *Torah*

Temple
Built by Solomon around 950 BCE, it was destroyed in 586 BCE. The second temple was dedicated in 516 BCE. Herod began a rebuilding in 19 BCE. This, the last temple, was destroyed in 70 CE

Tenakh
The Jewish Bible with three sections: *Torah*, *Nevi'im* and *Ketuvim*

Tefillin (also **T'filin**, **Tephilin**)
Phylacteries (two small cubic boxes of leather, fastened by straps to the forehead and arm for morning prayers on weekdays. They contain four Biblical texts written on parchment. Jewish men wear them

Tobit
The central figure in a book of the same name in Jewish Apocryphal writings

Torah
Hebrew 'Law', which applies particularly to the Law of Moses (the first five books of the Bible); in a general sense it can be translated as 'teaching'

Tractate
A section of the *Mishnah*

Trefa
Non-kosher food

Tzizit
Fringes on the corners of the *tallit* and on the undergarment worn by Orthodox Jewish men and boys

Yad
The hand-shaped pointer used in *Torah* reading

Yad vashem
'Eternal memorial' to the Holocaust. A bare room lit by a candle with names of concentration camps on the floor

Yadrzeit
'Year time': the anniversary of a death

Yahweh
The name of the Israelite God

Yamulkah
Skull cap worn during prayers and Torah study, which some Orthodox men wear continually (Sometimes also Capel and *Kippah*)

Yeshiva
College for Talmudic and Rabbinic studies

Yiddish
Mixed dialect of German, Slavonic (for example, Polish) and Hebrew

Yom Kippur
The Day of *Atonement*: A fast observed on *Tishri* 10, bringing to an end the ten days of penitence which start with *Rosh Hashanah*

Zaddikim
Lit: 'righteous ones', the leaders of the eighteenth-century Hasidim movement

Zeroa
Piece of lamb which is part of the seder plate to commemorate the Temple sacrifice

Zionists
Those who sought to set up a Jewish state in Palestine (Israel) and who support its continued existence

Zohar
The major work of Jewish mysticism, it was written by Moses de León in the thirteenth century, and is in the form of a commentary on the *Pentateuch*

Zemirot
Songs sung between the courses of the Sabbath meal

PART II

Christianity

Origins and definitions

6.1 Introduction

A Christian is a person who believes in Jesus Christ and follows him as Lord and Saviour. He was given the name Jesus to denote the object of his mission – to 'save'. For Christians it is important to live life as closely as possible to his teachings as set out in the New Testament.

The prophets had been silent for centuries until John the Baptist proclaimed Christ's ministry. John is seen as the Elijah figure that Malachi spoke of in chapter 4:5–6. Jewish tradition had long taught that one day God would send a **Messiah**, meaning a deliverer and King of the Jews. He would be from King David's family, an anointed deliverer (note that Messiah originally meant 'anointed'). It would be his purpose to restore the fortunes of Israel. So the name Christ means anointed or Messiah.

There had been many before Jesus who were called 'anointed': for example, Moses' brother Aaron, King David, and even Cyrus the king of Persia, who was non-Jewish. However, by the time Jesus appeared, 'Messiah' had come to mean someone sent by God to drive out the Romans who had made Israel a part of their empire. Prior to Jesus and for 50 years after his ministry, there were a number of 'Messiahs' who were unsuccessful.

Jesus stands out as special because he was a spiritual Messiah sent to restore the faith of Israel and lead the spread of God's covenant to the rest of the world. Most Jews rejected him, so he told his disciples to take his message to the Gentiles (non-Jews). So Christians believe that those individuals of whatever race who accept Jesus as the Messiah are the 'New Israel'; the new 'Chosen People' of God's Covenant.

6.2 How we know about Jesus

There is a reference in the writings of the Roman historian Tacitus, who was explaining the name of the 'Christians' put to death by Nero, and the standard history of the Jews written by Josephus towards the end of the first century CE also refers to Jesus. However, almost all we know comes from the four **Gospels** in the New Testament.

Christians believe that:

- Jesus was the **revelation** of God Himself
- he shows Christians what God is like
- he is the culmination of centuries of God's revelation recorded in scriptures that go back hundreds of years before His time.

Christians look for the authority of Christ and are thus led to the authority of the Bible – the two are inseparable:

- Jesus revealed God to people in a way that the Old Testament could never have done in that people saw him, touched him, spoke to him and so forth. Obviously people today were not there, so they have to turn to the New Testament to find the revelation of Christ.
- He intended this, because one of his important aims was to select and train disciples to preserve and pass on his teaching. The New Testament contains the record of what they taught.

6.3   Jesus and the Old Testament

Jesus explained that he had not come to abolish the law and the prophets but to fulfil them. He said that 'till heaven and earth pass away, not an iota, not a dot, will pass from the law until all is accomplished' (Matthew 5:17–18). He also explained that 'Everything written about me in the law of Moses and the prophets and the psalms must be fulfilled.'

- He believed it is the word of God.
- He believed its statements.
- He obeyed its commands.
- He said he came to fulfil the pattern of redemption it set down.

Jesus uses the Old Testament in a wide variety of episodes:

- to settle arguments with opponents
- in his battle with **Satan**
- teaching the disciples
- his ethical rules are drawn from the law of Moses
- when he was on the cross
- after the resurrection when 'beginning with Moses and all the prophets, he interpreted to them in all the scriptures the things concerning Himself' (Luke 24:27).

6.4   How the New Testament endorses the Old Testament

- It quotes and alludes to the Old Testament to show God's character and purpose.
- The writer of Hebrews says that God spoke through the prophets.
- Paul told Timothy that all scripture is inspired by God.
- The New Testament makes no distinction between what God says and what scripture says.

6.5   The life of Jesus

His Birth

Jesus was born in Bethlehem in Palestine, which was part of the Roman Empire. His parents, Joseph and Mary, had to return to Bethlehem because the Romans were holding a census which required everyone to go back to their home town. An angel appeared to Mary to tell her that she would give birth to a son called Jesus, who was the long-expected Messiah.

His ministry

The work of Jesus is known as his ministry. It began after He was baptised by John the Baptist in the River Jordan. This ministry began when he was 30 and lasted for three years. He chose 12 disciples to share his life and work and to continue to spread the Gospel after the **Ascension** (when he was taken up to Heaven). His work included healing the sick, restoring the sight of the blind, casting out demons, feeding the hungry, and preaching.

What Jesus taught

He travelled around Israel teaching about the coming of the *Kingdom of God*. To get into the Kingdom, a person must believe in the word of God. Earthly position, for example having a religious office, carries no weight. The Kingdom is open to tax collectors, prostitutes, the poor; anyone, as long as they have faith.

Jesus taught much of his message in **parables**. These are earthly stories with religious meanings. They can be found in the gospels of Matthew, Mark and Luke. Examples include the good Samaritan (Luke 10:25–37) and the sheep and the goats (Matthew 25:31–46)

The Last Supper

This was at the time of the Passover meal, and Jesus had arranged to borrow a room for this meal with the disciples. Judas Iscariot had gone to the chief priests, who wanted to arrest Jesus, and offered to betray him for 30 pieces of silver. At the supper, Jesus announced that he knew, and added: 'The Son of Man is going the way appointed for him in the scriptures ... ' This means that the Old Testament had foretold his birth and death. He had come to die to atone (pay for) the **sins** of those who believed in him. During the supper he took bread and gave it to the disciples with the words: 'Take this and eat; this is my body.' Then he took a cup of wine and they all drank from it. He said: 'This is my blood, the blood of the covenant, shed for many ... '.

He was teaching them that they were God's chosen people in a new way. It was not because they were Jews but because they loved Jesus. This was the beginning of the Christian ritual of Holy Communion. It is important because Christians believe that he is with them during **communion**, and that it acts as a bond between them, and with him.

The Crucifixion

The Jewish religious leaders did not like Jesus and they plotted to get rid of him. He was arrested and taken to Pontius Pilate, the Roman governor of Palestine. Against his better judgement, Pilate tried Jesus and had him crucified. This was on what is now called Good Friday. This particular period of time (a week) is known as Holy Week or *Passiontide* (see section 9.10). The crucifixion is vital to Christians, who believe that Jesus died on the cross to cleanse the sins of humankind. This is known as the **Atonement**. In the spiritual sense, Christians 'die to sin' and are reborn in the love of Christ; their spiritual life is resurrected because of Jesus' sacrifice.

The Burial

Joseph of Arimathea asked Pilate for Jesus' body. It was taken from the cross and wrapped in a shroud. Then it was buried in a tomb in a rock. The traditional site of the burial is the Church of the Holy Sepulchre in Jerusalem outside the city wall. Some think that Jesus was buried in the garden tomb.

The Resurrection

This was on what is now called Easter Sunday. The Gospel writers tell the story as follows.

Matthew
- Two women looked for the tomb.
- There was an earthquake.
- The stone at the entrance to the tomb was rolled away by an angel.
- The women were told by the angel that Jesus had been raised from the dead.

Mark
- Three women brought spices to anoint the body.
- They wondered how to roll away the stone.
- They found the stone already rolled away.
- When they entered the tomb they were alarmed.
- They were told by a man in white that Jesus was resurrected.

Luke
- Three women took spices to the tomb.
- They went into the tomb.
- The body was gone.
- Two men in dazzling garments told them about Jesus's resurrection.

John
- Mary Magdalene (one of the followers of Jesus) went to the tomb and found the stone rolled away.
- She told two disciples, who went back to the tomb with her.
- They found the wrappings from his body.
- The disciples went away, but Mary went back into the tomb and saw two angels. Then Jesus appeared to her.

Summary of points of agreement in the Synoptics

(1) The women went to the tomb.
(2) They found that it was empty.
(3) They were told about Jesus' resurrection.

Jesus's appearances after the Resurrection

(1) *Matthew* In Chapter 28 (from verse 9) he appears first to the two women named Mary and then to the disciples.

(2) *Mark* In Chapter 16 (from verse 9) he appears first to Mary Magdalene and then to the others.

(3) *Luke* In Chapter 24 (from verse 13) he appears to two of his followers on the way to Emmaus, and at Emmaus, and then later to Simon and then to all of them at Jerusalem.

(4) *John* In Chapter 20 (from verse 14) he appears first to Mary Magdalene and then to the disciples. The whole of Chapter 21 is about his appearances after the Resurrection.

(5) *The Acts of The Apostles* In Chapter 1 he appears to his followers and then ascends into heaven. In Chapter 9 Saul, while on the road to Damascus, finds a light from heaven shining around him. He falls to the ground and heard a voice say 'Saul, why do you persecute me?'. When Saul asks who it is, Jesus identifies himself.

(6) *1 Corinthians* 15.

The importance of the Resurrection

For Christians, the Resurrection is the greatest miracle and the ultimate sign of God's action in Jesus. It is the act of God that fulfils the scriptures, and which gives authority for believing in the living Christ. It means that God will act again in history through Christ's return (this is known as 'the second coming') and that this will happen at the end of the world. He will carry out final judgement and bring God's eternal reign in peace and justice. Paul relates that he was told that Jesus appeared to Cephas, the Twelve and to 'over 500 of our brothers at once ... ' Then he appeared to James and afterwards all the apostles. In the end he appeared even to me (verses 5–8)

The Ascension

After his post-resurrection appearances, Jesus went up to Heaven. This can be found in Mark 16:19; Luke 24:51 and Acts 1:9–11.

6.6 The birth of the Church

Pentecost

This is the Jewish harvest festival 50 days after the feast of the Passover. The Jews went from all over the Roman Empire to Jerusalem to celebrate the giving of the *Torah* to Moses on Mt Sinai.

The Acts of the Apostles say that the disciples were in the upstairs room where they celebrated the Passover meal with Jesus before his death just a few weeks before. They heard the sound of a powerful rushing wind, and little flames of fire appeared and came down on the head of each disciple. This was the Holy Spirit giving them the gift of tongues so that they could spread the Gospel to people of every race.

Peter went out and spoke to the crowd and by the end of the day 3000 people had come forward for baptism. This was the founding of the Christian Church. Peter and the others stopped calling themselves disciples (followers) and became instead 'apostles' (or those sent out to do the work). There were twelve of them.

Jesus had said that Peter was to be the rock on which the Church would be built, and Peter did lead the Church at first. He went on preaching tours, but he was not keen on Gentiles or non-Jews being welcomed as equal partners into the Church. Then Paul, a man who had ruthlessly persecuted Christians before he became one himself, became the dominant figure. Paul made three missionary journeys and wrote letters to the early Christian communities to advise and guide them.

Christians were often persecuted at this time and especially during the reign of Nero. Christians worshipped in each other's homes, or in synagogues in the early years. Churches were not specially built for centuries. The real turning point came when the Roman Emperor Constantine became a convert and made Christianity the official religion of the Empire, which at that time covered the entire Mediterranean region and what are today France and Britain.

The Early Church in the British Isles

Christianity was probably first brought to the British Isles by Roman soldiers, merchants and traders. St Alban, who was beheaded at Verulamium in the third century CE, is the first Christian soldier known to us.

St Patrick, who was an escaped slave from Ireland, arrived in England 200 hundred years later. He trained to be a priest before returning to Ireland in 431. Patrick's work was to make Ireland an important source of Christian missionaries.

A good example was *Columba*, who sailed with 12 companions to the Island of Iona, off the west coast of Scotland. It was from here that Christianity was spread across western Scotland and the English kingdom of Northumbria.

One of the Iona monks, *Aidan*, founded the monastery at Lindisfarne, off the coast of Northumbria, in 635.

St Augustine was sent by the Pope Gregory 1 in 597 to convert the English, but found that there was already an established Christian community. He converted the King of Kent, Ethelbert, who gave him land on which the first cathedral was built at Canterbury. Augustine was the first archbishop of Canterbury.

The Great Schism

This was when the Church split into East and West in 1054. There is more about this in Chapter 14.

The Inquisition

This began in 1233 when Pope Gregory IX ordered the trial and torture of anyone suspected of heresy. It was the job of the Inquisition to do this. Punishment for the guilty ranged from fines and prison to burning at the stake. Heresy means the denial or dissenting from Christian doctrine by someone who is a Christian.

The Reformation

The Reformers, led by Luther and Calvin in the sixteenth century, wanted changes in the Roman Catholic Church. This was rejected, so new Protestant Churches were set up (see Chapter 14).

The Reformation in England

Henry VIII made himself head of the Church in England (see Chapter 14).

The twentieth century

Important developments have been:

(1) the World Council of Churches set up in 1948
(2) the Second Vatican Council 1962 to 1965.

⑦ Christian beliefs

7.1 The Trinity

Christians believe that God shows Himself to humankind in three ways – as

- Father
- Son (Jesus Christ) and
- Holy Spirit.

This is known as the **Trinity**. It does not mean that there are three Gods: Christianity allows that there is only one God.

The Father sent the Son, Jesus, to Earth, and after the Ascension, the Holy Spirit has continued to work for God in human affairs.

7.2 God the Father

- Everything in existence has been created by God.
- God as Father cares for the whole of His creation, especially humankind, which He has made responsible for looking after it.
- God is directly involved in the affairs of the world. In other words, He did not create it with the intent of leaving it to its own devices.
- God loves unconditionally.

7.3 God the Son

- God lived on Earth as Jesus.
- Jesus was the promised Messiah, who would die on the Cross to save humankind from sin, as prophesied in the Old Testament.
- He was fully human and so could feel all the emotions that human beings can.
- He was conceived of the Holy Spirit and born of the **Virgin Mary**.
- After His death on the Cross he rose from the dead three days later as a sign that man can die to sin and live again in eternal life with God.
- God made Him the judge of all people.
- He will return one day in the **Last Judgement** and set up God's Kingdom on Earth.

7.4 God the Holy Spirit

- Jesus promised the disciples that he would always be with them, so when he ascended into Heaven, his Spirit was sent as their guide.
- This happened on the Day of Pentecost.
- The Spirit lives in Christians to bring guidance, strength, courage and inspiration.

7.5 The communion of saints and the forgiveness of sins

The communion of saints is made up of all the saints who, having died and gone to Heaven, are in a position to intercede on behalf of others. Sins are forgiven if people repent and try to change their ways. A saint is someone whose life on earth was exceptionally holy, and is given this status by the Pope. Protestantism does not believe in intercession.

7.6 Heaven

Christians believe that this is where Jesus is 'sitting at the right hand of God'. This is where the righteous will go as their reward when they die.

Some Biblical references to heaven

- Jesus calls it his 'Father's house' (John 14:2)
- 'the heavenly Jerusalem' (Galatians 4:26; Hebrews 12:22; Revelation 3:12)
- the 'Kingdom of Heaven' (Matthew 25:1; James 2:5)
- the 'eternal kingdom' (2 Peter 1:11)
- the 'eternal inheritance' (1 Peter 1:4; Hebrews 9:15)
- the 'better country' (Hebrews 11:14, 16)
- the blessed 'reign with Christ' (2 Timothy 2:11)
- Those who go to heaven have 'life everlasting' and 'an eternal weight of glory' (2 Corinthians 4:17)

7.7 Purgatory

Roman Catholics believe that all baptized souls who have died without repentance for venial sins (those sins which though serious do not destroy the relationship with God); or who have not paid their punishment for sins from which the guilt has been removed, go to purgatory. It is a place for those in receipt of Grace, and who are therefore saved, but who are not yet fit to enter heaven. Protestantism rejects the doctrine of purgatory for the following reasons:

- it is without scriptural foundation
- it retains the idea of punishment after forgiveness
- it implies that the **Satisfaction** of Christ (his death on the Cross to atone for the sins of the world) is insufficient
- it spoils the Gospels' promise of a complete forgiveness of sins.

7.8 Hell

In traditional Christian theology this is the place regarded as the state of utter and irrevocable damnation for the soul after death. There are three words for it in the Bible.

(1) *Sheol* This appears 65 times in the Old Testament. It is the place of disembodied spirits who are the 'congregation of the dead'. It is the abode of the wicked.
(2) *Hades* This is a Greek word found in the New Testament. It is a prison (1 Peter 3:19), with gates and bars and locks (Matthew 16:18; Revelation 1:18). The righteous and the wicked are separated. The blessed dead are in that part of Hades called paradise (Luke 23:43).
(3) *Gehenna* This is the place of the lost (Matthew 23:33). Jesus warns of an 'unquenchable fire of "Gehenna" ' (Mark 9:43–8).

7.9 The Last Judgement

This is the sentence that will be passed on our actions at the last day. The judge is Jesus Christ as mediator; all judgement is committed to him. Those to be judged are:

(1) the whole race of Adam (that is, all humans) without a single exception
(2) the fallen angels.

7.10 Creeds

A creed is:

• a formal statement of religious belief
• a confession of faith and
• an authoritative statement of certain articles considered essential to a religion.

By the end of the second century CE a summary of Christian beliefs had formed; it was called the 'Rule of Faith' and had two purposes:

(1) to preserve true teaching or doctrine
(2) to combat false teaching or heresy.

When the Emperor Constantine became a Christian, the Church was able to expand across the Roman Empire. The Empire had two capitals: Latin-speaking Rome in the West, and Greek-speaking Constantinople in the East. This led to disagreements about belief. From the discussions that followed, two important doctrines or teachings emerged;

• the doctrine of the Trinity – This is belief in God in three persons: Father, Son and Holy Spirit.
• the doctrine of the Person of Christ – This is also known as Christology. It involves the study of Christ's person, qualities and deeds.

Arius and the Arian Heresy

In 318 CE a priest called Arius, whose parish was Alexandria in Egypt, said that:

• only the Father is God
• Jesus is less than God, because he was created by him.

This became known as the Arian Heresy and led to the meeting of a council of bishops in 325 CE at Nicea. It was decided that Father and Son were 'consubstantial', which means both of one substance. By the time this and other decisions had been fully considered it was 381 CE, the official statement being made at the Council of Constantinople.

A later council at Chalcedon in 451 CE summarised the original Nicea decisions and has come down to us as the **Nicene Creed**. The words vary according to which service book is used.

The Nicene Creed established that Jesus is fully God.

The Nicene Creed

I believe in one God, the Father almighty, maker of heaven and earth, and of all things visible and invisible. And in one Lord Jesus Christ, the only-begotten Son of God, begotten of His Father before all worlds, God of God, begotten not made, being of one substance with the Father, by whom all things were made; who for us men and for our salvation came down from heaven, and was incarnate by the Holy Ghost of the Virgin Mary, and was made man, and was crucified also for us under Pontius Pilate. He suffered and was buried, and the third day he rose again according to the scriptures, and ascended into heaven, and sitteth on the right hand of the Father. And he shall come again with glory to judge both the quick (living) and the dead: whose kingdom shall have no end. And I believe in the Holy Ghost, the Lord, the Giver of life, who proceedeth from the Father and the Son, who with the Father and the Son together is worshipped and glorified, who spake by the prophets. And I believe one holy catholic and apostolic Church. I acknowledge one baptism for the remission of sins. And I look for the resurrection of the dead, and the life of the world to come. Amen.

The wording and English style is more modern in the latest service books.

The Athanasian Creed

This appeared in the middle of the fourth century but was rather too long to come into general use. Its opening words are a useful summary of why creeds are important:

Whosoever will be saved: before all things it is necessary that he hold the Catholic Faith. Which Faith except everyone do keep whole and undefiled; without doubt he shall perish everlastingly.

Athanasius, who produced this creed, was the Bishop of Alexandria. He defended the Council of Nicea and attacked the growth of Arianism, preventing an East–West split. This was despite the fact that he was banished five times by leaders who were in favour of Arianism.

Athanasius was convinced that if Jesus were less than God, then he could not be the saviour of humankind. It was largely due to his determination that the agreement of Nicea was confirmed.

The Apostles' Creed

This creed gets its name because it preserves the teaching of the first apostles. The original was a third-century question-and-answer baptism creed. The straight statement form dates from around 400 CE.

The Council of Ephesus (431 CE)

This looked into a number of beliefs:

Sabellius

Sabellius was a third-century teacher who said that God could not be Father, Son and Spirit at the same time. He could only be *one* of these at any given moment. This heresy was dealt with in the Nicene Creed.

Apollinarius

Apollinarius was the Bishop of Laodicea in Syria. He said that:

• Jesus could not have a human soul because of the corrupt nature of humanity;
• instead he had only his divine nature 'enfleshed in a human body'.

Nestorius

Nestorius was a theologian and deacon of Antioch who became Bishop of Constantinople in 428 CE. He believed that:

• Jesus was both God and man;
• these two natures were separate;
• God could never be a new-born baby, so the two natures must have remained separate when he became human in Jesus;
• Mary was the mother of the human Jesus, but not the 'bearer of God'.

Having looked into these beliefs, the Council of Ephesus decided to reaffirm the creed as it was. Nestorius was declared to be a **heretic**. Even so, he had a large following and his ideas continued. Nestorian ideas were challenged by Eutyches, a monk from Constantinople. Another council was called to debate the issues. It met at Chalcedon in 451 CE.

The Council of Chalcedon (451 CE)

400 bishops decided on the wording for the earlier creeds of 325 and 381 (Nicene Creed), plus a new confession which confirmed belief in the union of Jesus's two natures in one person.

Summary of Councils

(1) *The Council of Nicea (325 CE)* – dealt with the Arian Heresy: the ideas of Arius that only the Father was God.

(2) *The Council of Constantinople (381 CE)* – confirmed the Nicea decisions and tackled further heresy.

(3) *The Council of Ephesus (431 CE)* – dealt with Nestorius' ideas that Jesus was God and man but with separate natures; credal statements were confirmed.

(4) *The Council of Chalcedon (451 CE)* – said that Jesus was God and man with two natures which exist without separation. The wording of earlier creeds was finalized.
---

8 The Christian Bible

8.1 Some general points

- The Bible is the first and primary source of authority in Christianity.
- It is a library of history, letters, psalms, poetry and biography.
- The Christian Bible contains the Jewish scripture. Christians call this the Old Testament. It contains 39 books of Jewish scripture. The Old Testament is the root from which Christianity grew.
- The New Testament was added to this. It is the story of the life and teaching of Jesus and the growth of the early Christian Church.

8.2 The New Testament

The New Testament contains the following:

- the four Gospels of Matthew, Mark, Luke and John
- the Acts of The Apostles
- the 13 letters of St Paul
- eight other letters by early Christian leaders
- the Book of the Revelation of John the Divine.

8.3 The Gospels

For Christians, these are the most important part of the Bible. The word 'Gospel' comes from the Old English words for 'good news', which is a translation of the Greek 'evangelion'. This is why the Gospel writers are called **evangelists**; they are spreading the 'good news' about the Messiah.

The Gospels are written documents about the life of Jesus. Each gospel writer selected information and organised it to show Jesus in a particular way. The gospels of Matthew, Mark and Luke are similar, and so are known as the **Synoptic** Gospels (the name comes from 'synopsis', which means a summary or presenting an account from the same point of view).

The Synoptic Gospels were long thought to be based on Mark's Gospel, which was written around 60 CE. However, many scholars are no longer convinced that Mark was written first: a piece of manuscript held in the Bodleian Library has caused a stir, because it includes a fragment of Matthew's gospel and has been dated because of its style as having been written around 40 CE.

8.4 Why the Gospels were written

The Gospels were written by Christians for Christians and for non-Christians: Matthew wanted to convince his fellow Jews that Jesus really was their Messiah. They were written for a theological reason, in that they have information in the form of history and background plus interpretation. The information was handed on orally at first, and the preaching of the Apostles was added to it. The Gospels concentrate mostly on that period of the life of Jesus known as the ministry; that is, the three years leading up to the crucifixion, when he was preaching and performing miracles.

There are five main reasons why the Gospels were written:

(1)   To win converts to Christianity

In the early days there was an oral tradition based on the testimony of the many witnesses to the life of Christ. As long as they lived it was easy to correct any misunderstandings or inaccuracies. Gradually, of course, that generation would die out. Then, in 64 CE, the Emperor began the first major persecution of Christians, in which Peter, Paul and many other important Christians were killed. Clearly, the oral tradition had to be recorded before it was lost or before it became so distorted as to be useless.

(2)   To teach new converts and train new leaders

As the old leaders died or were killed, a new generation would have to take over the leadership. Paul's Letters reveal that Christian communities could lapse into their pre-Christian/un-Christian practice, leading to disagreement and strife. The written Gospels would show the way forward.

(3)   To clarify doctrine

There was a need to correct any misconceptions about points of doctrine. The Gospels could be used to instruct interested Gentiles.

(4)   To meet the need for readings during worship

(5)   To deal with the hostility of the Jews

It was hoped that a written account would help to win over Jews who so far had been unconverted.

8.5 Mark's Gospel

This was probably written between 60 and 70 CE in Rome, where the author heard it direct from St Peter. This would account for its vividness. It is the shortest Gospel and is ascribed to John Mark. It is thought that he wrote for a non-Jewish readership because:

- he takes the trouble to explain Jewish customs.
- words are translated from **Aramaic.**
- the emphasis on the suffering of Jesus and the possibility that his disciples may have to suffer too.

Mark displays five major themes in his writings:

- miracles
- parables
- conflict
- discipleship
- the arrest, trial and death of Jesus.

Mark shows the kind of Messiah that Jesus was. He explains the authority of his teaching and actions, and he reveals that something special happened through his ministry. He shows God at work through Jesus, emphasising the wonderful things done by him and the places he went to.

8.6 Matthew's Gospel

This was probably written around 10 years after Mark's Gospel. Matthew, who was an ex-tax collector and one of the apostles, wrote for his fellow Jews. He shows Jesus as the long-expected Messiah, and sets out to show how he fulfilled the Old Testament prophecies concerning the Messiah. So this Gospel more than any other is the link between the Old and New Testaments. The Jews expected a political leader to free them from the Romans, so Matthew emphasises that Jesus said that his was the Kingdom of Heaven.

Matthew collects Jesus' teaching in five sections which alternate with sections of the narrative. Jesus is portrayed as a second Moses, giving God's new law, just as Moses had given the old law. The old Israel is succeeded by the New Israel, which is the Church. There is a lot of teaching about the Kingdom of Heaven (God).

Episodes found only in Matthew

Parables
- The wheat and the tares 13:24–30
- Hidden treasure 13:44
- The pearl 13:45, 46
- The net 13:47–50
- The hard-hearted servant 18:23–35
- The vineyard workers 20:1–16
- The two sons 21:28–32
- The marriage of the king's son 22:1–14
- The wise and foolish virgins 25:1–13
- The talents 25:14–30
- The sheep and goats 25:31–46

Miracles
- The two blind men
- The possessed dumb man
- The coin in the fish's mouth

Incidents
- Joseph's dream
- The visit of the wise men

- The escape to Egypt
- Herod's massacre
- Pilate's wife's dream
- The death of Judas
- The saints resurrected in Jerusalem
- The bribing of the guard
- The great commission

8.7 Luke's Gospel

This is the fullest life story of Jesus, and was written around 85 CE. It is the first part of a two-part history of Christian beginnings: the second part is the Acts of the Apostles. Both parts are dedicated to the Roman, Theophilus.

Luke's Gospel shows the Gospel message as there for all people: sinners, the poor, and outcasts. As a biographer, Luke shows us Jesus the man, the Saviour whose coming is a world event.

The Gospel does not tell us the author's name, but the evidence suggests that it is Luke the doctor, Paul's companion on his missionary journey. He writes for non-Jews but is equally familiar with Greek and Jewish backgrounds. Archaeology also shows him to be an accurate historian. Luke's Gospel is put together from reliable first-hand sources. Luke knew Mark and worked with him – Mark's Gospel is one of his sources. Luke gives stories concerning women more emphasis in his account than Matthew and Mark did.

Luke's guidelines for those who would follow Jesus

(1) Be willing to 'take up his cross' day after day (9:23–7).
(2) Be the servant of all (9:46–8).
(3) Accept the possibility of homelessness: 'the Son of Man has nowhere to lay His head' (9:58).
(4) Put even family considerations second; as when Jesus told a man who wanted to bury his father to 'Leave the dead to bury their dead' (9:59–60).
(5) Do not be distracted by your family: a man wanted to say goodbye to his family and might have been persuaded to change his mind. Jesus said, 'No-one who sets his hand to the plough and then keeps on looking back to fit for the Kingdom of God' (9:61–2).
(6) Make known the message of God and He will judge those who reject it (10:1–24).
(7) To get eternal life 'Love the Lord your God with all your heart, with all your soul, with all your strength, and with all your mind; and your neighbour as yourself' (10:25–8).
(8) Be like the Good Samaritan (10:29–37).
(9) Do not be distracted from the Word of the Lord by everyday routine; this is shown in the story of Mary listening to Jesus while Martha rushed around the home doing her work (10:38–42).
(10) Be willing to give all if necessary (14:25–33).
(11) Forgive up to seven times seven (17:1–4)

(12) Sell everything to give to the poor 'and you will have riches in Heaven' (18:18–30).

(13) Give as willingly as Zacchaeus did (19:1–10).

8.8 John's Gospel

This was the last Gospel to be written, probably around 90 CE. It is very different from the others: it assumes that readers already know the facts of Jesus's life. It adds to the other accounts.

The emphasis is on interpreting and showing the meaning of what took place. John selects signs from Jesus's many miracles to show who he was. There are no parables in John. Most recorded events occur in and around Jerusalem. The main theme of this Gospel is Jesus as Messiah and Son of God.

John may have been Jesus' cousin (his mother Salome being the sister of Mary), or he may have been the brother of James, who with Peter made up the inner circle of three who were the leaders of the disciples. These were the three who were allowed to see the transfigured Christ. Jesus committed His mother to John's care as they stood at the foot of the Cross.

8.9 The main differences between John and the synoptic gospels

(1) The setting of Jesus's ministry

- John has Jerusalem rather than Galilee as the focus of the ministry.
- He records the early ministry in Judaea which preceded that of Galilee.
- The earlier Gospels only cover the last week of Jesus' ministry in Jerusalem.
- John recounts a three-year ministry, not a one-year ministry.
- His style and language differ greatly from the synoptics.

(2) John makes notable omissions from the story

He does not include:

- the birth narratives
- the temptation
- the transfiguration
- the mission of the twelve
- the institution of the Last Supper
- the prayer in the Garden of Gethsemane.

Also:

- Parables in the earlier Gospels are largely missing from John.

(3) The dating of Jesus' death

The Synoptics identify the Last Supper with the Passover meal, whereas John puts it before the Passover. So, the Crucifixion took place before the Passover meal, not after it.

(4) The character of the Gospel is different

Jesus's teaching and the miracles are linked

- The miracles are 'signs' through which the glory of Christ is seen and faith deepened.
- These signs are often the occasion of Jesus' teaching: for example, after the feeding of the 5000, he gives his teaching on the Bread of Life.

New concepts

- John brings in new concepts such as 'life', 'light', 'truth', and 'rebirth'.
- He uses contrasts such as truth and falsehood and light and darkness.
- There are important phrases used by Jesus to describe himself: 'light of the world', 'the good shepherd', 'I am the way, the truth, and the life'.

John's Gospel is more than history

- It reveals salvation from God.
- Jesus is the way to the Father because he has come from him.
- He announces that he is the revelation of God.

8.10 The Acts of the Apostles

This covers the 30 or so years from the birth of the Church at Pentecost to the end of Paul's imprisonment in Rome. It tells the story of the spread of Christianity westward through the Roman Empire. The 'Acts' described are mainly the work of saints Peter and Paul.

The book was probably written by Paul's 'dear friend Luke, the doctor'. He wrote the third Gospel, and Acts is its sequel. Luke is the only non-Jewish New Testament writer. He was present at many of the events he describes. This can be seen from the way he changes from 'they' to 'we' in Acts 16: 10; 20: 5 and 27: 1. He was with Paul at Philippi and went with him to Jerusalem. They spent two years together in Caesarea and went to Rome, sharing the experience of the shipwreck.

Acts was written at the end of Paul's two-year imprisonment in Rome in the early to mid-sixties. It was written to give the Roman, Theophilus, the facts about Christianity.

8.11 Paul's Letters

There are 13 letters, which make up a third of the length of the New Testament. They tell us what the apostles taught. They are a mixture of religious teaching and instructions on life and behaviour. The letters also tell us about the problems of the early Church and Paul's advice on how to solve them.

There are four groups:

(1) 1 and 2 Thessalonians are concerned about the return of Christ.
(2) Romans, Galatians and 1 and 2 Corinthians emphasise the gospel preached by Paul.

(3)   The 'captivity letters', which contain some of his best teaching. In all of them he mentions that he is a prisoner. They are Ephesians, Colossians, Philippians and Philemon.

(4)   The 'Pastoral Letters', 1 and 2 Timothy and Titus, deal with Church leadership and organisation.

8.12   The other Letters

These are:

- an anonymous letter (Hebrews)
- one by James
- two by Peter
- three by John
- one by Jude.

These letters are often grouped under the title of 'General Epistles' (the word **'epistle'** comes from a Greek word meaning something sent, a message). Except for Hebrews, which stands alone, they are addressed to a readership which is more general than Paul's. 2 and 3 John are for a specific person or Church.

8.13   The teaching of the Letters

God

- God is the pattern for Christian behaviour because he is a holy God who expects holiness.
- God is Father.
- He is the Creator and author of the new creation.
- The sending of Christ into this world has brought about the cosmic **reconciliation** of the world to God.

Jesus Christ

The letters reflect the fact that the early Christians explained their view of Christ in different ways.

- The title 'Jesus Christ' is used when showing Jesus as the Jewish Messiah. The use of 'Lord Jesus Christ' is used to acknowledge his sovereignty.
- Paul's letters show the nature of Christ:

  — he existed before the world was made;
  — he became poor for our sakes (2 Corinthians 8:9);
  — although equal with God, he humbled himself to be a man (Philippians 2:5–11);
  — he is the exact 'image' of God (Colossians 1:15).

- Hebrews 1 says that he is fully God.
- Hebrews 2 says that he is a man as well; this allows him to be the high priest of his people before God.
- Peter and John continue this theme.

- Through the Son the Father delivers salvation.
- Jesus Christ is the supreme expression of God's love.

The salvation of man

For Paul, the only answer to this corrupt and evil world is the new age ushered in by Jesus. The main theme of the Letters is the salvation, eternal life and the new creation. The old pagan ways cannot exist side by side with life in Christ because he demands a new morality by God's law. This must be lived in Church life and Christian community, and out in the wider world.

9 # Festivals and pilgrimage

9.1 The Church Year or Christian Calendar

The Church Year revolves around events in the life of Jesus.

In each week, Sunday is observed as a holy day. Other festivals and celebrations can be observed; saints' days and harvest festival are good examples. The observance of the Christian Year is simply a matter of either Church regulation or custom. It is not a matter of divine revelation – indeed, some sects regard festivals as sinful or at best irrelevant.

In the year there are three cycles:

(1) the Christmas Cycle, centred on Jesus' birth
(2) the Easter Cycle, based on his death and resurrection
(3) The cycle of saints' days commemorating notable followers of Jesus.

> The Christmas cycle starts with Advent.

9.2 Advent

Advent starts on the fourth Sunday before Christmas Day.

- The Christian Year begins with the First Sunday in Advent.
- Advent means the drawing near or coming of Christ.
- Christians remember Jesus' promise that he will come again in glory to judge the world.
- In many churches an Advent candle is lit. Another candle is lit on each following Sunday. The candles are a symbol to light the way for the Christ child. European Reformed Churches have the custom of the 'Advent Crown', which has four candles, one to be lit on each of the four Sundays.
- Children have Advent calendars to mark the days till Christmas.
- There are special hymns and readings in church. Sermons relate to the Advent theme.
- Christians examine their lives in preparation for the second coming of Christ, who warned that he would return unexpectedly 'like a thief in the night'.
- Some may fast during Advent.

Advent probably began in Gaul in the sixth century CE. Its length used to vary; one calendar began it six Sundays before Christmas.

The present practice of four Sundays dates from the time of Pope Gregory, who died in 604 CE. The Old Testament readings of Advent foretell the coming of the Messiah. The hymns and carols such as 'O Come, O Come Emmanuel', and 'On Jordan's Bank' reflect the message of the season.

9.3 Christmas

This is on 25 December in most Churches and is the most celebrated Christian festival. Some Churches, for example the Armenian Church, celebrate on 7 January.

- Churches are decorated with symbols of the story of the birth of Jesus (the crib and holy family, the star of Bethlehem, wise men, shepherds and angels).
- Special services are held (Christmas Eve and Christmas Day).
- Carols are sung and nativity plays performed.
- Lessons in church focus on the birth of Jesus and its meaning.
- Presents, cards and greetings are exchanged, and families and friends gather for merry-making.
- Homes and public places are decorated.
- The Christmas message is 'Peace on Earth and good will to all men'.

Christmas is widely celebrated in the secular as well as the religious fashion. The name derives from 'Christ's Mass' (Eucharist or communion).

The Romans had a festival of the sun on 25 December and Saturnalia on 17 December, and the Anglo-Saxons had a winter festival at about this time, when the god Woden was celebrated. They and the other Germanic peoples have given us the yule log, mistletoe, and holly. Mistletoe was also important in Celtic pre-Christian religion.

These were times for feasting and enjoyment. Many customs derive from the mid-winter solstice (21/22 December). The Christmas tree may derive from the Tree of Paradise in mystery plays and is also associated with the evergreen of Germanic custom. The custom of bringing trees indoors and decorating them was probably brought to Britain from Germany by Prince Albert, the husband of Queen Victoria.

Festivities continue because Christians believe that the birth of Jesus is the gift of the only son of God to mankind to save sinners.

Carols are a mixture of religious and secular music. At one time they were songs for dancing, hence the jauntiness of some of them.

The idea of Father Christmas or Santa Claus derives from the medieval feast day of St Nicholas of Myra, held on 6 December. In legend he dealt out rewards or punishments to children. This is perpetuated in the much-loved Christmas myth of Father Christmas bringing presents on a flying sledge pulled by reindeer.

The Christmas Day feast of roast turkey used to be a goose and before that swan was eaten in wealthy households. Britain has the custom of a Christmas pudding with coins hidden in it.

9.4 The Feast of the Holy Innocents

This festival is celebrated on 28 December and is in remembrance of the slaughter of all the boys in Bethlehem under the age of two because of Herod's fear that the birth of Jesus had produced a rival who would replace him. Its purpose is to remind Christians that the innocent suffer for the sins of men. It also show that there is much unfairness in the distribution of pain and happiness in this life, and that Christians have to trust God to make sense of it all.

9.5 Epiphany

This occurs on 6 January. 'Epiphany' means 'manifestation' (seen/obvious/apparent). In the fourth century CE it appeared in the Eastern Churches to commemorate three 'manifestations':

- Jesus' birth
- his baptism
- his first miracle at Cana.

Earlier than this it had meant the manifestation of Jesus as the Son of God at his baptism. When 25 December was adopted as the date to celebrate his birth, Epiphany came to commemorate the adoration of the magi or the 'manifestation of Christ to the Gentiles'. The twelve days of Christmas are the interval between Christmas and Epiphany. Celebrations may have processions centred around the magi or kings who brought gold, frankincense and myrrh to the Christ child. The visit from these Gentiles is seen as a sign that from his birth Jesus was Saviour and the Light of the World.

The Easter cycle

This celebrates the crucifixion and resurrection of Jesus Christ. He was crucified during the Feast of the Passover, on the day before the Jewish sabbath. The crucifixion is remembered on a Friday (Good Friday) and the resurrection on a Sunday (Easter Sunday) – the actual days of the week when these events happened. The first followers of Christ were Jews, so they added this new festival to the old one which takes place at the full moon of the first month of Spring. This is the reason why Easter does not have a fixed date. There is a period of preparation called Lent, which lasts for 40 days.

9.6 Shrove Tuesday

This occurs in February or March, and is the day before Lent begins.

- The name comes from the Middle English 'shriven', which comes from the practice of going to **confession** for **absolution** and penance before the start of Lent.
- The custom of eating pancakes arose because of the need to get rid of the fat in the home before the fast of Lent. The French name for Shrove Tuesday is **Mardi gras**, which means 'Fat Tuesday'. Mardi Gras, the New Orleans carnival, gets its name from this.

9.7 Lent

- 'Lent' is an Old English word for the season of Spring.
- This is the season of penitence and preparation for Easter.

- It lasts for 40 days, starting on Ash Wednesday, which may occur in February or March. The Eastern Orthodox Church calls it the 'Great Fast'.
- It was originally a period of instruction for baptism candidates; the baptism took place at Easter.
- Traditionally Christians give up meat and rich food, although now, other things may be substituted instead.

9.8 Ash Wednesday

Ash Wednesday is the Wednesday in the seventh week before Easter, so it may be celebrated in February or March.

- It gets its name from the custom of a priest making the sign of the Cross with ash on the foreheads of Christians during the Ash Wednesday service.
- Palm Crosses from the previous year may be burnt to provide this ash.
- This is a sign of penitence and a sign that Christians are no more than ashes before God, and are dependent on his grace.
- At one time people wore sackcloth as a sign of penance.

9.9 Mothering Sunday

- This is the fourth Sunday of Lent.
- It was once called 'Refreshment Sunday' because Christians would visit the 'mother' church (possibly a cathedral) for spiritual refreshment.
- The Lenten fast is suspended and, traditionally, simnel cakes are eaten.
- Modern practice has added the title 'Mothers' Day'.

9.10 Holy Week

This is the last week of Lent. It remembers Jesus' **Passion** – that is, his suffering and Crucifixion – so it is also known as Passiontide. Christians follow Jesus' progress from his entry into Jerusalem until his burial. A narrative of this is read each day in church and is taken from all four Gospels until they are read in full. This can be read by a narrator with others speaking the words of Jesus or others who were there, and there will be special choir presentations. These are the most important events in Christianity.

9.11 Palm Sunday

This is the celebration of Jesus riding into Jerusalem. It marks the start of Holy Week.

- Anglicans and Catholics sometimes also call it 'Passion Sunday'.
- Palm crosses are given out to remember that the crowd waved palm branches as Jesus entered the city.
- There are special readings and hymns in church.

9.12 Spy Wednesday

This remembers the betrayal of Christ by Judas Iscariot.

9.13 Maundy Thursday

This festival commemorates the celebration of the Last Supper by Jesus and His disciples.

- Maundy means 'command' or 'commandment' (from the Latin 'mandatum') remembering the command of Jesus to do 'this in rememberance of me'. This includes taking communion and feet washing.
- He also commanded that they love one another, so Christians give gifts of charity. The most famous symbol of this in Britain is the distribution of Maundy money by the Queen.
- Altars are stripped of their decoration.

9.14 Good Friday

This remembers Jesus' crucifixion.

- It is called 'Good' or 'God's' because Christians believe that out of Jesus' death came the redemption of mankind and the conquest of sin.
- Services may last up to three hours, ending at three o'clock, the time when Jesus died on the Cross.
- There are no decorations in church.
- There may be processions to remember the 'stations of the Cross' which are all the stages leading up to the crucifixion.
- Catholic churches have a service of 'Venerating the Cross' where the priest and congregation bow and kiss the Cross.
- Traditionally, hot cross buns are eaten to break the Lenten fast.
- Some churches have the Mass of the Presanctified, so called because there is no consecration of bread and wine. Instead, communion is given from the reserved sacrament, which is consecrated bread kept from a previous Mass. It will have been kept on a special altar surrounded by flowers and watched over all through the Thursday night by devoted Christians who are responding to Jesus' plea to the disciples in the Garden of Gethsemane: 'Could you not watch with me one hour?'.
- An example of local customs springing up is the 'procession of the penitents' in Seville. Those involved are hooded so that they cannot be recognised and so cannot have personal applause. This keeps the focus on Christ.
- Some other places have pilgrimages, during which a replica of the Cross is carried.

9.15 Holy Saturday

Ceremonies do not take place until the late evening.

In Romanian Orthodox churches, Christians remember that Jesus was in his tomb at this time by putting an icon of the dead Jesus flat on a table. Sometimes it will be a coffin. They then pass under the table from one side to the other to show the wish to die with Jesus and rise again through his death to a new life free from sin.

Roman Catholic and some Anglican churches also keep a vigil. Before midnight the people leave the church and the lights are put out. Then, at midnight, the **Paschal** candle is lit and carried into the dark building, whose opening doors are symbolic of the rolling away of the stone at the entrance of Jesus' tomb. The candle is the light of the Resurrection overcoming the darkness of death. Then, the Paschal candle is passed from person to person to symbolise that Jesus, Light of the world, has risen from the dead.

9.16 Easter Day

Easter Day celebrates the Resurrection. It is the most important festival in the Christian calendar, and is celebrated in March or April.

* Easter is observed on the first Sunday following the first new moon after the vernal equinox (21 March).
* The celebration of Easter lasts for 50 days, until Pentecost.
* Easter gets its name from the Old English 'easter' or 'eostre', meaning a festival of spring. Churches are decorated with flowers to symbolise Spring and new life.
* Traditionally, eggs are eaten as a symbol of new life. This is the origin of the custom of giving chocolate eggs.
* Some churches have a service at sunrise to celebrate the Resurrection.
* Roman Catholics have the Easter Duty, by which they must receive the sacraments of reconciliation and Eucharist.
* The Orthodox Churches begin Easter at midnight on Holy Saturday, when a light is passed round in the form of candles and lamps in the darkened church. The body of Jesus is looked for in an empty tomb with the cry of 'Christ is risen!' and the response 'He is risen indeed!' This custom has been adopted by some of the African Churches.

9.17 Ascension

Ascension always falls on a Thursday on the fortieth day after Easter. This is usually in May, but may be on 30 April or in the first few days in June in some years. It celebrates the return of Jesus to his Father after spending the 40 days following the resurrection appearing to His followers. They were told to wait in Jerusalem for the Holy Spirit's power to come to them (Pentecost).

9.18 Pentecost

This is celebrated on the seventh Sunday after Easter, which will occur in May or June. It celebrates the gift of the Holy Spirit to Jesus' disciples and the start of the Church and its mission.

* It became a popular time for the baptism of converts, who wore white robes to symbolise new life. These robes gave the festival the name of *White Sunday* or *Whitsunday*.
* Pentecost derives from the Greek 'pentecoste' (fiftieth day).

- Popular customs connected with Pentecost still exist in a number of places. For instance, in the North of England, the Whit Walk and Derbyshire has the translation of Well Dressing (when the well is decorated with flowers), although these are probably pre-Christian in origin.
- There are processions and Sunday services have hymns on the theme of the Holy Spirit.
- Clergy wear red vestments to symbolise the flames of fire in which the Spirit descended to the disciples.

9.19 Trinity Sunday

This is the Sunday after Pentecost, so it occurs in May or June. It is the culminating Sunday of the Christian year. It celebrates the glory of God as Father, Son and Holy Spirit and is one of the days set aside for the ordination of priests in the Western Church. The Orthodox Church celebrates the Festival of All Saints on this Sunday.

9.20 Corpus Christi

This is a Latin name which means 'the body of Christ'. It is the Thursday after Trinity Sunday and is kept by the Roman Catholic Church as a day of thanksgiving for Holy Communion. The principal celebration revolves around processions in which the consecrated bread is carried through the town in a monstrance, which is a silver vessel with a small glass container in its centre so that the host (bread) can be seen. Some Anglican churches also celebrate this festival.

9.21 The Sacred Heart of Jesus

This is on the Friday of the third week after Pentecost, falling in June or July. It is a feast of the Roman Catholic Church. The symbol of Jesus's heart is used to show his love for mankind. Pictures of Jesus with a superimposed heart are widespread in Catholic homes and schools.

9.22 The Transfiguration (6 August)

This remembers the time when the resurrected Christ was seen transfigured (changed in appearance) and talking to Moses and Elijah.

9.23 Feasts of the Blessed Virgin Mary

There are six of these:

(1)   the Nativity of the Blessed Virgin Mary (8 September)
(2)   the Immaculate Conception of the Blessed Virgin Mary (8 December)

(3)   the Annunciation of the Lord (25 March)
(4)   the Visitation of the Blessed Virgin Mary (31 May)
(5)   the Assumption of the Blessed Virgin Mary (15 August)
(6)   the Solemnity of Mary, Mother of God (1 January).

9.24   Saints' Days

The origin of these commemorations lies in the days of persecution faced by Christians before Constantine became Roman emperor. At first there were simple memorials to the martyrs. These churches were built over the tombs of martyrs and the anniversary of martyrdom was kept as a special day.

Some of the principal saints' days

- St Joseph of Nazareth (19 March)
- The Birth of John the Baptist (24 June)
- St Peter and St Paul (29 June)
- All Saints (1 November) (Originally All Martyrs)
- The Conversion of St Paul (25 January)
- St Barnabas (11 June)
- St Stephen (26 December) – he was the first martyr
- St Mary Magdalene (22 July)

The four evangelists have their own days, as do the 12 apostles.

9.25   St Michael and All Angels

This is on 29 September. Catholics celebrate saints Michael, Gabriel and Raphael in their calendar. The Orthodox Church celebrates angels on 8 November.

9.26   Pilgrimage

This is not compulsory in Christianity and many Christians never even contemplate pilgrimage. However, many do go to holy places and return spiritually refreshed and with their faith strengthened. Christianity often uses the imagery of pilgrimage to describe life's journey; the inner pilgrimage of the soul in the quest to find and to know God.

From the earliest times people have undertaken pilgrimages to the places associated with Jesus and the saints. Pilgrimages were very popular in the Middle Ages and people would make a vow to go on a pilgrimage if their prayers were answered or to make amends for some misdeed they had committed.

Apart from the obvious attraction of the Holy Land or Israel as it is today, there were hundreds of minor places that attracted pilgrims because of miracles or healings that had happened there.

Some of the best-known places to visit

- the Holy Land – especially Bethlehem, Jerusalem and Nazareth
- Rome – especially St Peter's Church
- Canterbury and the tomb of Thomas à Becket
- Lourdes, where St Bernadette had visions of the Virgin Mary; this site is noted for its spring which is associated with healing by its holy water
- Walsingham in Norfolk
- Lindisfarne and Iona, which have been monastic sites since the early days of Christianity in Britain
- the tomb of St Cuthbert in Durham
- Downpatrick in Ireland, the traditional site of St Patrick's tomb
- St David's in Wales, the site of St David's tomb
- Santiago de Compostela in Spain, for the tomb of St James

The denominations of the Christian Church

10.1 Introduction

The Church in Rome became important because it had begun in the capital of the Roman Empire. By the third century CE there were 40 000 Christians there, and it had become wealthy, owning much property.

The Great Schism

The five main churches of the Empire were Rome, Alexandria, Antioch, Jerusalem and Constantinople, and the leaders of these churches were called **patriarchs.** Problems arose because they disagreed about matters of faith and the government of the Church.

This led to meeting of the first world-wide or ecumenical council at Nicaea in 325 CE. The differences were not settled, but the Nicene creed was produced. Further councils were called to settle outstanding issues, but the row came to a head when the patriarch of Constantinople condemned the *filioque* clause of the Nicene Creed, which means literally 'and the Son'.

Simply, the Church in the West says that 'the spirit proceeds from the Father (God) and the Son (Jesus)'. The Eastern Church claims that 'The Spirit proceeds from the Father' and did not want the *filioque* clause (the 'and the Son' part).

So in 1054 the Church split between East and West.

10.2 The Roman Catholic tradition

- Roughly six out of ten Christians are Roman Catholics.
- Their leader is the Pope, or Bishop of Rome.
- St Peter was the first Bishop of Rome. Jesus gave him the 'keys of the Kingdom of God'. Most Catholic beliefs go back to Peter.
- These beliefs have been handed on to each new Pope by the 'laying on of hands'. This is called the Apostolic Succession.
- The Pope has the power to proclaim new doctrines when he speaks '*ex cathedra*' (literally 'from the throne').
- He is regarded as infallible because Catholics believe that he is speaking with God's authority.

- There is a hierarchy with authority vested in the bishops. Countries are divided into dioceses, each being headed by a bishop. The figurehead in each country is a cardinal.
- There is a strict code of law called canon law. It covers all Church matters, and there are canon lawyers to interpret it.
- Priests cannot marry.

The Second Vatican Council

The First Council took place in 1870 and involved all the cardinals and bishops of the Church. Pope John XXIII called the Second (1962–5) and the following were decided.

(1) The importance of prayer, worship and sacraments in the life of the Church can never be replaced. (Note that there are seven sacraments in Catholicism: baptism, the Mass [holy communion], confirmation, marriage, penance, ordination as a priest, and anointing the sick with oil.)

(2) The Mass should be said in the language of the congregation (the vernacular) instead of Latin, and there should be new prayers and music.

(3) Worshippers should be encouraged to play a part in services.

(4) Cardinals, bishops, priests and ordinary members of the Church (the laity) should have a part in running the Church.

(5) New links should be established with other Christian denominations, non-Christian religions and those with no religion at all.

(6) There should be a rethink on issues such as abortion, birth control, and euthanasia (there was no change here).

10.3   The Orthodox tradition

The main facts

- In 1054 the Eastern Orthodox Church split from Rome because the pope's representative went to Constantinople and excommunicated the patriarch (the leader of the Church there), who promptly excommunicated the Pope in revenge.
- The two areas had grown apart, especially on matters of authority. The Pope regarded himself as supreme, and the eastern bishops regarded all bishops as equal.
- Other areas of dispute included the wording of the creed (the Eastern Church used Greek, the West used Latin, thus causing difficulties of interpretation), the use of different types of bread (the East used ordinary bread; the West used unleavened bread). Also, the status of priests was in dispute (the East allowed married men to become priests).
- There are 75 million members of this Church and 300 bishops.
- The leaders are called patriarchs, with one for each country; the Patriarch of Constantinople being the senior one.
- Its main area is in Eastern European countries such as Russia and Bulgaria, and in the Mediterranean countries of Greece, Cyprus and Turkey.
- Britain has approximately 4000 members of the Orthodox church.

Marriage and the priesthood

Bishops are not married and have been a priest first. A man must be 30 before he becomes a priest and cannot be married afterwards, although he can marry before. Married priests cannot become bishops. If a married priest's wife dies, he cannot marry again unless he abandons his vows and gives up the priesthood.

10.4   Protestantism

Luther

Protestantism gets its name from the protest against the beliefs and practices of the Roman Catholic Church.

In 1517 CE Martin Luther put forward 95 theses or points of protest for discussion about corruption in the Church, in particular the sale of 'indulgences'. An indulgence was given by doing penance to gain the forgiveness of sin. The problem arose when Christians were allowed to buy them to cut out the need for penance. Luther was a German monk (1483–1546 CE).

Some people wished to avoid penance because it involved fasting, wearing sack-cloth and going on pilgrimages. Luther said that forgiveness and salvation or 'justification' came through faith and prayer as St Paul had said in his letter to the Romans. He also said that the Bible, being the Word of God (which is infallible), was the only source of authority for Christians; not the Church.

He refused to stop saying this, so he was excommunicated by the Pope. This meant that he was no longer a member of the Church. Many people liked his ideas though, and by the time of his death in 1546, North Germany, Denmark and Sweden had developed a form of Christianity called Lutheranism.

Calvin and Knox

Jean Calvin in Switzerland and John Knox in Scotland took up Luther's ideas about the Bible's authority. The Scottish Church became known as **Presbyterian**, because the ministers in Calvinist churches are called presbyters. Presbyters were originally Elders or Senior figures in the Church.

These Protestant Churches were far removed from the Roman Church, having no images and subordinating tradition to the authority of the Bible.

10.5   The Church of England or Anglican Church

This was formed because Henry VIII (1509–47) wanted to divorce Catherine of Aragon so that he could marry Anne Boleyn. This divorce was not allowed by the Pope, so Henry made himself head of the Church in England (by the Act of Supremacy of 1534). Thomas Cranmer prepared for the Church of England the Book of Common Prayer, which included material from the European reformers.

This process was taken much further under Edward VI (1547–53), and although Mary I (1553–8) tried to make England a Catholic country again, it was too late. Elizabeth I (1558–1603) made herself head of Church as well as state with a policy of uniformity which meant that people not attending the Church of England were fined. She took the title 'Supreme Governor of the Church of England'.

Some important points

- The Church of England is not just an English Church and can be found in every continent.
- The 'mother' church is Canterbury Cathedral.
- The Archbishop of Canterbury is unofficial leader.
- It is the 'established' or official Church of England.
- The sovereign must belong to the Church because she or he is head of the Church and must swear an oath to protect it at the coronation ceremony. The monarch is crowned by the Archbishop of Canterbury.
- Anglican bishops and archbishops can sit in the House of Lords; other Churches cannot do this.
- The Church is governed according to the 39 Articles of the Church of England.
- Priests can marry.

There are four main beliefs that Anglicans should hold:

(1) The Scriptures contain all things necessary for salvation.
(2) The creeds contain all that Anglicans should believe.
(3) The two sacraments of baptism and Holy Communion should be celebrated using the words of Jesus (as written in the Bible).
(4) Bishops lead the Church, but their line cannot be traced back through Peter to Jesus Christ.

10.6 The Nonconformist or Free Churches

These began because many people thought that the Church of England did not go far enough in its move away from the Catholic Church. They wanted a 'pure' Church and so were called 'Puritans'. They were called free or nonconformists because they were (and are) Protestants who did not conform to the established church or Church of England.

Nonconformists believe that:

- the state has no right to interfere in church matters
- the Church must be free to organise its own worship
- the authority of the Church is in the church, not in the government
- lay people should take the services in church
- a council of lay people makes decisions and policy.

The main Nonconformist or Free Churches are as follows.

The Presbyterians

Presbyterians follow the form of church government laid down by Calvin, the Swiss Protestant Reformer.

The Church is governed by Christ and a hierarchy of church courts. The authority of the Bible is paramount. The importance of the local congregation is emphasised. Worship is centred on Bible readings, a sermon on the reading, hymns and spoken prayers by the minister.

The Congregationalists

The Congregationalists formed a congregation with their own elected leaders. They believe that Church and state must be separate. They believe that each congregation is governed by Christ's Spirit, because where Christ is, there is the Church.

The United Reform Church

This was formed in 1972 when the Congregationalists and the Presbyterian Church of England joined together.

The Baptist Church

Baptists believe that only when a person is old enough to make a conscious commitment to Christ should they be baptised. The Church is governed by the Holy Spirit. This church emerged in the seventeenth century, and has 40 million members worldwide today.

The Quakers (Society of Friends)

This group was founded by George Fox in the seventeenth century. He wanted a return to the faith and simple lifestyle of the early Christians.

The name 'Society of Friends' arose because Fox wanted his followers to be Friends of Christ and of each other. The name 'Quakers' comes from the judge who was trying Fox in 1650 and was told by Fox to 'tremble [quake] at the voice of the Lord'. Quakers believe that religion means to follow personal conviction. The Holy Spirit is the sole inspirer of faith and operates freely without any church structure. They are total pacifists.

The Methodists

Methodism was founded in the eighteenth century by John Wesley, who was a Church of England clergyman. The name comes from Wesley's days as an Oxford student, where small groups called the Holy Club were very methodical in their daily devotions and Bible study. The present Methodist church was formed in the twentieth century from the Primitive Methodists, Bible Christians and Wesleyan denominations.

The Salvation Army

This was founded in 1865 by William Booth, a former Methodist, to take the Gospel to the poor in a healing and helping ministry (it was called the Christian Mission at that time; the name Salvation Army was adopted in 1878). It is organised on military lines. Today it holds outdoor meetings for worship, provides food and shelter for the needy, helps ex-prisoners, searches for missing persons and carries out a wide range of other forms of social work.

The Pentecostal Churches

These appeared in the twentieth century, mainly from the USA. They preach the gospel 'through the fire of the Spirit'. They have grown in popularity in Britain during the last few decades.

The House Churches

In recent years some Christians have rejected the traditional denominational churches. At first they started worshipping in each others' homes, but as numbers have grown, schools, halls and other places have been rented. Most are **charismatic**, emphasising the gifts of the Holy Spirit, and displaying a more free, uninhibited approach to worship.

10.7 The World Church

The Ecumenical Movement

This is a movement which seeks the unity of the various churches. Church leaders meet from time to time to find shared beliefs and use them as a foundation to look for further unity. There are shared services, and in remote areas, shared churches, plus joint church schools.

The World Council of Churches

This was formed at Amsterdam in 1948 when 146 different Protestant Churches formed a council. Many others have joined since. The modern HQ is in Switzerland. It has five main divisions:

(1) Faith and Order
(2) Dialogue with people of living faith
(3) World mission and evangelism
(4) Theological education
(5) Church and society.

The Roman Catholic and Eastern Orthodox Churches are not members but they send observers and co-operate wherever possible.

The British Council of Churches

This is formed by the Church of England and the Free Churches to deal with those aspects of church affairs where co-operation is possible. Non-members send observers to the meetings. Also, different churches worship together and share charitable and other social work.

Other United Churches
The Church of South India

This was formed in 1947 by the union of the Anglican South Indian dioceses, the Presbyterian and Congregational churches and the Methodists.

The Church of North India

This dates from 1970 and is made up of the Anglicans, Baptists, Congregationalists, Methodists and Presbyterians.

Places of worship

11.1 Introduction

The Christian place of worship is a church or chapel.

Every diocese of the Anglican and Catholic Church has a cathedral church, usually shortened to cathedral. Cathedrals are large and are the focus of all diocesan services. They are the headquarters of the bishop of the diocese.

Most Anglican parish churches as found in villages and towns were built before the Reformation to a standard pattern.

Chapels are smaller and simpler in design, and are preferred by Nonconformist Christians.

A diocese is an area controlled by a bishop.

A parish is an administrative sub-division of a diocese and has its own church.

11.2 Anglican churches

Most of these were mostly built before the Reformation and are either rectangular or cross-shaped (Figure 11.1). There is a door at one side and a belfry, bell tower or spire, at the end of the nave at the opposite end to the altar. There may be paintings on the walls, put there in earlier times to teach the life of Jesus and other Bible stories because many people were illiterate. Stained glass windows were once put in for the same purpose, but were later decorative or symbolic. It was also common for wealthy people to pay for a stained glass window as a memorial to themselves, their family or a long-serving clergyman.

The main parts of the church

The nave

This is the central part of the church where the congregation sits. It used to be compared to a ship (Latin *navis* means ship), the congregation being on the journey of life with the clergy as the sailors of the ship.

The Chancel

This is raised above the floor level of the nave, and is made up of the *sanctuary* at the end, and the *choir*.

Figure 11.1 A traditional medieval-style church, now used for twentieth-century worship

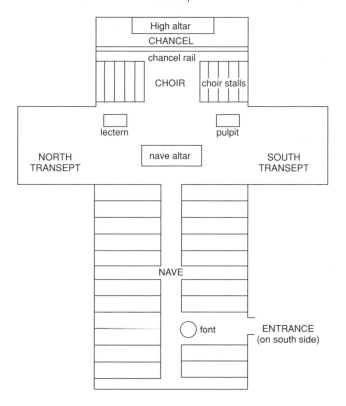

The altar

In traditional churches this is found at the eastern end of the chancel. Essentially, it is a table used to make an offering to God. Holy Communion is delivered from here. Designs vary from ornate to simple, with embroidered cloths appropriate to the time of the Church year. On the altar will be found a cross and candles. There are altar rails between the altar and the rest of the church because it is the focus of the church, and is the most holy place within it.

The lectern

The Bible stands on this for readings during the service. It is usually made from brass or wood and is often in the shape of an eagle with outspread wings to symbolise the spread of the Word of God.

The pulpit

The sermon is delivered from the pulpit. It is made of wood or stone and often has ornate carvings.

The font

This is where baptism takes place. It looks like a basin on a pedestal, and may be ornately carved. The wooden cover dates from the days when it was thought necessary to stop people from taking the holy water which was believed to have healing properties.

11.3   Roman Catholic churches

Roman Catholic churches have an altar for the celebration of mass as the focal point of the church. There are normally pictures of the Holy Family and the stations of the Cross (14 pictures of scenes from Jesus' journey to Calvary) on the walls around the inside of the church, plus statues of the crucified Christ, the Virgin Mary, Joseph, and any saint particularly favoured by that church. There are wide altars where candles can be lit and prayers offered. These are often dedicated to the Virgin Mary or one of the saints, and the worshipper may ask that they intercede with God on their behalf.

Other features

The Confessional

This is for the priest to hear confession and give absolution before a person can have communion. It is a booth with a partition which the priest sits behind to hear the person confess their sins.

The sacristy

The priest puts on his robes here and it is also where artefacts are kept.

The Lady Chapel

This is dedicated to the Virgin Mary.

The font

This is at the side or near the back of the church, and if there is no font then for baptisms the priest will bring a bowl of water to the altar.

The tabernacle for the Blessed Sacrament

This is where the bread and wine for mass are kept.

11.4   Eastern Orthodox churches

These are either in the shape of a Greek cross or they are square. Either way, there is a large dome over the center. The *hieron* is where the liturgy is celebrated. The *naos* is where the congregation meets. The *iconostasis* is a solid screen between the two parts. It has three doors and is covered with pictures.

- The north door is the *servers' door*
- the centre door is the *royal or holy door,* and
- the south door is the *deacons' door.*

There are three areas behind this:

(1)   the *diaconicon*, where priests put on their robes. Equipment is kept here too.
(2)   the *chapel of prothesis* where the bread and wine are prepared
(3)   the *domed sanctuary* where communion takes place

The only seats are reserved for the elderly and the weak. There are *icons* (holy pictures) and niches for candles on the walls. On the east side is the altar, with a bishop's throne behind it. The altar is covered by a white cloth, and on that is a seven-branched candlestick, a copy of the gospels, and a painting of Christ. The *narthex* is at the entrance to the church. This is the stage crossed by novice Christians.

Symbolism in Orthodox churches

- The square of churches so shaped represents order and equality.
- The floor of the nave represents the Earth.
- The four corners stand for the evangelists (Matthew, Mark, Luke and John).
- The dome stands for eternity.
- The candlestick represents the seven gifts of the Spirit and the seven sacraments.

11.5   Nonconformist or Free churches

These are very simple in design, having no status or artefacts, and tend to be more modern. They are usually rectangular and may double up with non-religious uses.

The pulpit is quite near the centre, with the communion table in front of it. There is a cross on the table – and this can be a Latin cross; a Celtic cross, which has a circle around the point where the cross beam meets the upright; or a Calvary cross, which has three steps to represent faith, hope and love.

12 The family and rites of passage

12.1 Introduction

Christians see their lives as a journey to be with God. There are important events or rites of passage that punctuate this journey; hence the word 'passage'. They do not travel alone but are part of the community of Christians making the same journey. The journey is from birth to death and another life with God.

12.2 Baptism

This is normally the first rite of passage and infant baptism is combined with the naming of the baby.

- The priest pours water from the front on to the baby's head and says 'I baptise you in the name of the Father and of the Son and of the Holy Spirit' (Figure 12.1). The baby now belongs to the Christian Church, which is the family of Christ.
- Since a baby is too young to understand, there will be a number of godparents, to make the vows for the child.
- First, the priest asks the parents and godparents if they know what they are doing. Then they have to make three vows which will be *confirmed* in a later ceremony.
- Water is used because Jesus was baptised in water and so it has come to mean the start of a new life in Christ.
- A candle is given to the parents and godparents to show that the child has passed from darkness into light.
- This service is often called a 'christening', which is an Old English world meaning 'to make someone a Christian'.

Orthodox baptism

The main steps

The baby is immersed in water and is then dressed in white.

Next comes *chrismation* or anointing with oil, the priest making the sign of the Cross on the forehead, eyelids, nostrils, ears, lips, chest, hands and feet, as he says: 'the seal of the gift of the Holy Spirit'.

Figure 12.1 Anglican baptism, St Bartholomew's, West Ham, London (Carlos Reyes-Manzo Andes Press Agency)

A lock of the baby's hair is cut as a sign that he or she is now committed to Christianity. The baby is also given a crucifix to wear.

The child is now a full member of the Church and can have Holy Communion.

The meaning of the symbolism

- Chrismation takes the place of Protestant confirmation
- Water symbolises the cleansing of sin and a new life in Christ.
- The oil (chrism) symbolises healing and confirms that the baby will grow strong in Christ.

Anglican baptism

The minister reads from the gospel account about how Jesus cared for children. The child is brought to the font and is attended by the parents and godparents (usually three) while the minister prays and then tells the parents about their responsibility for the Christian upbringing of their child. The baby is then baptised with water in the name of the Father, Son and Holy Spirit. Lighted candles are given to those present. The baby is blessed and is then seen as a member of the Church.

Roman Catholic baptism

Again, membership of the Church is by baptism. The parents and godparents (usually only two) affirm their faith and renounce evil on behalf of the child and themselves. Using oil of catechumens the priest makes the sign of the Cross on the baby's head. Holy water is poured over the baby's head while the priest says: 'I baptise you in the name of the Father and of the Son and of the Holy Ghost (or Spirit)'. The baby is anointed with oil of chrism on the chest. There is also a white baptismal shawl for the baby. The parents are given a candle lit from the Paschal candle. One or more of the Christian names of the child will be that of a saint, whose qualities it is hoped will be followed by the child as he or she grows up.

The meaning of the symbols

- *Chrism* – a symbol of healing, showing that the child is called to share in God's Kingdom
- *oil of catechumens* – used to welcome new members
- *white shawl* – the baby is pure and sinless
- *candle* – Christ is the light of the world; this is why it is lit from the Paschal candle.

Adult baptism

Some of the Protestant churches (for example, the Baptists) are opposed to infant baptism and have what is called believer's baptism. The person is totally immersed in water and is baptised in the name of the Father, Son and Spirit. Immersion in water symbolises drowning or dying to sin, and being born again in Christ (see Romans 6: 3–11 and John 3: 3–8). This is where the term 'Born Again Christian' comes from. Of course, many Christians who were baptised as a baby may wish to be baptised again as believers.

Dedication

Some believe that a child should decide for itself whether or not to become a Christian. They hold a dedication service instead of a baptism after the baby's birth. This can also be called a 'Service of Thanksgiving'. This service involves thanking God for the gift of a child, the promise to bring it up in the Christian way, and that they will dedicate their child to God.

12.3 Confirmation

This completes the act of baptism by renewing the vows made for a person by others when he or she was baptised. The person is confirmed – strengthened to live a Christian life.

- The candidate for confirmation is prepared by a priest and is then confirmed by the bishop.
- In the Catholic Church this can happen from the age of seven, after which they can take their first Holy Communion. Other Churches prefer to wait until the child is older.
- Having received the Holy Spirit at baptism, the person is now given power for work in the Church.
- In the Orthodox Church, confirmation and baptism are a single act.

12.4 Confession/Penance/Reconciliation

This is a sacrament of the Catholic and Orthodox Churches. Originally, the sinner acknowledged or confessed his or her sin to God through a priest. The priest has the power to grant absolution or forgiveness in the name of God, provided that the person had repented. The emphasis is now on reconciliation because sin creates a barrier between people and God. Sorrow and commitment to change brings this reconciliation through the forgiveness and love of God. Confession is also found in the Anglo-Catholic/High Anglican tradition. Sometimes confession is called an act of contrition.

12.5 Communion

- This receiving of bread and wine (Figure 12.2) celebrates the Last Supper of Jesus and the Disciples.
- It is called the Body and Blood of Christ.
- Catholics must first attend confession and say prayers of repentence for the forgiveness of their sins so as to be in a state of **Grace** before they can receive Communion. A child must be aged seven or above before this can happen, because this is regarded as the age of reason.
- In the Orthodox Church any baptised member of that faith can have Communion.
- Some Protestant denominations have confession.

12.6   Marriage/matrimony

This is the union of a man and a woman in the sight of God.

Anglicans read the Banns on each of the three Sundays before the wedding so that anyone with an objection can make it.

The ceremony

The groom and his family and guests arrive at the church first, to wait for the arrival of the bride. Traditionally she wears white and there will be a great deal of fuss in her preparation (Figure 12.3). She is led to the front of the church by her father, whose job it is to 'give her away' (if she has no father then another man of her choice, perhaps an uncle, will substitute).

The priest talks to those present about the meaning of marriage. The bride and groom promise to 'love, cherish, for better for worse, for richer for poorer, in sickness and in health till death do us part'. The priest blesses the ring(s) which are slipped on to the third finger of the left hand, both saying: 'With this ring I thee wed'. With the words: 'Whom God has joined together let no man put asunder', the priest pronounces them man and wife. Hymns are sung and prayers are said at various points in the service, and there is a sermon.

The Orthodox tradition calls the marriage ceremony 'crowning' and the words 'The servant of God (name) is crowned unto the handmaid of God (name). In the name of the Father, and of the Son, and of the Holy Spirit.'

The failure of marriage

Divorce is not allowed by the Roman Catholic Church. However, if couples separate, they can use an agency such as RELATE or the Catholic Marriage Advisory Council (CMAC) to find reconciliation. Anyone of any religious belief, or none at all, can ask for help. Anglicans accept divorce.

Annulment

Sometimes there may be circumstances which make a marriage invalid. The Roman Catholic Church may, for example, appoint an official to examine such a claim. If substantiated, the marriage will be declared null; it is annulled (cancelled). This means that when the couple have a legal divorce as well they will be free to marry someone else. Circumstances for annulment include the following:

- The marriage was not consummated, which means that sexual intercourse has not taken place.
- One or both partners was not competent to make vows.
- One or other partner conceals the fact he or she is unable to have children.
- One partner refuses to have children after having agreed to before marriage.
- Any sort of compulsion or pressure behind either person marrying.

Remarriage

Once divorced, neither partner, if Roman Catholic, is allowed to remarry in church and will have to undergo a civil ceremony in a registry office. They are also considered to have cut themselves off from the sacraments of the Church, though in practice this rule is not strictly adhered to.

In the Church of England the decision about whether to allow remarriage in church is up to the vicar or rector of the parish concerned. The decision will depend on the reasons for the breakdown of the first marriage. Some clergy may only be willing to perform a service of blessing after a civil ceremony in a registry office.

Figure 12.3 A wedding in Westminster Cathedral
(Carlos Reyes-Manzo Andes Press Agency)

12.7 Family

Christianity teaches that marriage and the family are the natural flowering of the Christian religion. Its purpose is to provide a stable, loving setting for the bringing up of children. The Ten Commandments say that children should honour their parents. The New Testament says that parents should not alienate their children, and should regard them as gifts from God.

Many churches and Christian groups run youth clubs and parent and toddler groups, plus other social events to bring Christian families together in a sense of community and fellowship. Also, there are family services in church specially designed to appeal to parents with young families.

Birth control

Many couples choose to limit the number of children they have: this might be for financial reasons; or it might be that the health of the woman would be at risk if she had too many children. Whatever the reason, artificial contraception, such as condoms and the pill, are popular and are accepted by most Christian denominations.

The Roman Catholic Church only permits natural methods (such as abstention from sexual intercourse when the woman is fertile), though many Catholics ignore this ruling.

12.8 Death and burial

Death for the Christian means leaving this earthly life for an everlasting life, in which the soul goes to live with Christ in heaven.

The dead person is prepared for the funeral by being washed and placed in a coffin. A service will be held in a church, chapel, the home, or at a crematorium chapel.

In this service there is often a sermon explaining the Christian view of death, and a eulogy, which is a speech in praise of the deceased. There will be appropriate readings from the Bible, and favourite hymns will be sung.

Burial can be by cremation or in a grave, though cremation used not to be accepted in the Catholic or Anglo-Catholic traditions. This was because the body is supposed to reunite with the soul on the Day of Resurrection, when it is believed that Jesus will come back and judge the living and the dead.

Questions

1. (a) What is meant by 'baptism'? [2]

   (b) Describe what happens at a Christian baptism service [6]

   (c) Explain how parents might bring up their children to live a Christian life [7]

   (d) 'All Christians should have their children baptised.'

   Do you agree? Give reasons to support your answer and show that you have thought about different points of view. [5]

   (*MEG Sample Paper 1998*)

2. (a) Choose *either* Christmas or Easter.

   Give an account of:
   (i) a special service of worship held only during the festival.
   (ii) the Christian beliefs on which the festival is based.

   (b) Explain how *either* Christmas or Easter shows the importance of family life.

   (c) 'Easter is a more important festival for Christians than Christmas.'

   Do you agree? Give reasons for your opinion, showing that you have thought about more than one point of view. (*Total 20 marks*)

   (*NEAB Paper 2, Short Course, 13 June 1997*)

3. (a) What is Holy Communion? (*2 marks*)

   (b) Describe the role of the priest at Mass. (*6 marks*)

   (c) Explain why the Eucharist is important to Christians. (*8 marks*)

   (d) 'It is not necessary to go to Mass in order to be a good Catholic.'

   Do you agree? Give reasons for your answer showing that you have considered another point of view. (*4 marks*)

   (*Total 20 marks*)

   (*London (1479) Specimen Paper for May/June 1999*)

4. (a) Describe how the followers of Jesus received the Holy Spirit on the Day of Pentecost. (*7 marks*)

(b) Explain:

    (i)   the importance of this event; *and*

    (ii) what Christians believe about the Holy Spirit.

(c) Christians claim that the Holy Spirit is active in the world today.

    Do you think this claim can be proved? Give reasons for your answer.

(Total 20 marks)

(SEG SYL A, Paper 2, June 1993)

5.   Questions (a)–(d) can be answered in a single word, phrase or sentence.
    Question (e) requires a longer answer.

(a) Give **one** other name for the eucharist.   *(1 mark)*

(b) Name **one** of the four gospels.   *(1 mark)*

(c) What is the word for the Christian belief that God is three persons in
one?   *(1 mark)*

(d) Name **two** people who visit Jesus' tomb and find it empty according to
Luke chapter 24.   *(2 marks)*

(e) 'Any set pattern for worship will always end up being lifeless and boring.'

    How far do you agree with this statement? Give reasons to support your
answer and show that you have thought about different points of view.   *(5 marks)*

(Total 10 marks)

(SEG Paper 14801/1, Section A, 1998 Short Course Specimen Questions)

Christianity: a glossary

Absolution
The pronouncement by a priest of the forgiveness of sins
AD/CE
AD = Anno domini, 'In the Year of Our Lord': The Christian era dates from the birth of Jesus. (CE = Common Era)
Advent
'Coming': the period observed as the preparation for Christmas
Agape
The New Testament word for 'love'; also used for the common meal of Christians, a love feast
Altar
A table made of wood or stone, used for the *Eucharist* or *Mass*
Anglican
The Fellowship of Churches, including the Church of England, in full communion with Canterbury and its historic tradition
Anointing
See *Unction*
Apocalyptic
Derived from a Greek word meaning 'revelation', it refers to a type of literature that reveals God's purposes, often concerning the end of the world, as well as the present. The revelations were made to prophets and seers. Examples include the Book of Daniel in the Old Testament, and the Book of Revelation in the New Testament
Apocrypha
Derived from a Greek word meaning 'hidden', it is often used to describe books in the Old and New Testaments that are non-canonical: that is, those included in the Septuagint but excluded from the Hebrew Bible (for example, Ecclesiasticus). Some early Christian writings are sometimes described as Apocryphal New Testament, for example the Gospel of Thomas
Apologists
Christian writers of the first two centuries CE, who set out an apology (a reasoned argument), for their faith; for example, Tertullian and Justin Martyr
Apostasy
In the Septuagint apostasy relates to rebellion against God, as in Joshua 22:22. In the New Testament it means deliberate turning away from God, or abandoning religious customs and duties, as in Acts 21:21
Ascension
This marked the last appearance of Jesus in human form. Luke 24 and Acts 1 tell of his ascension into heaven to assume full divine authority. Ascension day is the sixth Thursday, the fortieth day after Easter

Atonement
The reconciliation between God and humanity (at-one-ment): it restores a relationship broken by sin. New Testament doctrine is that Jesus Christ through his life, death and resurrection is the Saviour who brings about the atonement

Baptism
The rite of initiation into the faith, it involves immersion in or sprinkling with water. There are two symbolic meanings: (1) purificatory, the washing away of sin; (2) regenerative; the death of the penitent is seen in the immersion in water, followed by the rebirth in their emergence from the water

Baptistry
A building or pool used for baptism, especially by immersion

Baptists
Members of a Protestant denomination which practices adult baptism by total immersion as the rite of entry into membership

Beatific vision
For Roman Catholics this is the ultimate goal of human existence; it is the intuitive knowledge of, and union with, God which constitutes the supreme joy of heaven

BC
The time before the birth of Christ

BCE
Before the Common Era

Benedictine
A monastic order founded by St Benedict of Nursia c.530 CE

Benediction
The blessing at the end of a service; also a late afternoon service (Roman Catholic) including the blessing of the congregation with the consecrated host

Bible
A collection of sacred writings: the Massoretic text (Hebrew) of the Jewish Bible contains 39 books, and is also called the Old Testament; the Greek text of the New Testament has 27 books. The Old and New Testaments make up the Christian scriptures as translated in the Authorized and Revised Versions. The Latin Vulgate text and its translations has an extra 15 books known as the *Apocrypha*

Calvinism
A school of Protestant theology, based on the teaching of Jean Calvin, with the emphasis on *predestination, election, original sin* and total depravity: this theology is followed by the Baptists, Presbyterians and Reformed Churches of France, Holland and Switzerland

Catechumens
One who is being taught the principles of Christianity

Catholic
'Universal': the catholic faith seen as the universal church throughout the world

Charismatic
A modern movement in the Church, its emphasis is on spiritual gifts such as healing and speaking in tongues

Chrism
Mixture of oil and balsam consecrated by a bishop and used for anointing in various church sacraments such as baptism

Chrismation
Anointing with oil

Church
A community of Christians, or a building in which they worship

College
The order of Roman Catholic Cardinals responsible for electing a new Pope

Confirmation
The rite of admission into full communicant membership of the Christian Church; Roman Catholics regard it as a *sacrament*

Consubstantiation
Luther's teaching concerning Christ's presence in the *Eucharist*

Contrition (also *penance* or *confession*)
One of the seven sacraments of Roman Catholicism
Council
An assembly of bishops for the maintenance of discipline and the declaration of doctrine
Covenant
An agreement between God and an individual or group of people; God promised to grant certain blessings if they kept his laws. So in the Old Testament there was a Covenant with Noah, and with Abraham and Israel at Sinai. The New Testament has a new Covenant made through Christ with the Church
Creed
A statement of religious beliefs, for example the *Nicene Creed*
Crucifixion
Roman method of executing criminals by nailing or tying them on to crosses till they died: used to execute Jesus
Diocese
Area ruled by a bishop
Dominicans
A Roman Catholic monastic order founded by St Dominic at Toulouse in 1212 CE
Easter
The most important Christian festival, in memory of the crucifixion and resurrection of Christ
Ecumenical
World-wide
Ecumenism
A movement within the Church towards co-operation and eventual unity, it started at the Edinburgh Missionary Conference in 1910. It established the World Council of Churches
Election
This is a doctrine which states that from the beginning of creation, God elected some of humanity to eternal life. The rest were passed by or condemned to eternal damnation. It is particularly associated with Augustine and Calvin
Episcopacy
A system of Church government by bishops
Epistles
New Testament letters, for example, by Paul and John
Eschatology
(Lit: 'the doctrine of last things') The doctrine that there will be an end to this world, probably in judgement, its concern is for the destiny of humanity
Eternal Life
A term used in the Fourth (John's) Gospel, which is almost synonymous with the Kingdom of God in the *Synoptics*. It refers to the special quality of life experienced by those who commit themselves to Christ as Lord
Eucharist
(Lit: 'thanksgiving') The central liturgical act of the Church, originating in the *Last Supper*: the bread and wine focus attention on the sacrificial death of Jesus Christ. It can also be called *Mass* or *Holy Communion*
Evangelical
A group or church emphasising the gospel and the scriptures as the path to salvation
Evangelist
A gospel writer: a preacher of the gospel
Excommunication
Cut off from, excluded from the Church
Font
The receptacle holding water for use in the *baptism* of infants
Franciscans
An order of friars founded by St Francis of Assisi in 1210 CE, they are dedicated to absolute poverty and the renunciation of worldly pleasure, and to preaching the Gospel and caring for the sick and needy

Free Churches
Non-conformist denominations, free from state control
Gehenna
Hell
Gnosticism
From the Greek word for knowledge, this refers to systems of belief that claim to impart special knowledge of God, of his relation to the world and humanity, and their redemption. Only the enlightened who go through initiation ceremonies can gain such knowledge. Leaders such as Marcion, Valentinus and Ptolemaus developed different schools. There was strong opposition from the early Church because they minimized the importance of faith in the journey to salvation
Gospel
'Good news': of salvation through Christ; also refers to accounts of his life and work as found in the New Testament (Matthew, Mark, Luke and John)
Grace
The favour and mercy of God given to people in this life, and shown in the death of Jesus Christ, his son, as the *atonement* for the sins of humankind, Grace brings about the forgiveness of sins and the *justification* of the sinner. Protestant theology holds that Grace comes through faith alone. Catholic and Orthodox theology emphasises the part of the Sacraments as 'efficacious signs' of Grace. They also see Grace as an essential transformation of a person by a new God-like quality
Hades
The place of dead. Righteous & wicked are separated. The good go to the part of Hades called Paradise
Heaven
The habitation of God and his angels, this is where the souls of the righteous will go after death
Heresy
Denial or dissension from **Christian** doctrine by a **Christian**
Hell
The place where damned souls go after death. Also Sheol and Gehenna
Holy Communion (also *Eucharist* or *Mass*)
Central liturgical (public worship) act of the Church
Holy Spirit
The third person of the Holy Trinity: through the Holy Spirit, God the Father continues his redemptive work shown in Jesus Christ. The Spirit is active in the church and the world
Holy Week
The week before Easter, when the last week of Christ's life is remembered
Icon (also *ikon*)
Painting or mosaic of Christ or one of the saints, used in the Orthodox faith as an aid to devotion
Iconostasis
A screen separating the sanctuary from the nave in Orthodox churches
Immortality
Christian theology holds that the survival of the soul after the death of the body is dependent on the resurrection of Christ, believing that by faith in him, the believer is saved from the death of sin to experience the fullness of *Eternal Life*
Incarnation
This is the doctrine that the eternal word of God, the second Person of the Trinity (Christ), became flesh. The New Testament says that he lived a human life, with all the difficulties that people suffer such as hunger, tiredness, doubt and so on, but that his deity was not reduced or lessened in any way
Indulgences
Gift of money to the Roman Catholic Church who defines it as a 'remission of the temporal punishment which often remains due to sin after its guilt has been forgiven'
Jesuits
The Society of Jesus was founded by the Spanish knight Ignatius Loyola. Papal approval was granted in 1540. The stress is on missionary and educational activity. Members take the three monastic vows, plus a vow of absolute obedience to the Pope

Jesus Christ
The central figure of Christianity, the Son of Man, born to Mary; also the Son of God, the incarnate Word, one with God the Father, the second Person of the Trinity
Justification
God's gift to individual Christians, this is the event by which the sinner passes from a state of condemnation to being declared just or righteous. Christian theology says that humanity is sinful and in wrong relation to God, but unable to put things right. Protestantism teaches that justification is by faith alone. Catholicism says that Justification is by faith reinforced by the grace that is mediated through the sacraments
Kerygma
Early church preaching (as distinct from exegetical or analytical/critical teaching)
Last Judgement
This is the belief that humankind is under the judgement of God. Some believe it is a process that continues throughout life and after death. Others believe in the judgement of the individual at the end of earthly life. Yet others believe that at the end of history there will be a Last Judgement by Jesus Christ when the saved and the damned will be separated
Lectern
A stand on which the Bible is placed in church
Lectionary
A list of scriptural passages for systematic reading throughout the year
Liturgy
Divine service according to a prescribed ritual – for example, the Eucharist, Matins, Evensong
Logos
A Greek noun meaning 'word': in John 1:1 it is the naming of Christ as the eternally pre-existing and creative word of God. As the Incarnate Word, he is one with the Father, perfect God and perfect man in John's teaching
Lord's Supper
The term used by St Paul for the *Eucharist* or *Holy communion* (1 Corinthians 11:20)
Lutheran Church
A Protestant denomination which follows the teachings of the German monk, Martin Luther, who started the Reformation
Mass
Roman Catholic term for the *eucharist* or *Holy Communion*, it is probably derived from the closing words of the Latin liturgy, 'Ite, missa est'
Matrimony
The rite of marriage, it is one of the seven sacraments in the Roman Catholic Church
Messiah
'The anointed one', an early Christian title for Christ
Methodism
This is a Protestant Christian denomination, which was founded by John Wesley (1703–91). His followers were called Methodists because of their methodical practice of prayer and Bible study
Missal
A book containing words and ceremonial directions for saying mass
Montanism
A Christian movement founded by Montanus in the second century, its members expected the immediate fulfilment of the prophecy concerning the pouring out of the Spirit in the last days
New Testament
The 27 books forming the central section of the canon of Christian scriptures
Non conformist
Protestant denominations that do not accept the teachings of the Church of England
Old Testament
The 39 books of Jewish scriptures included in the canon of Christian scriptures
Order
A brotherhood of monks, friars or nuns – for example, Benedictines, Dominicans and Carmelites; also, in the priesthood of the Roman Catholic, Orthodox and Anglican Churches, the three divisions of bishop, priest and deacon

Original sin
This is the doctrine that there is a connection between the sin of Adam and Eve and the sin of all people since. Apart from Genesis, this is mentioned in Psalm 51:5 and Romans 5:12. It is believed that baptism cleanses the baptized person of this original sin

Orthodox
This was the Church of the Eastern Roman Empire which separated from the Roman Catholic West in 1054 CE. It has five major Patriarchates: Constantinople, Moscow, Greece, Cyprus and Jerusalem

Papacy
The papacy is the doctrinal and administrative office of the Bishop of Rome, the central organization of the Roman Catholic Church. The Pope is the successor of St Peter and the Vicar of Christ on earth, and as such is the guardian of the faith in the Roman Catholic Church

Parable
From Greek: placing beside; a comparison; equivalent to Hebrew 'mashal' used by Jesus to teach. Earthly stories with religions meanings, e.g. the wheat and the tares

Paraclete
A term used for the Holy Spirit

Paradise
From the Iranian word meaning 'a walled garden': it is a place where the righteous live with God. Christ used the word to explain the place where the repentent thief would be with him after dying at the crucifixion (Luke 23:43). Revelation 2:7 describes it as the dwelling place of God, in the middle of which is the tree of life

Parousia
From Greek: 'presence' or 'arrival': the second coming or return of Christ

Parish
An administrative subdivision of a diocese with its own church

Paschal
Derived from **Pesach**, the Hebrew word for the Passover; the Paschal candle lit on Holy Saturday symbolizes the resurrection light. The paschal lamb is a title applied to Christ

Passion
The sufferings of Christ

Patriarch
The main Eastern Orthodox bishops; also the early Hebrew leaders such as Abraham and Isaac

Paul of Tarsus (*St Paul*)
He was a Jewish scholar who set out to destroy Christianity. On the road to Damascus he was converted when a blinding light dazzled him and Jesus spoke to him (Acts 9). His Letters have made him accepted as a source and an interpreter of Christian doctrine

Pentecost
The day the early Christians received the gift of the Holy Spirit: it is usually called *Whitsun*

Pope
The chief bishop, the Head of the Roman Catholic Church

Predestination Church
The belief by theologians such as Augustine and Calvin that some (but not all) Christians are chosen or elected by God for salvation

Presbyters
Elders or senior figures in the Church

Presbyterianism
A Protestant Christian form of Church government based on the ideas of Calvin, it teaches that the church leaders should be presbyters or elders, and rejects the system of bishops and prelates. It also emphasises the importance of the local congregation

Priest
A priest is a person authorized to officiate in public worship and religious ceremonies. The term '*presbuteros*' (lit: elder) has been translated as 'priest' in the Catholic and Anglican Churches to refer to those, ordained by bishops, who are authorized to administer the sacraments

Protestant
A major division of the Church protesting against the belief and practice of the Roman Catholic Church, and who do not follow the Orthodox Church, it originates from the Diet of Speyer in 1529 when Luther's supporters 'protested' against the Catholic Church
Pulpit
An elevated stand from which sermons are preached
Purgatory
An intermediate state after death for those not yet ready for the reward of heaven, and not guilty of such serious sin as would condemn them to hell, but who still have a debt to pay for sin; this is a Catholic doctrine ratified by the Council of Trent in 1563
Quakers
A Christian society which arose in seventeenth-century England from the teaching of George Fox, their formal title is the Religious Society of Friends. They have no paid ministry, refuse to take oaths, and reject war. Their meetings for worship are silent unless someone feels that they have to speak
Ransom
A term applied to his death by Christ (Mark 10:45); some of the early Church leaders interpreted it as a ransom paid to Satan for the release of humanity from his power
Reconciliation
This is an important word in the theology of St Paul. Christ was the perfect, sinless sacrifice which redeemed humanity from sin, and so achieved reconciliation with God, bridging the gulf between a righteous God and sinful humanity
Redemption
Salvation through the death of Christ: this is a key word in St Paul's theology and is closely linked with *reconciliation*. Christ's death and resurrection makes it possible, delivering the human race from sin, death and the powers of darkness
Reformation
The sixteenth-century reform movement that led to the formation of the Protestant Churches, it is considered to have been started by Martin Luther when he pinned up 95 Theses against Indulgences
Reformed Churches
The Churches founded after the *Reformation*; This term is now used for the French Protestant Church, and the Calvinist Churches of Holland and Switzerland
Resurrection
A central doctrine of the Christian Church which says that Christ rose from the dead on the third day after the crucifixion. Also the rising from the dead of believers on the Last Day
Revelation
This term indicates a knowledge of God derived from what He himself reveals, as distinct from any thoughts about God which are the result of meditation and contemplation. Also the title of the last book of the bible
Roman Catholic
A major division of the Church, led by the Pope in Rome
Sacrament
This is an outward visible sign of an inward spiritual blessing obtained through the rites of the Church. The Anglican and Reformed Churches have two: baptism and eucharist. The Roman Catholic Church has seven: baptism; confirmation; matrimony; orders; eucharist; penance and extreme unction
Salvation Army
A Protestant organization founded by William and Catherine Booth, it is very evangelical, has open-air services with military-style bands, and emphasizes social work as an important aspect of the Gospel
Sanctification
This is the purification and dedication of life through the grace of God. In Catholic theology, sanctification comes through the grace that comes through the sacraments. Protestantism stresses the importance of faith alone

Satan
(Hebrew 'the accuser') In the New Testament, he is the leader of evil spirits who oppose God. Also, the chief of devils of fallen angels
Satisfaction
Doctrine of Anselm of Canterbury, that the death of Christ offered to God the satisfaction (apology) due for the offence by which man's sin had offended God's divine majesty
Sheol
See Hell
Sin
Act of disobedience or rebellion against the known will of God; the human condition assessed as disordered and needing transformation
Society of Friends
See *Quakers*
Soteriology
A branch of theology concerned with the salvation of humankind – this includes: the fall of man and sin; God's redemptive work and the atonement in Christ; grace and eternal life
Spirit
In the New Testament the Spirit of god is referred to as the Holy Spirit. It represents a special power of God. It can also be another word for the soul
Stations of the Cross
14 pictures of Jesus' journey to Calvary
Synoptic
A common viewpoint – for example, the first three Gospels by Matthew, Mark and Luke
Tabernacle
A receptacle for the vessels containing the Blessed Sacrament, the bread and wine for the Mass
Thirty-Nine Articles
The accepted doctrines of the Church of England
Transfiguration
The visionary transformation of Christ after the resurrection
Transubstantiation
The Roman Catholic view of the Eucharist, it says that the substance of the elements of bread and wine is transformed by God's power into the substance of the body and blood of Christ directly upon the words of the priestly consecration of the Mass
Trinity
One God in three persons; Father, Son and Holy Spirit
Unction
This is the anointing with oil in a religious ceremony. In the British coronation service the monarch is anointed by the Archbishop of Canterbury before being crowned. The sick can be anointed in a special service with prayers for healing. Extreme Unction is a preparation for death, and is a sacrament in the Catholic Church. It can also be for the restoration of the sick to health
Universalism
This is the doctrine that God's purposes are not limited to the Jews, but will ultimately include all nations. Also, the doctrine that at the end if time, all of humankind will be saved and will share eternal salvation
Vatican
The Pope's residence in Rome, it is the administrative centre of the Roman Catholic Church
Viaticum
Holy Communion given to a person near to death
Vicarious suffering
The concept that one person without fault can suffer for another person who is guilty; Christ the sinless victim suffered in the place of the guilty, thus atoning for them
Virgin Birth
The doctrine that Jesus was born of the Virgin Mary by the power of the Holy Spirit, having no human father
Virgin Mary
The mother of Jesus Christ

PART III

Islam

Origins and definitions

13.1 Introduction

The word, '*Islam*', in Arabic means 'submission (to **Allah** – God)'. Islam is much more than the usual Western idea of 'religion'. It is:

- a religious tradition
- a civilization
- a total way of life.

Islam sets out patterns of order for society in:

- civil and criminal law
- business
- family life
- etiquette
- personal hygiene
- food
- dress.

The Western distinction between religious and secular life is not acceptable to traditional Islam. Islam believes that individuals, societies and governments should conform to the will of God.

The word '**muslim**' (small 'm') is someone who submits to the will of God in any age or time. The word '**Muslim**' (large 'M') is one who follows the religion of Muhammad.

Muslims believe that Islam has the answer to the religious problems and questions that have beset mankind since the beginning. **Surah** 3.19 in the **Qur'an** declares, 'Truly, religion with Allah is Islam'. This is because, for the Muslim, Islam 'religionises' humanity properly.

Other religions have some elements of ultimate religion but, for the Muslim, Islam contains and corrects them all, thus bringing religion to a climax in Islam. There have always been 'muslims' who have submitted themselves to the will of Allah, and Muslims would include Abraham, Moses, David and Jesus. However, it is the religion of Muhammad that perfects the process. So Muslims see themselves as the people of the point of what religion should be.

13.2   Historical background

Islam dates from the last ten years of the life of the Prophet Muhammad. It began in Makkah around 610 CE. The main religion in Arabia at that time was a form of the old Semitic religion which had shrines to a variety of gods and goddesses in a multitude of places. There was also a widespread acceptance of a supreme God (Allah). The other gods were often regarded as angels who could be asked to intercede with Allah on behalf of the person praying. There was a strong belief that Fate or Time controlled human fortunes and that this was not something that needed to be worshipped. Christianity was spreading and there were Jewish communities in Madinah and in other parts of western Arabia.

13.3   The Prophet Muhammad

Muhammad was born in Makkah around 570 CE, after the death of his father Abdullah, and was part of the Bani Hashim, one of the nobler but poorer clans of **Quraysh**. His mother died shortly after his birth, so he was brought up by his uncle, Abi Talib, in conditions of some hardship.

Muhammad married the widow Khadijah, to whom he was in service (she was prosperous and involved in commerce), and although they had a happy marriage with children, none of their sons survived childhood. She was his only wife while she lived, but later he had several more marriages.

He was religiously inclined from an early age and often went to Mount **Hira** near Makkah for religious vigils and meditation at night. Soon after his fortieth birthday came the call to prophethood when, while he was meditating, an angel appeared and told him to 'recite' in the name of Allah. He did not, so the angel took him by the throat and repeated the command. He still did not obey, so the angel choked him until he did.

This was the start of a series of revelations which are the most important mark of his prophethood. The record of these makes up the Qur'an, which is Islam's most important scripture.

Muhammad found all this disturbing and feared that either he was insane or had demonic possession. It was made worse by a long gap between revelations. Eventually he realised that this mission was as the agent of Allah's message to his generation. Thus began his career as preacher, reformer and prophet.

13.4   Muslims in the UK

The first Muslim migrants

The first arrivals came at the time of the expansion of the British Empire into the sub-continent of India, when sailors who had been recruited along the sea routes of the Empire began to settle in British ports. At first they were from West Africa and India, but after the opening of the Suez Canal in 1869, they came increasingly from the Yemen.

Large-scale migration

This really began in the twentieth century; firstly, students came in the early part of the century and then ex-servicemen came after the world wars.

Figure 13.1 The Regent's Park Mosque, London
(Carlos Reyes-Manzo Andes Press Agency)

When the British Indian Empire became independent in 1947–8, the rate of migration to Britain really increased, especially during the 1950s, when many came from India and the Turkish part of Cyprus. These were followed by further waves from Pakistan and later from East Africa. The last major group to date has been from Bangladesh and the Middle East in the 1970s.

Muslims in the UK today

Most of the post-war immigrants were what are known as economic migrants – people looking for work. Muslims have settled in most of Britain's larger cities, and many of the smaller cities have a Muslim community as well. The Muslims from North Africa have settled mostly in London and the South East, while Pakistanis have concentrated further north in Birmingham, Manchester and West Yorkshire, especially Bradford. This is still a young community, over half of whose members were born in Britain.

Over 50 per cent of British Muslims are of Pakistani origin, while seven out of ten originate from the Indian subcontinent in general. The overall figures for the size of the nationwide community is uncertain, and figures vary from 1.5 million to 2.5 million, while the number of British converts to Islam amounts to just a few thousand.

Mosques

The first mosques opened in Woking, Surrey and Liverpool in the 1880s, and an Islamic Cultural Centre was set up in London in the years between the two world wars. In the 1940s, King George VI gave a plot of land in Regent's Park to the Muslims in exchange for land in Cairo, where an Anglican cathedral was built. In the 1970s a mosque was built on the Regent's Park site (Figure 13.1). At present there are around 400 mosques spread throughout Britain, and these vary from converted factories, warehouses and disused chapels, to purpose-built structures.

14 Scriptures

14.1 The Qur'an (Koran)

- The name 'Qur'an' means 'the Recital' and each separate revelation making up the book is called a Qur'an.
- The Qur'an is understood by Muslims to be the final, the ultimate scripture; that is, it is the last edition of God's Will.
- It is the basic religious document for Islam.
- It was pre-existent in Heaven, inscribed on a 'preserved tablet' (85:22).
- It is the written collection of the revelation to the Prophet Muhammad by the Angel Jibra'il (Gabriel) starting on 'The Night of Power'. The Revelation continued piece-meal over 20 years, read by the angel from the heavenly tablet.
- It was made to 'descend' on Muhammad in **tanzil** (downward flow).
- Islamic theology gives the term 'Qur'an' a sequence:

  — the eternal Qur'an with God
  — the Qur'an in the Prophet's hearing
  — the Qur'an in the Prophet's speaking
  — the Qur'an in his hearer's hearing
  — the Qur'an in their reciting after him
  — the recording of the hearing and reciting in the earthly book.
- It is an infallible source of authority for all matters of doctrine, practice and law.

The structure of the Qur'an

The Qur'an is about the same length as the New Testament in the Bible, containing 114 chapters or **surahs**.

It begins with a short surah called '**al Fatihah**', meaning 'The Opener', which is in the form of a prayer to Allah for guidance. This is the most frequently recited part of the Qur'an and is used in daily prayers and on all sorts of religious occasions.

The following surahs are loosely arranged in order of length, with the longest first (286 verses) and the shortest (3–5 verses) at the end. Each surah has a name derived from something mentioned in it.

Every surah except one starts off: '**Bismillah al rahman, al rahime**', which means 'In the name of Allah the Compassionate, the Merciful'. (The ninth surah, which starts differently, is called 'The repentance', and traditional commentators regard it as a continuation of 'The spoils'.)

All surahs are assigned in their heading to either one or other of the cities of Makkah or.Madinah. Chronology is ignored, with Makkan and Madinan surahs mixed, because order is by length. Even inside Makkan and Madinan surahs, the contents come from different times and circumstances.

The Qur'an is divided into before and after the **Hijrah** (Arabic: 'migration') in 622 CE, when Mohammad and 100 followers left Makkah for Madinah. This marks the start of the Islamic calendar.

The opening surah

Islam believes that:

(1)   the whole Qur'an is within this chapter;
(2)   the whole of this chapter is within the *Bismillah* which opens it;
(3)   the whole of the *Bismillah* is within the initial 'bi', the preposition which invokes;
(4)   the initial letter is understood in the point or dot below. In Arabic, it makes it the letter it is.

So in the mystical sense, Muslims are 'the people of the point' invoking Allah's name. It is their whole religion.

To invoke His name is sure protection for the believer because it has the double quality of mercy:

- it is Allah's essentially: *Al Rahman* (the compassionate)
- it is Allah's operatively: *Al Rahim* (the merciful).

In short, believers confess Him by pleading what He is as the pledge of how He will deal with them – that is, He will be merciful.

14.2   The Hadith

Hadith means 'saying'. The sayings record the **Sunnah**, which are the rules of life. These are based on things that Muhammad said, did or approved of in others. There are two headings for the Hadith:

(1)   the Prophetic Hadith – these are the sayings of Muhammad which reveal his wisdom and compassion. They concern matters of everyday living.
(2)   the Sacred Hadith – these have authority because they go back through the Prophet to Allah. They are insights that Allah revealed through the Prophet but which are not in the Qur'an. They cover matters of belief and worship.

The sources of the Hadith

A chain of narrators kept sayings orally and in writing, simply because Muhammad did not write anything himself. Because of the number of sayings in circulation, it became necessary to sort out the genuine from the false. Two genuine collections resulted:

(1)   the Bukhari collection (2762 sayings/traditions), filling 97 books
(2)   the Muslim collection (4000 sayings/traditions).

Al-Bukhari's collection is called the **Sunna**.

The Hadith's value compared to the Qur'an

- The Qur'an carries greater weight as the revealed Word of Allah, so it is not open to discussion.
- The Hadith comes directly from Allah, but the way it is recorded comes from Muhammad, and so can be discussed.

- **Sunni** Muslims have six collections of Hadith.
- **Shi'ah** Muslims have five collections of Hadith.

14.3 The Sunna

This is the custom by which Islamic belief and practice is regulated. In the early centuries of Islam principles of interpretation of the Qur'an evolved which are still used today. The **Shari'a** or 'Highway' of divine command the guidance covers every aspect of life. This was important because there were matters not covered by the Qur'an and the Hadith because they did not exist at the time they were written.

The classification of sunnah

(1) sound (**Sahih**)
(2) good (**Hasan**)
(3) weak (**Da'if**)
(4) infirm (**Saqim**)

Classification depends on how likely they seem when examined by scholars.

Islamic beliefs and the Five Pillars of Islam

15.1 Allah

- Allah is the only god.
- Allah is One (this belief is called **Tawhid**).
- Allah is beyond human understanding. He is unique and incomparable.
- He is the First and Last, the One and Only Creator.
- All of creation owes its existence to Allah.
- All living things draw their breath because of His power and authority, so that if it is withdrawn, then the person or creature dies.

15.2 Angels

- Angels were created by Allah and are His servants.
- Because of their nature they obey Him perfectly; human beings do not, because He has given them free will. This is the only difference between them.
- Angels are the messengers of Allah; they take His revelations to the prophets and they strengthen the good in every person.
- There is at least one angel for every person.

15.3 Satan

Only one angel ever disobeyed Allah. This was Satan (or **Iblis** as the Qur'an calls him). He is sometimes known as Shaytan.

When Allah created the first man, Adam, Satan became jealous and refused to serve him as Allah commanded; so Allah expelled him from heaven. Satan decided to destroy humanity by leading it away from Allah so that it would be damned for eternity. He does this by whispering lies which will make them do wrong.

He tempts Muslims to disobey the laws of the Qur'an, and they in turn persuade others to follow Satan. These are the 'false prophets'. The only defence is to keep the words of the Qur'an constantly in mind.

15.4　The Day of Judgement

On this day, the graves will be opened and the dead will be resurrected (brought back to life). This is when everyone will be sentenced depending on how they lived their lives. The dead will be questioned by two terrible angels, after which they are to be presented with a book. If it is placed in their right hand, then they are saved, but if in the left hand, then they are damned for eternity. The saved pass over the narrow **Assirat Bridge** to heaven, with its beautiful gardens. Here will be found heavenly food, and lovely maidens. Those allowed in are the charitable and humble, and anyone persecuted for the sake of God, or who has fought for and in the name of Allah. The wicked will fall off the bridge into hell (**jahannam**). There, they will suffer everlasting fire and torment. They will suffer physically and experience 'fire in their hearts'. On the Day of Judgement Allah will abolish death itself so those who suffer hell will do so eternally; those who go to Paradise will do so for ever.

15.5　Serious sin

Shirk

This is the sin of seeing any thing or person as comparable or equal to Allah. Other gods or idols are forbidden. This includes film, sport and pop stars.

Sihr

This is magic. The spirits (**Jinn**) must not be given authority. To do so will mean the misinterpretation of Allah's Will.

Qatl

This is murder, which is a sin and a crime. All life is Allah's gift and is therefore sacred.

Riba

This is usury, or money-lending for profit. Anyone who can do so must help those who are less fortunate.

Sariqah

This is theft, which is punishable by the chopping off of the hands unless the person is in desperate economic need. Islam wants to help people so that such a situation cannot arise.

Jubn

This is cowardice. It is an obligation for Muslims to fight **Jihad** for society. Anyone deserting the battlefield is committing a sin.

Qadhf

This is slander, which is a sin that includes gossip and bad language.

Adultery

This is a crime as well as a sin. It is punishable in Islamic countries. The Qur'an recommends 100 lashes, but punishment does vary from country to country.

Consuming Intoxicants

Drugs and alcohol cause people to lose control of themselves, and this is condemned by the Qur'an. Strict Islamic states give severe punishments for this. Non-Muslims living and working in Islamic countries are asked not to corrupt Muslims in this way.

15.6   The Five Pillars of Islam

These are the principal factors in the worship of Muslims. They are duties which are part of a Muslim's **ibadat** (ibadah) or obligations to God. They are:

(1)   **shahadah** – confession of faith
(2)   **salat** – ritual prayer
(3)   **zakat** – alms for the poor
(4)   **saum** – the fast during Ramadan
(5)   **hajj** – pilgrimage to the Kaaba in Makkah.

15.7   The Shahadah

The way into worship, the beginning and essence of being a Muslim, is to recite the *Shahadah* or confession (alternatively known as the Kalimah). It is the 'word of witness'. This must be done with sincere 'intention' (**niyyah**), as is the case with all the Pillars of Islam. It is the conscious focus of purpose that precedes all ritual acts in Islam. Merely to recite the words of the creed does not make the speaker a Muslim. It is the 'intention' that counts; it must be a deliberate focus of the conscious will.
There are two statements:

• There is no god but Allah.
• Muhammad is the Messenger of Allah.

Both occur in the Qur'an, but not together. They are recited by new converts as part of the ceremony of becoming a Muslim.

Note that Muhammad is the last and the greatest of the prophets. He is the model, the archetype of all true religions, faith and practice.

In later parts of the Qur'an, the title 'messenger of Allah' is used synonymously with 'Prophet'.

15.8   The Salat

This was the earliest Islamic practice to emerge. It is the ritual or liturgical (public worship) prayer in Islam (Figure 15.1). It was required only of Muhammad until some time after the *Hijrah* in 622 CE, when Muhammad and his followers went from Makkah to Madinah.

ISLAMIC BELIEFS AND THE FIVE PILLARS OF ISLAM   125

It was performed twice a day at sunrise and sunset, but at Madinah all Muslims had to perform the *Salat*. Possibly because the Jews performed their prayers three times a day, a third or 'middle' *Salat* was introduced.

For the first year after the Hijrah, Muslims faced towards Jerusalem to pray. At the time of the 'break with the Jews' the direction of prayer (**qiblah**) was reorientated towards Makkah, and this has been so ever since. Parts of the later Salat are mentioned in the Qur'an; for example, the bowing (**ruku**), and the prostration (**sujud**). The three daily *Salats* performed by all Muslims in Muhammad's time are mentioned by name in the Qur'an.

The number of *Salats* had risen to five within a century of Muhammad's death, and a number of hadiths (traditions) arose supporting this number.

Salats are announced by a public call to prayer (**adhan**) by the **muezzin** ('caller').

The call has seven statements

(1)   Allah is most great. (repeated four times)
(2)   I testify that there is no god but Allah. (twice)
(3)   I testify that Muhammad is the Messenger of Allah. (twice)
(4)   Come to prayer. (twice)
(5)   Come to salvation. (twice)
(6)   Allah is most great. (twice)
(7)   There is no god but Allah. (repeat once)

In the call to morning prayer, the statement 'Prayer is better than sleep' is inserted after the fifth statement, or in one of the legal rites at the end. Shi'ites insert 'Come to the best work' after the fifth statement, and recite the final statement twice.

Ritual purification

Without this preliminary purification, prayer is invalid. Every mosque has its pool or fountain if possible. Failing that, taps, bottles or an artificial water supply is used. Sand can be used instead of water if there is a drought. This ablution, called **wudu**, is performed before prayer because of the need for inward purity. Hands, forearms, and legs below the knees must be washed. The face, nose and mouth must be rinsed.

The positions and postures of Salat

After purification, word and posture move together. It is important to understand that these postures are both a 'sacrament' of personal worship and of corporate devotion. *Salat* takes the hands, knees, and joints from other use and takes them for worship. This worship is not just thought and said; it is done as well, because the Qur'an says 'perform the prayer'.

No matter where the *Salat* is performed, the personal immediacy is the same, because there is no rite depending on another, no external agency, no substitute; whether the person prays alone or in the mosque it makes no difference. In other words everyone is his or her own 'doer'. This is vital, because the prayer act is the celebration of God's being, which includes His power, mercy, unity and revelation.

15.9 Zakat

Zakat means 'purification'. Purification can be achieved by giving charitably. The amount is 2½ per cent (a fortieth) of disposable income. It is a religious duty.

Zakat can be given to relatives, the poor, or to an Islamic charity. It must be paid every year, and it must be given sincerely and willingly.

No one should refuse it or feel ashamed to get it. The spirit of solidarity and kindness reflects Muhammad's generosity during his lifetime.

15.10 Saum

Saum is fasting and is observed during Ramadan: see Chapter 17.

15.11 Hajj

Hajj means pilgrimage to Makkah and must be undertaken at least once in a lifetime by any physically fit Muslim who can afford to do so. It is undertaken in the twelfth month of the year. It reminds every Muslim that earthly prejudices and personal pride mean nothing because all will be equal on the day of Judgement. (See also 'The Day of Arafat' in Chapter 17.)

(16) The mosque

The word **mosque** is from the Arabic '**masjid**', meaning 'to prostrate oneself'. A mosque is a building where Muslims bow before Allah to show their submission to His will.

It is not necessary to have a building to do this. Muhammad said that 'Wherever the hour of prayer overtakes you, you shall perform the prayer. That place is the mosque'. In his early days in Makkah there was no mosque, so he and his friends would pray anywhere.

16.1 The building

- The mosque is usually rectangular.
- The sacred area is established by the walls (Figure 16.1).
- Shoes must be removed before entering.
- There will be a place to wash, either at the entrance or in the courtyard. Face, hands and feet must be washed before prayer.

Figure 16.1 Diagram of a mosque: *A* Site of fountain; *B* Hall of worship; *C* Mihrab; *D* Qiblah wall; *E* Entrance; *F* Minaret

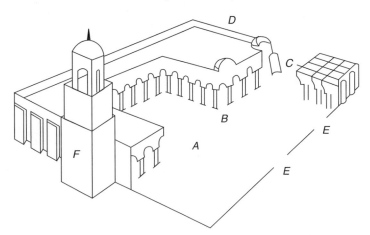

- If the mosque has a roof, it may have a dome as well, to symbolise the universe and enhance the imam's voice.
- Prayers are said in the main room, which may have carpets, and lines to help the congregation to form neat rows.
- Buildings are plain, because Islam does not allow idolatry; so there are no stained glass windows, statues or pictures. The reason is that only God is worshipped, and there can be no likeness of him because he is pure spirit. Beautifully elaborate Arabic inscriptions *are* permitted and calligraphy is a highly developed art.

16.2   The minaret

This is a high tower, from which the faithful are called to prayer five times a day; a mosque will have at least one. The call is made by the muezzin, who stands in the top of the tower. Prayer times are fixed by the sun, and the muezzin will judge when it is time for the next session.

16.3   The qiblah wall

This gets its name from the word meaning 'direction'. It shows the Muslim where Makkah is because it is built in the direction of the city, towards which Muslims face to pray. This wall is different from the others: in hot countries there may not be a roof, so it may be that one wall is higher than the others. Or there may be a niche, known as the **mihrab**, which points towards the Ka'bah. Elsewhere it points in the direction of Makkah, so the prayer leader stands before it when leading worship. In some places the *qiblah* wall is a covered colonnade, and the *mihrab* is a majestic ornamental arch. Examples include the Blue Mosque at Isfahan in Iran, and the great mosque of Lahore in Pakistan.

16.4   The pulpit

This is usually found in front of the *qiblah* wall, to one side of the *mihrab*. It can be a raised platform, or may be at the top of a flight of stairs. It is from here that addresses are made on Fridays.

Festivals and food

17.1 Introduction

Islamic festivals are called **eid** (or **id**), an Arabic word from a root which means 'periodically returning'. These festivals are times for reducing tension and for establishing new relations in an atmosphere of festivity and happiness. It is vital that strangers, the poor and the lonely feel at home. Broken relations must be mended, quarrelling must end and orphans must experience the love of others. The two major festival days are:

(1) the festival of Breaking the Fast after Ramadan
(2) the Festival of Sacrifice after the pilgrimage.

Some general points about festivals

- Festivals begin with an act of devotion and prayer.
- Individual Muslims remember Allah at the mosque, at home, at school, at work; in short, wherever they are.
- On the two major festival days, a larger gathering is held for the whole community, either in the biggest mosque or outside.
- Muslims celebrate many of the events of Muhammad's life and the history of Islam.
- Festivals will be celebrated by Muslims according to their country's customs, but all agree on the importance and spiritual significance of the events that they are celebrating.

17.2 The annual fast: Ramadan

This is the annual fast of the ninth month of the lunar year. Ramadan moves through the seasons because the lunar year is shorter than the solar year.

It is the fourth 'pillar' or duty of Islam.

It is linked with the great events in Islamic history such as the revelation of the Qur'an to the Prophet, and three important battles.

It involves total abstinence from food and drink from dawn till sunset for the whole month. The Prophet's tradition is followed by breaking the fast each day at sunset with dates and water at the mosque. Then the faithful say the **maghrib**, or sunset prayer, before returning home for the main meal.

The custom in Makkah is for people to take food to the Grand Mosque of the Ka'aba before sunset. The food is shared when prayer is complete and the cannon signalling the end of the fast for the day has been fired. A prayer is said after eating.

Ramadan is the month of forgiveness and charity, so Muslims must pay *zakat-ul-fitr*, which is a charity given as an act of purification. It is the price of one good meal for each member of the family and is for the relief of the poor.

The aim of Ramadan is to fulfil Allah's commands of discipline, piety and collective worship.

Mosques and minarets are lit up, and restaurants and coffee bars are closed during the daytime.

Exemptions at Ramadan

The following categories of people are exempt from fasting at Ramadan:

- the very old
- those under the age of 12, who gradually build up to a full fast by going without a little more food and drink each year
- the sick
- women who are menstruating, pregnant or breastfeeding
- those who are travelling.

Compensation must be made by fasting on an equal number of days at a later date.

Why the fast is beneficial

- The fast produces an immense sense of solidarity.
- The rich realise what it is like to be poor.
- As everyone is hungry, everyone is equal while it lasts.
- Spiritual benefits and merit are acquired because prayer and charitable donations go hand in hand with the fasting, the contemplation, and reading the Qur'an.
- Passion is checked, the will is denied, and the material world's preoccupations are set aside.
- The self-discipline learned brings the faithful nearer to the angels, whose behaviour is perfect in Allah's presence.
- The feast which ends the fast is the peak of communal consciousness because the whole of Islam celebrates its fulfilled obedience, and the merit which it brings.

Islam does not seek to justify Ramadan, because it is ordained by God. In other words, it is an obligation which people owe to God. Ramadan is not asceticism, because Islam does not approve of that. Rather, it is discipline, not denial, because the world is to be enjoyed. It teaches restraint and the mastery of desire.

17.3 The Festival of Breaking the Fast: Eid-ul-Fitr

This festival ends the fast of Ramadan. It falls on the first day of the following month, *Shawwal*, and lasts for three days.

It is also called the Small Festival or *Eid-ul-Sagheer*. Two other names for it are *Eid Ramadan* and *Bairam*.

It is a time of thanksgiving for having the strength to complete the fast and so fulfil their duty. There is also celebration and rejoicing in God's favour for His revelation of the Qur'an.

Id-ul-fitr is a festival of alms-giving, and those Muslims who have not paid *zakat* during Ramadan must do so before the *Id* prayer, which begins the festival. This is the purification act which allows the poor and needy to participate in the festivities.

The festival begins with *salat-ul-fitr*, the festival prayer, an hour after sunset. This is an essential requirement of the festival, and it is like the Friday prayer, having two *rakas* or prostrations in congregation and without *adhan* or **iqamat** (major or minor calls to prayer). Bowing and prostrating before God like this links the spiritual experience of the Ramadan fast with the enjoyment of the festival. There is a sermon after prayer, during which there will be some mention of charity.

Customs associated with this festival are based on the Pillars of Islam, and stem firstly from the rules of the Qur'an and the tradition of the Prophet, and secondly from the national variations in *Eid* traditions.

Procedure

- The Muslim bathes and puts on best or new clothes.
- There is a meeting with fellow Muslims at the mosque.
- The night of *Eid* is spent in meditation and prayer.
- Families go to the mosque for news of the new moon.
- Others remain at home to prepare for the feast day.

17.4 The Day of Arafat

The day of Arafat falls on the ninth day of the twelfth month (**Dhul-Hijjah**).

It commemorates the end of the Qur'an's revelation to the Prophet on Mount Arafat, 12 miles east of Makkah. The revelation ended shortly before the Prophet's death with a verse which can be found in surah 5:4 of the Qur'an. Umar ibn al-Khatab was told that if this verse was revealed to any community, they would celebrate the day of its revelation to Muhammad as a festival. Umar said that he knew that the verse was revealed on Friday at Arafat, so that both Friday and the Day of Arafat are festivals for Muslims.

The main features of Arafat

Arafat is the climax of *hajj* (the pilgrimage to Makkah). Observances are concentrated on the eighth, ninth and tenth days of the month.

There are four main ceremonies:

(1) walking round the Ka'bah seven times (Figure 17.1)
(2) walking between the hills of al-Safa and al-Marwa
(3) the afternoon assembly on Mt Arafat on the ninth day
(4) sacrifices of sheep, goats or camels at Mina on the following day, the Festival of Sacrifice.

Figure 17.1 The act of Tawaf, the circumambulation of the Ka'bah
Hulton Library

The state of ihram

Just as the worshipper must wash according to the prescribed ritual before prayer, pilgrims must be in the physical and spiritual state of ihram before making the pilgrimage. The state of *ihram* involves four things:

(1) consecrating oneself to God
(2) wearing the two plain unsown sheets which are the garments of *ihram*
(3) the shaving of the head for men
(4) no sexual relations until after the sacrifice at Mina

The Mount Arafat service

The pilgrims set out from Makkah after sunrise on the ninth day and head for the mountain. It stands on a plain large enough to hold the entire assembly of about two million pilgrims. It is on the mountain that the pilgrims examine themselves and repent. They break camp after sunset and move to Muzdawfah, five miles away. Here, the night is spent in prayer and meditation. The Festival of Sacrifice which is held on the following day ends the pilgrimages. Anyone who has completed the pilgrimage is now known as a *hajji* if a man; *hajja* if a woman.

17.5 The Festival of Sacrifice: Eid-ul-Adha

This festival, known as *Eid-ul-Adha*, is the culmination of the pilgrimage to Makkah. Celebrations last for four days, which is a day longer than the other major festivals of Islam. Animals are offered at the small village of Mina on the way back to Makkah from Arafat. This is to celebrate Ibraham's (Abraham) willingness to sacrifice Isma'il (Ishmael), his only son, to God. (Islam teaches that Ishmael, not Isaac, was prepared for sacrifice by Abraham.)

There are three stone pillars near the village, representing the places where the Devil tried to tempt Isma'il to rebel against his father who was taking him to be sacrificed. Pilgrims stone these pillars in rejection of evil promptings.

An animal is sacrificed by each pilgrim after the stoning of the first pillar. This is to follow Ibraham's example when he sacrificed a ram after God spared his son. This festival symbolises the submission and commitment of each Muslim to the Will of Allah.

The Festival of Sacrifice for those not on pilgrimage

Muslims not on pilgrimage will celebrate the occasion with much festivity and rejoicing. The following are the main points:

- An animal is bought for the sacrifice.
- The night before the festival is one of prayer and meditation.
- The festival prayer begins the day.
- Then there is a sermon during which sacrifice is mentioned.
- Afterwards the animal is sacrificed in the name of Allah.
- A portion of the meat is given in charity as an act of purification to enable the poor to join in the festival.
- The celebrations may extend until those on pilgrimage have returned.

The four names for the Festival of Sacrifice
(1)   The Great Festival (*Eid-ul-Kabir*)
(2)   The Festival of Immolation (*Eid-ul-Nahr*)
(3)   The Festival of Offering (*Qurbani Eid*)
(4)   The Festival of Sacrifice (*Eid-ul-Adha*)

The Prophet's farewell sermon

The Day of Sacrifice is also a time to celebrate the Prophet's farewell sermon, which was delivered on that day three months before his death, in the tenth year of the Hijrah (the migration from Makkah to Madinah). The sermon is important because it sums up the principles of Islam as laid down by the Qur'anic revelations. It concludes with the demand that Muslims follow the teachings of the Qur'an and the tradition of the Prophet.

17.6 The New Year festival

New Year's Day is on the first day of the month of *Muharram* and is very important for Shi'ite Muslims, who commemorate the death of Hussain, the grandson of

Muhammad, in the Battle of Karbala. They make this a time of mourning and extra time is spent in prayer. Symbols are set up in the streets and the Shi'ites dress in black.

Gatherings are held to recall stories about Muhammad, Ali and Hussain. At the end of this period, when the members of the sect have eaten the 'food of sorrow', a passion play is formed to re-enact the martyrdom of Hussain.

The tenth day of Muharram is a public holiday for Shi'ites everywhere. Special mention is made of the departure of Muhammad from Makkah. He had intended to settle in Saif to the south, but opposition from the leaders of the old religion was too strong, so he had to go to Madinah for safety. This city came to be known as the 'city of the Prophet'.

17.7 Muhammad's birthday: Maulid an Nabi

Muhammad's birthday is celebrated on the twelfth day of the third month (*Rabi'ul-Awwal*). This, the last of the festivals to evolve, was introduced by the Abbasids of Baghdad during the tenth century CE, a time when the Abbasids were the rulers of Islam.

The whole month may be kept as the 'birth month', but the birthday is a public holiday in only a few countries. The celebrations include the following:

- singing the praises of Muhammad
- readings from the Qur'an
- processions and feasting
- bright clothes being worn and homes being decorated
- lectures on the Prophet's way of life
- meeting places being decorated with lights and flags.

17.8 The festival of the Prophet's night journey and Ascension: Al-isra

This festival (*al-isra*), on the twenty-second of *Rayab* (the seventh month), is celebrated throughout the Islamic world, and mosques and minarets are lit up in honour of the night journey from Makkah to Jerusalem, known as the Hadith, when Muhammad was led by the Angel Jibra'il (Gabriel). From the remains of Solomon's temple the Prophet ascended into Heaven (*al-miraj*) and led all the other prophets in prayer before ascending through the Seven Heavens to Allah. He was told by God that all Muslims must pray five times a day after ritual purification achieved by washing.

Prayer is the only direct link between the Muslim and Allah, and so it is the central pillar of Islam. This particular commandment was repeated more than 80 times in the revelation of the Qur'an.

17.9 The Night of Forgiveness: Lailat-ul-Bara't

This is the fifteenth of the eighth month (*Sha'ban*). The night is spent in prayer, because a person's life for the coming year is determined by God during this night, so

His guidance is vital. Many will fast on the previous day in preparation. Some places have firework displays, charity is given and Muslims pay respect to dead relatives by visiting the cemetery.

17.10   Food

Introduction

To eat the pure and wholesome foods given by Allah, in a spirit of thankfulness, is seen as an act of worship. A healthy, moderate diet is a religious duty.

Food banned by the Qur'an

The following foods are banned:

- pigs because of their general filth, and their diet of offal and rotting food: swill. Their meat is also rather fatty and they are prone to disease;
- meat, if its method of slaughter is unknown;
- meat which still contains the blood of the animal;
- an animal killed in the name of any but Allah;
- intoxicants (alcohol).

Important points to remember

- Islam teaches that Allah is protecting the minds and bodies of Muslims by setting out these laws.
- If a Muslim has to choose between eating these banned foods and starving, then he or she must eat.
- Lawful food must be killed according to strict rules (**halal**). Animals must be killed with compassion. The throat of the animal is cut with a sharp knife, so that death is as quick and painless as possible. The animal must not see the knife, and the killing should not be seen by another animal. It is taken comfortably to the place of slaughter and left free to move about while it bleeds to death.

Alcohol

Allah has provided the bounty of nature for human enjoyment, but Satan encourages the misuse of these gifts; alcohol being an excellent example. The date palm and vine provide fruit, date-honey and vinegar but the rotted, fermented fruits produce the alcohol which corrupts individuals and societies.

In strict Muslim countries the buying, selling, making and drinking of alcohol is dealt with by the use of severe corporal punishment.

The family and rites of passage

18.1 The family

The family is the living symbol of Islamic society, and it is in the family that the values of Islam are upheld. The ground rules for the running of the family are set out in the Qur'an.

- The family must be united for the sake of the children, who are its pride and joy.
- Children must be brought up in the faith and the *Adhan* (call to prayer) is whispered to babies so that they hear the words that 'God is great' from the very beginning of their lives.
- Parents must be kind and nurture their children.
- Children must be loyal and obedient to their parents. They must also love their parents and be caring and supportive as they grow old.
- The father is the head of his family; the mother is the heart. He provides for the material needs; she creates an Islamic home true to the principles of the Faith.
- Muslims have extended families so that all rites of passage involve all of a family's members.

18.2 Birth

All babies born into a Muslim family are the gift of Allah. Therefore they are welcomed into the **Ummah**, which is the worldwide family of Islam. Within minutes of birth, the father of the child whispers the *Adhan* to it. Then a tiny piece of sugar or date is put on to the baby's tongue by an older member of the family in the hope that the child will grow up to be obedient and kind. Food, clothes and money are given to the poor in thanks.

18.3 Aqiqah

This ceremony takes place seven days after birth. It involves shaving the baby's head, symbolising the removal of misfortune. It also removes the uncleanliness of birth and encourages the hair to grow more quickly.

Gold and silver of a weight equal to the shaven hair is donated to the poor. A sheep or goat will be sacrificed if the child is a girl. Two animals must be sacrificed if it is a boy. A third animal is given in charity. Relatives receive a third of the meat which is sweetened while cooking; the poor get the other two-thirds.

The child is named, and this is done with much thought. Most names are taken from those of Allah (who has 99), Muhammed or one of the great Muslim leaders of the past. The word *Abd* (servant) is added.

Abu Musa asked Muhammad for a name for his son, so parents may ask the **imam** to choose a name for the baby. Fashionable names are not used because Muslims believe that the name influences the personality and character.

Muhammad stated that Allah liked names such as Abdullah (servant of Allah) or, for girls, one of the 99 beautiful names of Allah.

18.4 Circumcision

Boys can be circumcised when eight days old, although this can be done at any time up to the age of 10. Circumcision is known as '*khitan*' and is carried out because the Sunnah says it is a practice of all prophets, even though it is not mentioned in the Qur'an.

18.5 The Bismillah *ceremony*

This takes place when the child is four years, four months, and four days old. It remembers the first time that the Angel Jibra'il appeared to Muhammad, and is the start of the child's religious education. The father gets the child to repeat the first lesson from the Qur'an: 'In the name of Allah, the Compassionate, the Merciful', and this is followed by further verses from the Qur'an. Sweetmeats are shared by everyone at the ceremony.

18.6 Aqd Nikah *(marriage)*

The Qur'an says that marriage is a natural state. It is a righteous act though not a sacrament. Sexual relations are allowed in marriage.

The creation of a family is a natural part of Islamic life. Marriage is a public commitment between the two people. The woman must state her willingness and her father must give his permission. A man can have up to four wives, but in practice this does not happen. (In the UK the law does not allow this anyway.) Marriage is for life, so great care is taken over choosing a partner, and parents and relatives are involved in the choice; this is known as arranged marriage.

A man wishing to marry a woman presents himself to her family and asks the conditions for her hand in marriage. When agreement is arrived at, the engagement is announced. Sex before marriage is banned and is punished by the *shari'ah* law. In a Muslim country, marriage can take place anywhere, typically the bride's home is used; in Britain it is usually undertaken in the mosque. The ceremony has readings from the Qur'an (usually the fourth surah: 'The Woman') and the Hadith read by the *qadi* (legal official).

There is a spoken and written contract; there must be three copies of the latter so that the husband and wife have one each, the third being for the officials. The contract is between the bridegroom and the bride's male guardian in front of two male witnesses.

The Qur'an demands that the husband gives his wife money or property (*mahr*) to keep, the *qadi* announcing the amount of dowry being given (this belongs to the wife).

The ceremony can be conducted by any male Muslim, but it is usually the *imam*. Rings are exchanged by the couple, the one put on the man's finger cannot be gold.

There is a feast afterwards, in which dates are shared. Then the bride and groom go to their home. The next day, family and friends come to the marriage celebration (*walima*).

Divorce

Muhammad said that divorce is the most hateful of permitted things. The marriage contract is terminated only if the marriage has totally broken down; even then it must be done amicably. In the event of divorce, Islamic law protects the rights of the wife, although the children usually go to the custody of the father. Remarriage is encouraged.

18.7 Death

Muslims believe in the resurrection of the body and life after death. After death, a soul is reunited with friends and family who have already died. Death should be faced without fear and with a spirit of hope.

Preparation for death

As death approaches, the creed (*shahadah*) is recited and the Qur'an is read, especially surahs 36 and 55. Prayers are said for forgiveness. The last statement before death is, 'There is no god but God and Muhammad is His messenger'. When the person dies, Muslims say 'To Allah we belong and to Allah we return'.

18.8 Burial

The procedure

- After death the body is washed by a member of the same sex, as before prayer, in scented water. The mouth and nostrils are perfumed.
- Male corpses are dressed in three robes, females in five. If the dead person was lucky enough to have been on the pilgrimage to Makkah and returned with the sheets that they wore, then they will be wrapped in these sheets, especially if they had been washed in the holy well at Zam Zam.
- Rich and poor must be treated the same; everyone is equal in the sight of God.
- The body is taken to the mosque or open space for the funeral prayer, which is led by the *imam* or by a family member.
- There are no strict rules about how long a body should wait for burial, as long as it is not kept in a house for too long.
- The body is taken to a cemetery for burial, because Muslims do not believe in cremation. In Muslim countries, a coffin is not used and the grave is dug to fit the size of the body; it is important for the body to be in actual contact with the soil.

- More prayers are said, and then the body is placed in the grave with the right side facing Makkah; the head is turned in that direction as well. Surah 20:25 is recited.
- The ground is left raised and without monuments.

Mourning

This lasts anything from seven days to three months. Islam teaches that the grave is visited by two angels to question the deceased to establish whether or not he or she is fit for the next life and the Day of Judgement. Graves are visited as a reminder of the ultimate fate of everyone. Muslims are not ashamed about weeping because Muhammad wept when his son died. Muhammad said that all a person can leave is charity given, knowledge passed on and pious children to pray for them.

Questions

1. *Zakat* (giving of charity) is one of the 'pillars' of Islam.

   (a) Describe:

       (i)   the practice of *Zakat*;
       (ii) who should receive *Zakat*.   *(7 marks)*

   (b) Explain the meaning **and** importance of charitable giving for Muslims.   *(8 marks)*

   (c) 'You should give to charity because you want to, not because your religion says you should.'

   Do you agree? Give reasons in support of your answer.   *(5 marks)*

                               (Total 20 marks)

   (SEG SYL A Paper 2, June 1995)

2. Questions (a)–(d) can be answered in a single word, phrase or sentence. Question (e) requires a longer answer.

   (a) During which month should Muslims obey the command to fast?   *(1 mark)*

   (b) What is *Tawhid*?   *(1 mark)*

   (c) What does the word *Qur'an* mean?   *(1 mark)*

   (d) Name **two** groups of people who are excused from making the pilgrimage to Makkah.   *(2 marks)*

   (e) Explain the importance of prayer in Islam.   *(5 marks)*

                               (Total 10 marks)

   (SEG Paper 148011, Section A, 1998 Short Course Specimen Questions)

3. Birth, marriage and death are important family occasions in Islam. Select **one** of these.

   (a) (i)   Describe the religious customs associated with the occasion you have chosen.   *(5 marks)*

         (ii) Explain the importance to the family of these customs.   *(5 marks)*

   (b) Who do you think benefits most from these customs – the individual, the family or the community? Give reasons for your answer, showing that you have thought about more than one point of view.   *(10 marks)*

   (NEAB Short Course Paper 4, 19 June 1997)   *(Total 20 marks)*

4. (a) How many times a day do Muslims pray? [1]

   (b) Describe **three** of the Five Pillars of Islam. [7]

   (c) Why are these rituals and beliefs important in a Muslim's life? [7]

   (d) 'Prayer is the most important part of a believer's life.'

   Do you agree? Give reasons to support your answer and show that you have thought about different points of view. You must refer to Islam in your answer. [5]

   (*MEG Sample Paper, Summer 1998*)

5. (a) What does the word '*wudu*' refer to? (*2 marks*)

   (b) What do Muslims mean by the word *ibadah*? (*6 marks*)

   (c) Describe and explain how Ramadan makes a difference to a Muslim's daily life. (*8 marks*)

   (d) 'If religious people were really generous, there would be no poverty.'

   Do you agree? Give reasons for your answer showing you have considered another point of view. (*4 marks*)

   (*Total 20 marks*)

   (*London (1479) Specimen papers for May/June 1999*)

Islam: a glossary

Abd
Arabic, meaning 'slave (or servant) of Allah', as in Abdullah; it indicates the status of human beings as doers of God's will

Abu Bakr
The first *Khalifah* or successor to the leadership of the Muslim community when the Prophet Muhammad died

Adam
The first man and the first prophet of Allah; this is the same Adam who, with Eve, lived in the Garden of Eden until God sent them away for sinning

Adha
A feast held to coincide with the annual sacrifice which takes place at Makkah, near the end of the *Hajj*

Adhan
The call to prayer, made five times a day to Muslims from every mosque; it is from the same root as 'Mu'adhin', one who makes the call to prayer

Ahmadiyyah
A reform movement founded by Mirza Ghulam Ahmad (1839–1908), who announced that he was the expected *Mahdi* of Islam (see under *al-Mahdi*)

Aishah
One of the wives of the Prophet Muhammad, daughter of *Abu Bakr*

Akhirah
Everlasting life after death

Akhlaq
Attitudes, ethics and behaviour

al-Amin
The 'Trustworthy': a name used to describe the Prophet Muhammad

al-Aqsa
Al-Masjid al-Aqsa, 'The Farthest Mosque': it is in Jerusalem

al-Fatihah
'The Opener – *surah* 1 of the *Qur'an*; it is recited at least 17 times daily during the five times of *salat*. It is also known as 'The Essence' of the Qur'an

al-hamdul-li-Llah
Lit: 'Praise belongs to Allah'; it is often used as an expression of thanks to Allah

Al-isrd
The Festival of The Prophet's Night Journey and Ascension

al-Kafi
Lit: 'Enough' or 'Sufficient'; this is the title of the books of *Hadith* compiled by Muhammad ibn-Yaqub Koleini, a *Shi'ah* scholar

al-Khulafa-ur-Rashidun
Lit: The 'Rightly-Guided' *Khalifahs*: they were the first four successors to the leadership role of the Prophet Muhammad. They were *Abu Bakr*, Umar, Uthman, and *Ali*

al-Madinah
The 'City of the Prophet', the name given to Yathrib after the Prophet moved there in 622 CE and founded the first Islamic state; note that it is a shortened form of *Madinatu'n-Nabiyy*

al-Mahdi
Lit: 'The guided one': he will appear towards the end of time to restore righteousness. This is the expected and promised Messiah

Al-Miraj
The ascension into Heaven by the Prophet

Ali
Cousin and son-in-law of Muhammad, he was the husband of *Fatimah* (al-) Zahrah, and the father of Hassan, Hussein, and Zainab – the fourth '*Al-Khulafa ur-Rashidun*' according to *Sunnis* and the first successor accepted by *Shi'ah* Islam

Allah
Derived from the Arabic '*al-ilah*', this is the name of the Supreme Being. The Arabic term has no singular, plural or gender. Allah is the sole deity with no associates, and no images of him are permitted. The attributes of Allah are rehearsed in the 99 Most Beautiful Names, which are often recited with the aid of prayer beads

Allahu Akbar
Allah is most great

Ansar
Lit: 'supporters', they were the Muslims of Madinah who welcomed and supported those Muslims who came from Makkah

Aqd Nikah
Marriage

Arafat
A plain a few miles from Makkah where pilgrims gather to worship, pray and ask for forgiveness on the ninth day of the Islamic month of *Dhul-Hijjah*

Asr (salat-ul-Asr)
Mid-afternoon *salat*, which is any time from mid-afternoon until half an hour before sunset

As-Salamu alaykum
An Islamic greeting, literally 'Peace be upon you'

Assirat Bridge
The entrance to Heaven

Ayah
Lit: sign; a unit within a *Surah* of the *Qur'an*

Barakah
Blessings

Bilal
The first *Mu'adhin* of Islam, who was once an Abyssinian slave

Bismillah
'In the name of Allah'

Bismillah-ir-Rahman-ir-Rahim
'In the name of Allah, most Gracious, most Merciful', the preface to all *surahs* of the *Qur'an* except the ninth

Caliph
See *Khalifah*

Da'if
Weak; one of the classifications of Sunnah

Dar ul-harb
Lit: 'the house of war', or those areas of mankind that Islam has not yet subdued

Dar ul-Islam
Lit: 'the house or abode of Islam', this means the lands under Islamic rule

Da'wah
Inviting people to Islam, literally or by preaching and the example of good actions

Dawud
The prophet to whom the Zabur (psalms) were revealed

Dhikr
Lit: 'remembrance', it means to remember Allah by mention of His names, and His reminder to men, which is in the *Qur'an*, the relevant sections of which should be recited

Dhimmi
A non-Muslim living freely under the protection of an Islamic state

Dhul-Hijjah
The month of the *hajj*, last month of the Islamic year

Din
Religion in general and religious duties in particular; it includes the five basic obligations of the Muslim. It also means divine judgement

Din ul-fitrah
Description of Islam as the 'natural way of life'

Du'a
Varying forms of personal prayer and supplication

Eid
See *Id*

Eid-ul-Nahr
Festival of Immolation

Fajr (salat ul-Fajr)
The dawn *salat*, performed at any time from dawn until just before sunrise

Fana
In *Sufi* Islam this is a term meaning the passing away of the self, either momentarily or permanently

Fard
An obligation under Divine Law, such as the five daily times of *salat*

Fatihah
The title of the first *surah* of the *Qur'an*; see *al-Fatihah*

Fatimah (al-) Zahrah
Muhammad's daughter and the wife of *Ali*, the mother of Hassan, Hussein and Zainab

Fatwa
A legal opinion given by a Muslim *mufti*, by which the *Shari'ah* is applied to cases or issues so that its authority and precedents may be upheld

Fiqh
Islamic jurisprudence; it is the legal order as exercised in the courts and expounded by the several schools of law

Fitnah
Originally trial or persecution borne by believers in Muhammad, it was later used to describe sedition or conspiracy against the Islamic state

Five Pillars of Islam
Five duties incumbent on all Muslims: (1) *Shahadah* or the profession of faith and confession of the Unity of God; (2) *Salat* or prayer; (3) *Zakat* or almsgiving; (4) *Saum* or fasting; (5) *Hajj* or Pilgrimage to Makkah

Ghusl
Greater ablution; the formal washing of the whole body before worship

Hadith
Tradition in Islam from the sayings and deeds of Muhammad as reported and recorded by his household and companions, this is a major source of *Sunnah* or obligatory law

Hafiz
Someone who has learned the *Qur'an* by heart

Hajar
The wife of the Prophet *Ibrahim* and the mother of the Prophet Isma'il

Haji (Hajji)
A Muslim male who has completed *Hajj*

Hajiah (Hajja)
A Muslim female who has completed *Hajj*

Hajj
Pilgrimage to Makkah in the sacred month; the fifth pillar of Islam

Halal
Any action which is permitted or lawful; for example, meat that is slaughtered according to Islamic requirements

Hanif
A seeker after true religion; in the *Qur'an* Abraham is an example of a God-fearer before the coming of Islam

Haram
Anything unlawful or forbidden

Hasan – good; one of the classifications of Sunnah

Hijab
Lit: 'curtain' or 'veil', used to describe the headscarf of modest dress for women. This involves covering everything except the face and hands in front of anyone other than the immediate family

Hijrah
Lit: 'migration, emigration, departure or exit'; in 622 CE Muhammad and 100 followers left Makkah for Madinah which is about 300 km away. A new community was set up there. This date is the beginning of the Islamic calendar

Hira
The name of the mountain near Makkah where the Prophet Muhammad used to go for solitude and to worship. This is where he received the first revelation of the *Qur'an*

Ibadah (Ibadat)
This covers all acts of worship and covers any permissable action performed with the aim of obeying Allah. It comes from the verb 'Abada' (to serve), and 'Abd' (a slave)

Iblis
The Angel who defied Allah by refusing to bow to Adam, and later became the tempter of all mankind. See also Shaytan

Ibrahim
Abraham, a prophet of Allah to whom the 'Scrolls' were revealed

Id (Eid)
Lit: 'recurring happiness', this is a religious holiday, a festival and feast for thanking Allah

Id mubarak
A greeting on Islamic festivals: 'Happy Id!'

Id-ul-Adha
Festival of the Sacrifice commemorating the Prophet Ibrahim's willingness to do Allah's will by sacrificing his son Isma'il. It is also known as *Id ul kabir* – the 'Greater Id' and *Qurban Bayram* or Feast of Sacrifice in Turkey

Id-ul-fitr (Eid-ul-Fitr)
This is the day after Ramadan ends, and is also the first day of Shawwal, the tenth month. It is also known as *Id Eid-al-asaghar* or the 'Lesser Id', and it is the Turkish *Sheker Bayram* or 'Sugar' feast

Ihram
The state of ritual purity necessary for *hajj* or *umrah*; it also refers to the plain white garments worn by male pilgrims to show the equality, brotherhood and purity of the pilgrim

Ijma
The general consensus in *Sunni* Islam on matters of law, practice and usage

Ijtihad
The initiative of experts and pioneers in facing and responding to new situations in Islam

Ikhlas
Religious sincerity as an ethical ideal in Islam as set out in the *Qur'an*, *surah* 112, named *Ikhlas*

Imam
Lit: 'leader'; someone who leads communal prayer/public worship in a mosque or elsewhere. The *imam* is not a priest and has no authority. The *Shi'ites* gave the title to their leaders, descendents of the Prophet through his daughter *Fatima*

Imamah
Religious authority in *Shi'ah* Islam as successor to the Prophet as leader of the Muslim community

Iman
Faith

Injil
Gospel
Iqamah
The call to stand up for *salat*
Isa
Jesus, who in Islam is seen as a prophet of Allah who had a virgin birth and to whom the *Injil* was revealed
Isha (salat-ul-Isha)
The evening *salat*, which can be performed from an hour after sunset until midnight
Isma'il (Ishmael)
The son of Ibrahim (Abraham) and Hajar (Hagar), described in the *Qur'an* as a prophet (xix.55), he is seen as the father of the Arabs. He helped Ibrahim to build the *Ka'bah*, and placed the Black Stone in it (ii.119–25). Islam teaches that Isma'il, not Isaac, was prepared for sacrifice by Ibraham
Islam
Lit: 'Peace through willing obedience to Allah's divine guidance', it is an Arabic word based on the letters S-L-M, in which there is also the root of the word 'Salaam' meaning 'peace'. It is the religious teaching, faith, obedience and practice, and the widespread religious community founded by the prophet Muhammad, and based on the *Qur'an*. Without a capital letter, *islam* indicates the quality of submission or surrender to the Divine word as taught by Islam
Isma'ilis
A branch of the *Shi'ah* Muslims, sometimes called the 'Seveners', because they believe that the seventh Imam was the last and the greatest
Isnad
The chain of transmission of each *hadith*
Jahannam
Hell
Jahiliyyah
The time of ignorance in Arabia before Islam
Jibra'il
The Angel Gabriel, who delivered Allah's messages to His prophets
Jihad
'Striving' or 'Holy War', this is the duty imposed by the *Qur'an* on every Muslim to fight against polytheists (viii.39), or Christians and Jews (ix.29) in order to advance the faith. A *Jihad* must be carefully defined and led by an *imam* or Islamic head of state. The *Sufis* say that the true *Jihad* is against personal sin
Jinn
Demons and spirits mentioned in the *Qur'an*, Muhammad was sent to preach to them, and some repented
Ka'aba
This an Arabic word meaning 'cube'. It is a cube-shaped structure in the centre of the grand mosque in Makkah. It is a sacred shrine in the courtyard and is 12 metres long × 11 metres wide × 5 metres high. It is towards this that all Muslims turn to pray. It is covered by a black cloth into which the confession of faith is woven, and it is renewed annually. The Black Stone is set into the east corner. Tradition holds that it was built by *Ibraham* and *Isma'il* as the first house built for the worship of Allah
Kalimah
This is the title of the *Shahadah* or confession made by Muslims that: 'There is no god but God; Muhammad is the messenger of God
Khadijah
The first wife of the Prophet Muhammad
Khalifah
'Successor, inheritor, custodian, viceregent', it refers to the chief defender of the Islamic faith. *Sunni* Muslims regard *Abu Bakr* as the first in Madinah. *Shi'ah* Muslims reject the first three and start from *Ali*. The Abbasid Caliphate was founded in Baghdad in 750 CE and remained there until they moved to Cairo in 1258. In 1517 the Turks forcibly removed the Caliphate to Istanbul, which was its home until 1924 when the Turkish National Assembly abolished it

Khitan
Circumcision
Khums
The additional contribution to *zakat* of one-fifth of surplus annual income paid by the *Shi'ah* Muslims as demanded in *surah* 8:41
Khutbah
'Speech': a talk delivered on special occasions such as the *Jum'ah* and *Id* prayers
Kufr
The ultimate evil; disbelief in Allah and His signs, rejection of revelation and thanklessness (Compare with *Shukr.*)
Labbaika
It means 'Here I am before Thee' and is the cry of greeting of the Muslim pilgrim in Makkah
Laylat al-qadr
The Night of Power when the first revelation of the *Qur'an* was made to the Prophet Muhammad during the last ten days of *Ramadan*
Maghrib (salat ul-Maghrib)
Sunset *salat*, which can be performed after sunset until daylight ends
Mahr
Dowry given by husband to wife
Maryam
The virgin mother of the prophet *Isa*
Masjid
Lit: Place of prostration; mosque
Makkah
The city where Muhammad was born, it is the spiritual centre of Islam and is in Arabia. In the centre is the sacred Mosque, and the *Ka'bah* with the Black Stone. Legend links its foundation with Adam and its development with *Ibraham* and *Isma'il* (Ishmael)
Madinah
The tomb of the Prophet is there, and it is still a place of pilgrimage second only to *Makkah*. (See also *al-Madinah*.)
Mihrab
The niche or alcove into which the *imam* prays, it indicates the direction of Makkah, of the *'qiblah'* for those worshipping in the mosque
Mina
A place near Makkah where pilgrims stay on the 10th, 11th and 12th of *Dhul-Hijjah* and perform some of the activities of the *Hajj*, including stoning three pillars
Minaret
The tower near a mosque from which the *muezzin* calls the faithful to prayer, five times a day; it was probably a fire tower or beacon originally
Minbar
Rostrum, platform or dais: the stand from which the *imam* delivers the *khutbah* or speech in the *mosque* or place of prayer
Miqat
Lit: A 'place appointed' at which the pilgrims enter into the state of *ihram*
Mosque
Building for Muslim public worship, it is normally in the form of a square, with an open court-yard containing a watertank for ritual washing. It has an area for prayers, with a pulpit, and a recess in one wall which shows the direction of Makkah. This word is derived from the Arabic *'Masjid'*, meaning a place of prostration
Muezzin (Mu'adhdhin)
The man who calls the faithful to prayer; he does this five times a day from the *minaret* of the *mosque*. The name is derived from the Arabic word *Mu'adhdhin'*: the *adhan* caller
Mufti
Islamic lawyer who gives judgements or **fatwa** based on the *Shari'ah* or religious law
Muhajirun
Those who took part in the *Hijrah* when Muhammad and his followers migrated from *Makkah* to *Madinah* in 622 CE

Muhammad

Lit: 'Praised': he is the final Prophet and was born in Makkah around 570 CE. At the age of 40 he experienced visions and revelations which form the basis of the *Qur'an*

Muharram

The first month in the Islamic calendar which is reckoned from the time of the migration to *Madinah*

Mumin

A person who wholeheartedly yields to Allah's guiding wisdom and so is in harmony with His will and at peace with himself and all creatures

Munafiqun

This is the term used in *surah* lxiii of the *Qur'an* to describe hypocrites

Murid

This is the first stage in *Sufi* discipleship; the would-be seeker

Muslim

Someone who submits to the will of God in any age or time

Muslim

One who has submitted to the Will of God, and has accepted Islam

Muzdalifah

Place where pilgrims camp for the night after standing at Arafat during *hajj*

Nabi

Prophet of Allah

Nifaq

A Muslim term for hypocrisy, or pretended belief in the *Qur'an* which is devoid of sincere faith

Niyyah

Lit: 'intention'; the statement of intent made before all acts of worship such as *salat, hajj* or *sawm*

Pilgrimage

The fifth pillar of Islam is the duty to undertake a pilgrimage to *Makkah (Hajj)*, at least once in a lifetime

Prophet

The *Qur'an* identifies many figures in the Old and New Testament as prophets (this includes Jesus), but believes that Muhammad is the final prophet of Allah. *Qadi* – Muslim judge

Qadar

Allah's complete and final control over the outcome of events or destiny. (See also *Laylat al-qadr*.)

Qiblah

The direction to which Muslims must turn in prayer towards the *Ka'bah* in Makkah. (See also *mihrab*.)

Quraish

The tribe to which Muhammad belonged; the ruling authorities in Makkah

Qurbani Eid

The Festival of offering

Qur'an

That which is read or recited; it is the Divine book revealed to the prophet Muhammad on the Night of Power. It is Allah's final revelation to mankind. It has 114 *surahs* or chapters

Rabb

Lit: 'Lord', the title most frequently for Allah

al-Rajim

The Muslim name for Satan ('the accursed one', see also *Iblis*), it means 'one who is stoned', and is derived from the stone-throwing ceremony at Makkah

Rak'ah

A unit in *salat*, made up of recitation, standing, bowing and two prostrations

Raka'at

The Muslim ritual of repeating several prayers with obligatory bodily positions in a specified sequence

Ramadan

The ninth month of the Islamic calendar, which involves fasting during the hours of daylight, it celebrates the month when the *Qur'an* was 'sent down'

Rasul
Messenger of Allah
Ruku
Bowing in Salat
Sabr
Patience and fortitude under adversity; the staying power which is the fruit of firm reliance on God
Sa'y
Walking between Safa and Marwah as part of *Hajj*, in remembrance of *Hajar's* search for water for her son *Isma'il*
Sadaqah
A voluntary payment or good action for charitable purposes
Safa and Marwah
Two hills in Makkah, near the *Ka'bah*; now next to the grand mosque
Sahih al-Bukhari
The title of the books of *Hadith* compiled by Muhammad ibn Ismail al Bukhari, a *Sunni* scholar, this collection is described as *Sahih* or 'Authentic'
Sahih Muslim
The title of the books of *Hadith* compiled by Abul Husayn Muslim ibn al-Hajjaj, a *Sunni* scholar, the collection is described as *Sahih* or 'Authentic'
Salat (salah)
This is ritual or liturgical prayer in Islam, and is the second Pillar of *Din*; it is performed five times a day
Salat ul-Jum'ah
The weekly congregational prayer and attendance for the *khutbah* performed at middays on Fridays
Salik
The second stage of *Sufi* discipleship, the journeyer
Saqim
Infirm; one of the classifications of Sunnah
Sawm (also *Saum*)
Fasting, especially during *Ramadan*, it lasts from dawn till sunset every day during the ninth month of the Islamic calendar. This includes all food, drink (including water), smoking and sexual relations
Seveners
Muslims who accepted the seven *Imams*, and in 765 CE accepted the leadership of *Isma'il*, thus becoming the ancestors of the *Isma'ili* Muslims
Shahadah
The declaration of faith, the witness and confession of the *Kalimah*; the first Islamic Pillar of *Din*: 'There is no god except Allah, Muhammad is the Messenger of Allah'
Shari'ah
Canon Law of Islam based on the *Qur'an* and *Sunnah*, but more commonly used to mean all the commandments of God concerning human actions
Shaytan
The 'accursed'; a name given to *Iblis* or Satan
Shi'ah
The Islamic sect which regards *Ali* as the first true *Khalifah*, they believe in the successorship of Ali and the eleven of the most pious knowledgeable descendents of his after the Prophet Muhammad. It is the official religion of Iran, and has subdivisions such as the *Imamis* and the *Isma'ilis*
Shirk
Lit: 'association', this is the cardinal sin of idolatry or deification. This applies to any deviation from the exclusive worship of the one true God
Shukr
Gratitude for divine mercy
Sirah
The career or biography of Muhammad

Sufi
A Muslim mystic
Sujud
Prostration in Salat
Sunnah
From the Arabic for 'custom'; the path of tradition; the theory and practice of orthodox Islam, following the standards of Muhammad
Sunni
The broad mass of Islam who rely on the *Qur'an*, the *Sunnah* and the community. They reject the *Shi'ah* Imams
Surah
Division or chapter of the Qur'an
Tanzil
The descent or downward flow of inspiration that came to Muhammad
Taqlid
Authoritarianism, unquestioning adherence to a traditional school of teaching in Islam
Tariqah
The *Sufi* way of discipline and initiation into divine knowledge through self-transcendence and self-mortification
Tawhid
The driving motive of Islam: the doctrine of divine unity, that God is one; let God be God alone
Ulama
Islamic doctors of theology or law. They are the guardians of Islamic teaching
Ummah
The world-wide family of Islam
'Urf
Customary law, from which the content of Islamic *Shari'ah* is derived
Wahhabis
An Islamic community which has been the main influence in Saudi Arabia since 1924, it was founded by 'Abd al-Wahhab (1703–92)
Wahy
The state of mind and spirit in which Muhammad received and communicated the *Qur'an*
Walima
Marriage celebration
Wasil
The final stage of *Sufi* discipleship
Wudu
Washing before prayer: the hands, forearms and legs below the knees must be washed, the face, mouth and nose must be rinsed
Zakat (zakah)-ul-fitr
Almsgiving; the third of the five Pillars of Islam
Zawiyah
A local Muslim community or 'cell' sharing devotion and spiritual exercises
Zuhd
The call to abstinence or a religious life

PART IV

Hinduism

Hinduism: origins and definitions

19.1 Introduction

The year 1829 saw the first-known use of the word 'Hinduism' in English. Definition is not easy because Hinduism is at least 3000 years old and is followed by hundreds of millions of people. 'Hindu' is in fact a Persian word meaning 'Indian', and strictly, Hinduism refers to the civilization of the Hindus, the inhabitants of the land of the River Indus. Indian law tells us that a Hindu is a citizen of India who is not a Muslim, Christian, Parsi or Jew. Presumably, this must include Buddhists, Jains, and Sikhs as well; but what of the followers of Hinduism who are citizens of the United Kingdom and other countries?

We can say that Hinduism is the worship of the gods **Vishnu** or **Shiva**, the goddess **Shakti**, or any of their various forms, incarnations, spouses or offspring. This includes the cults of **Rama** and **Krishna**, who are incarnations or **avatars** of Vishnu; and **Durga**, the wife of Shiva, and their sons Skanda and **Ganesha**. The important benchmark is that any teachings do not deny the authority or supremacy of the sacred scriptures of the **Veda**. This is vital because every Hindu pays homage to the Veda, even though few read or follow it today.

Hinduism is made up of a vast number of cults and sects which are more or less closely connected with the high tradition which influences them, and gives them a quite recognisable Hindu form. This high tradition has formed over the centuries by absorbing the gods, rites and philosophies of each tribe and locality. The secret of understanding Hinduism is to focus on this high tradition and its literature, and the **Brahman** priests and scholars who are its guardians.

Interestingly, Hinduism is an ethnic religion, unlike the more recent missionary religions such as Buddhism, Christianity and Islam. It is the religion of a single cultural unit, like Judaism, and has not strained to attract converts from outside that unit. It is sharply distinguished from Western religions by its belief in *transmigration*. It shares this characteristic with Buddhism and Jainism. Briefly, this means a belief that the soul inhabits many bodies in rebirth after rebirth, until it reaches its ultimate goal of complete freedom from rebirth.

Hinduism has a huge range of popular belief, elaborate ritual and philosophy. There are many stages of transition, magic, animal worship, belief in demons, a multitude of gods of varying degrees of power, mysticism, asceticism, abstract theology, some of which is very profound, plus a variety of esoteric doctrines. It includes all sorts of belief and worship without the need to select or remove any. In Hinduism no religious belief ever dies or is succeeded because any new idea is combined with existing ones.

Hindus respect the Divine in any form and tolerate other beliefs as suit them best. They can follow another religion without giving up Hinduism. It is believed that the different religions and divine powers complement each other. Hindus distinguish themselves from others on the basis of practice (or *orthopraxy*) rather than doctrine (or *orthodoxy*). They call their religion the '*sanatan dharma*' or 'eternal dharma'. 'Dharma' in simple terms means 'law' and 'religion' (this will be dealt with in more detail below, see Section 20.4).

19.2 An evolving religious tradition, not a separate religion

Its characteristics

It has few of the characteristics normally associated with a religion.

- It has no founder
- It is not prophetic
- It does not have a creed
- It has no particular doctrine, dogma or practice
- It is not a system of theology
- It is not a single moral code
- The concept of God is not central to it
- No specific scripture or work is uniquely authoritative
- It is not sustained by an ecclesiastical organization.

Its diversity

It has had an astonishing diversity since historical times.

- It is the mainstream of religious development in the Indian subcontinent going back thousands of years.
- It has input from other races and cultures.
- India is vast and has huge regional variations in climate, resources, terrain, communications, people, culture and language.

Three important features

Three important features of Hinduism give it a distinctive form and consistency:

- the six *Darshanas* or philosophical schools at the intellectual level
- the Epics and **Puranas** for legend and mythology
- the **caste** system for day-to-day behaviour.

19.3 Hinduism in the UK

Since the break-up of the British Indian Empire in 1947–8 there has been a steady stream of Hindus to Britain, but not in any numbers until the late 1950s onwards. They were encouraged to come to fill vacancies in British industry, transport and in the Health Service. In the late 1960s and early 1970s a new wave of Hindu immigration came from East Africa, where the 'Africanisation' policies of Kenya, Uganda and Malawi forced them to leave.

The progress of Hindus in the UK

The main concentrations of Hindus are to be found in London, and in the industrial cities and towns of the Midlands and the North. Clearly, they have been economically successful, especially as they can escape the restrictions of caste in this country. Even so, caste is still important in matters such as marriage, which is still arranged to a large extent. The first generation immigrants had the difficulty of coping with language and customs, but generations born in Britain, on the other hand, have the problem of retaining their sense of Hindu identity.

The main characteristics of Hinduism in the UK

- The traditional extended family is the norm.
- Marriage outside Hinduism is rare.
- Hindu rites of passage are observed.
- The home is the stronghold of Hindu practice in Britain and it has a special shrine room with pictures of favourite gods.
- Major festivals such as **Divali** and **Holi** are celebrated but not on the sort of scale that they would be in India.
- The National Council of Hindu Temples provides a link for local temples throughout Britain, and The Hindu Centre in London provides information for non-Hindus who have to deal with Hindus in such matters as the care of the dying, blood transfusions, and funerals.
- Temples provide schooling for children in the language of their ethnic group.

Associated movements

The Ramakrishna mission

This was established in Britain before the main migration of Hindus to this country, and it has had little impact on the general Hindu community. In any case, its mission is to mankind in general and not just Hindus.

The Hare Krishna movement

This is a Hindu movement and it works with Indian Hindus. It has centres for visitors and produces literature for use by the Hindu community. It has an annual **yatra** (pilgrimage) procession through London every year.

The Swami Nariyan movement

This is active in bringing Hinduism to the attention of non-Hindus.

20 Hindu beliefs

20.1 Three purposes in Hinduism

(1) Coming to terms with this life

Bringing up a family and earning a living is difficult at the best of times because of natural and supernatural challenges. Hinduism has to deal with everyday problems such as sickness, the need for a successful harvest, fending off ghosts and the 'evil eye' or pleasing a troublesome minor god.

(2) Gaining merit and a good rebirth

Hindus must keep to their *dharma* to avoid sin and gain merit. *Dharma* requires that every being must live by the laws that affect its particular nature. People, for example, have to obey the rules of their particular caste. It is concerned with the ultimate purposes of humankind, and the fate of souls when people die. It also includes the upholding of social order.

There are rules and regulations to allow people to find and pursue a way of life and observance that will let them gain the merit needed for an improvement in their rebirth.

So, there are two main aims. Firstly a proximate aim: to gain merit by appropriate living and observance. Then the ultimate aim, which is to acquire a better lot in life in a future rebirth earned by merit achieved in this life. Of course, merit brings incidental benefits in this life – for example, a good name and prosperity.

(3) The search for liberation and salvation

This is a very personal quest and concentrates on liberation, salvation and union with the Supreme Being. It is to be free from the cycle of rebirth. It is 'to be carried safely across the ocean of existence'. This is what is called a '**Transcendental Complex**'; in other words, it aims to rise above worldly matters. There are two ways that this affects religion in village life: asceticism and the sect.

Asceticism

Asceticism, or renouncing the world, is taken up by the **sannyasin**, who stands outside the caste system in searching for liberation from **samsara** and the laws of **karma**. Wandering ascetics are a familiar sight in India and from time to time one will live on the outskirts of a village. The *sannyasin*, who has renounced worldly affairs and is on the last of the four stages of life, is very influential and is honoured and respected for pursuing the quest for **moksha** (salvation) in this way.

The sect

This is more common and more influential, and the numbers, beliefs and practices of sects seem boundless.

Of greatest importance are those who seek living salvation by loving devotion to God. This is known as **bhakti**. This third form of religious motivation is highly personal and is completely concerned with the next world in matters such as liberation, salvation and union with God.

20.2 Samsara, Heaven and Hell

Samsara is the transmigration of the soul and its continual rebirth by the law of *karma*, by which our deeds determine our fate in this life, and after death and in rebirth. The soul goes to heaven or hell until its merit or sin runs out, after which it is reborn. There are various heavens, and **Indra, Shiva, Vishnu** and **Krishna** each have one.

20.3 The doctrine of Atman Brahman

Hindus believe in an Ultimate Reality which they call *brahman*. It is in all things and is the 'self' (*atman*) of all living creatures. *Brahman* is uncreated eternal, infinite and transcendent and includes absolutely everything. It is the only reality, the only source and the purpose of all existence. This *Brahman* is impersonal because it has no qualities or attributes. Hindus see it as a personal high God; normally Vishnu or Shiva. The belief in, and quest for this Ultimate Reality has remained the focus of Hindu spiritual life, practically unchanged for 3000 years.

20.4 Dharma

Some definitions of dharma

Generally, *dharma* means religion, duty, law, righteousness and eternal order.
  Dharma is a mode of Hindu religious motivation, acquiring merit and having good rebirth. To keep to dharmic rules means to avoid sin and to acquire merit.

- Hindu *dharma* is the *dharma* of the Hindus.
- *Sanatan dharma* is the eternal *dharma* which is the unchanging universal law of order which says that every being in the universe must act according to the laws that apply to its own nature.
- *Sadharan dharma* is the general code of ethics that applies to everyone. This includes pilgrimage, giving to charity, honouring **brahmins**, not lying, not injuring and so forth; all bring merit.
- **Varnashrama dharma** is accepting and following customs and rules of caste.
- **Jati dharma** decides how and which **samskaras** (or rites of passage) are celebrated by each caste or subcaste.

Why dharma is important

Dharma is at the core of Hinduism because by fulfilling it individual Hindus gain merit and achieve the goal of their religious quest. They learn the rules in their families and these will affect nearly all aspects of their life. Probably the best example is that they follow the rules of their caste and subcaste, and in matters of purity, purification and pollution. The *Samskaras* depend on caste and family customs, and mark the major life changes. *Sadharan dharma* is concerned with carrying out these rites properly.

Sadharan dharma

This is so important that it warrants a more detailed examination at this point. It contains two categories of principles.

First category

- This bans murder, violence, cruelty and incest.
- There must be respect for *Brahmans*, the Vedas, parents and elders.
- The gods and the cow must be honoured.
- One should be honest and moral.

Second category

This is for the pursuit of extra merit and moral advancement; for the next rebirth and for the prestige attached to being righteous now. This includes the following:

- Increasing divine knowledge by reading scriptures and by meditation and contemplation.
- Performing acts of worship and sacrifice to the gods.
- Giving alms to *brahmans*, mendicants (those who live by alms), temples and the poor.
- Building temples, cow shelters, wells, tanks, and bathing places on rivers.
- Visiting the major spiritual centres of pilgrimage and bathing in the Ganges to wash away sin.

The three methods of learning dharma

(1) This is through *scripture*. In the village setting this means finding someone who knows texts; recitals with explanation; and professional wandering preachers.

(2) *Myths and stories* are used for moral instruction and explaining festivals. These are passed down from generation to generation.

(3) This is by *custom and example* in both caste and family. Custom not only makes a practice acceptable, it sanctifies or makes it sacred.

20.5 Transmigration and karma

Transmigration is the passing of a soul or form of existence into another body after death. *Karma* literally means 'deeds' or 'doing' and is the sum of a person's actions in successive lives. These actions determine fate or destiny in future lives after a stay in heaven or hell. The process of continual rebirth is called *samsara*.

20.6 The characteristics of samsara

- It is cyclic or recurring and all worldly life is subject to it.
- It has no beginning and normally no end.
- It is a state of never-ending attachment.
- It is not a cycle of progress.
- It is not a process of purification.
- It is like self-perpetuating clockwork in that while running down, it winds up again.
- As a result, the *atman* or self is trapped in a permanent cycle of death and rebirth.

Any social interaction, especially involving food or sexual relations, means the mutual exchange of good and bad *karma* for the believer. Misfortunes are the direct result of *karma* resulting from one's actions. Furthermore, world history is the result of collective *karma*. So people should strive towards ending this mechanism of *karma* and *samsara* and to achieve *moksha* or liberation, because worldly life is not true existence. This can be achieved by knowledge, works and devotion leading to the integration of the soul with *Brahman* (the ultimate Reality).

20.7 The three margs, or paths to salvation

(1) *The Karma Marg* – This is 'The Path of Duties'; it is the disinterested performance of ritual and social obligations.

(2) *The Jnana Marg* – This is 'The Path of Knowledge'; it uses yoga's long and systematic training, plus meditation, to secure revelation and an insight from higher consciousness into one's identity with Brahman.

(3) *The Bhakti Marg* – This is 'The Path of Devotion'; it means devotion to a personal god. It can also mean the integration of the self with Brahman.

The three paths are presented in the **Bhagavad Gita** or 'Song of The Lord' which dates from around 200 BCE. It tells us that it is not acts themselves but the desire for their results that produces *karma*. Only a small minority of Hindus pursue *moksha*, but liberation is an ideal that affects all Hindus. Its purpose is to discuss what must be done to gain true fulfilment, and what must be realised in the light of experience to escape *samsara* or bondage. This will bring spiritual liberation. For millions of ordinary Hindus, life's daily path consists of following social and ritual duties. There are traditional rules for personal conduct for every caste, profession and family. All of this makes up *dharma* for the individual. It is all part of the broader picture of order, society, nature and basic equilibrium in creation.

--- **Summary** ---

Religion for Hindus is:

- a tradition
- a heritage
- a way of life
- a mode of thought
- the right application of methods for securing welfare in this life and a good condition in the next life.

20.8 Bhakti

This is the devotional way of achieving salvation and is open to everyone of either sex and any caste. It means 'love' or 'devotion'. It is used as a general name for the system of *bhakti*. *Bhakti* has led to a huge increase in the number of sects. Here the divine is no longer a multitude of gods as in ordinary religion, but is a unique and personal God, with whom the devotee can identify, and in whom that person may participate. In fact 'participation' is another meaning of *bhakti*. Love and total devotion to the Lord brings salvation. Divine grace is given to the pure and humble heart.

The importance of bhakti

- It is a revolutionary doctrine because it rises beyond both caste and renunciation.
- It is an easy road to salvation open to everyone without distinction.
- Love allows a person to give up the need for renunciation by becoming detached and disinterested. This is called 'internalisation', because the process goes on within the believer, so inactivity is not necessary.
- Thus devotion takes the place of deliverance.

The two principal types of bhakti

- *Nirgun Bhakti*: devotion to the Divine as seen without attributes
- *Sagun Bhakti*: devotion to the Divine seen as having attributes such as an *avatar* or incarnation (Krishna is a good example).

20.9   The role of the guru in Hinduism

The role of the guru in the quest for salvation is worth mentioning at this stage.

Meaning

The word 'guru' comes from '*gu*', meaning darkness, and '*ru*' meaning light. So a guru dispels spiritual darkness and gives light to the disciple. Another meaning links the name guru with a word meaning 'heavy'. In other words, the guru removes the burden of doubt and ignorance from the disciple, leading from the unreal to the real.

The four qualities of the guru

The guru must:

- be knowledgeable in scriptures
- have achieved the spiritual goal
- be free from desire
- be pure and without cunning.

The work of the guru

The guru:

- guides the seeker in:
  - which action to take
  - which food to eat
- advises from his knowledge of mantras and techniques of meditation.

The guru acts as a helmsman to steer the disciple across the ocean of birth, life, death and rebirth.

20.10   The four stages of life

Introduction

The four stages are:

(1)   the celibate student (**brahmachari**)
(2)   the householder (**grihastha**)
(3)   the hermit (**vanaprasth**)
(4)   the homeless religious beggar (**sannyasin**).

Few Hindus at any one time have strictly kept to the above categories, but it is an ideal for them to consider. Even today, elderly men tired of a life of worldly struggle may devote their remaining years to meditation and worship.

Stage one

The age of the initiate varies from eight to twelve when he leaves homes to begin his studies with a guru or master. His way of life will be severely simple and economical, and he will learn how to perform the domestic devotions of the brahmin, as well as studying the Vedas. By the time his studies are complete, the student will have become a young man. He then goes home to his parents to marry.

Stage two

As a householder, a man's life is spent pursuing the 'Three Aims' which are:

(1)   religious merit
(2)   wealth
(3)   pleasure.

Hindu law books point out that the first is most important, and that the first two are more important than the third.

Stage three

This begins when a man's hair is grey and he has grandchildren. He should then give up his home, and he and his wife go to live in a hut in the forest. This stage of life is devoted to the welfare of the soul through penance and religious exercise.

Stage four

The aged man breaks all worldly attachments and becomes a penniless wanderer.

20.11 Caste

In simple terms, castes are divisions or groups in Hindu society. They are not the same as the four classes or **varnas** and there are hundreds of castes and sub-castes throughout India. A person gets his or her caste by being born into it.

Some basic facts about caste

- A caste is a separate hereditary group.
- Castes protect their overall purity by restricting contact with other castes which are polluting and impure. To some extent 'pure' and 'impure' depends on the status of the caste making that judgement. So, for example, the Brahman caste is the highest and is most in danger of pollution.
- The other three castes are the **Kshatriya** (the ruling or warrior division), **Vaishya** (merchants and farmers) and **Sudra** (the lowest division).
- Marriage usually takes place only within the caste.
- Food is a serious problem when it comes to pollution, because it so readily carries pollution. There is an elaborate set of rules concerning which castes can accept water, cooked food, raw food and so on from any other caste.
- Another area is physical contact with the so-called 'untouchable' castes, who are now called **Harijans**, and who, incidentally, are still bottom of the hierarchy.
- The lowest castes are those who handle dead animals and skins and who do funeral work.
- Discrimination is greatest in villages and weakest in towns.
- If one person breaks the purity rules, then his whole caste is affected. He or she will then have to perform a number of ritual acts of purification before being allowed full caste rights again.
- A person's ritual status depends on his or her caste's status.

20.12 Pollution

Involuntary pollution

Everyone becomes polluted no matter what their caste, so purification is constantly necessary. Human emissions such as urine, faeces, saliva, semen, menstrual flow and afterbirth are all polluting. Death and decay are the most powerful cause of pollution. The whole household and other members of the family, plus those who handle the dead body, are deeply polluted. This polluted state lasts until the funeral rites are completed several days later. The polluted family are subject to various restrictions depending on their caste.

Voluntary pollution

This comes about when the purity rules of the caste are broken by contact with the impure. Examples include:

- touch
- taking food from an impure person

- eating with an impure person
- sexual intercourse
- serious sins; for example, killing a cow pollutes the whole village.

Coping with pollution

At a social level

There are specialist castes to deal with polluting situations such as toilet excretions, washing polluted clothes and dealing with the corpse at a funeral.

At a personal level

This is by purification. Some examples are:

(1) *the Indian-style bath* – this is the commonest. It involves pouring water over oneself because running water is a very effective purifying agent. Bathing and washing covers all involuntary and voluntary situations;

(2) *penances* – verbal, pilgrimage, giving a feast, or giving a gift to a brahman if, say, a cow, calf or ox is killed. A person may have to pay a penalty to his caste, or in the case of marriage to a non-caste person the marriage would have to be dissolved. If that caste was of a different status, then this would be more serious, and a heavy penalty would be involved;

(3) *cowdung* is a purifier because the cow is a pure animal. Dung is smeared on the floor where a ritual is to take place;

(4) a new mother is made to drink *cow's urine* to purify her because the act of giving birth is considered to be polluting.

20.13   Aspects of village religion

Ghosts

Hindus have a strong belief in ghosts. Different regions have their own names for ghosts, and in northern India, for example, the word for a ghost is **bhut**.

Bhuts can be a problem for villagers because they are believed to seek revenge against a person or family if they have a grievance, or if they have died in abnormal circumstances such as murder, suicide or drowning, and it is believed that someone is responsible.

At funerals meticulous care is taken over the ceremonial to make sure that the soul of the dead person is not angered. Every soul remains a *pret* (a lingering shade) until these ceremonials are completed 13 days after death. If it is not done properly, then the *pret* will become malevolent. Another problem is the need to prevent *bhuts* from touching the corpse in order to make it a *bhut* also. It is thought that *bhuts* often take the form of wasps to make it easier to slip through the mourners who surround the body to protect it. The mourners keep a piece of iron next to the body because it is thought that iron will make the *bhut* burst into flames and vanish. The best protection is not to be afraid.

If anything bad happens to someone, then *bhut* possession is often suspected. Examples include odd behaviour and movement, and unexplained illness and death.

Some general points about ghosts

- In the daytime they look dreadful.
- At night they have a human form but can be recognised because they do not have a shadow and their feet are back to front.

- House *bhuts* are less of a problem and can be quite harmless.
- Those outside the house are most feared, especially in the vicinity of water where someone might have drowned, or near trees where someone might have fallen.
- The **curail** is the prominent female type, especially those that died childless or in childbirth. They seduce men and cause impotence, and they attack other women.
- The *brahm* or Brahman ghost is the most powerful male type, and is often made a *devata* or minor god.
- Numerous other types of spirit threaten crops, livestock and villagers.
- Demons are such a problem in some areas that every village will have a demon temple and devil dances.

Magic

Witches and wizards in India follow a procedure similar to those in the west. This subject is a source of constant discussion and attention in rural India, and accusations of witchcraft are often used against personal enemies. There are experts who will interpret the effects and enable the afflicted to take countermeasures. Witchcraft is believed to be the cause of much misfortune.

The Evil Eye

This is greatly feared as an ever-present threat and great effort goes into countering it. No one is immune because there is always someone worse off than oneself. Villagers attribute misfortune to the Evil Eye just as they do to witchcraft. The death of a child, for example, could be attributed to a childless woman asking to see it.

Astrology

Astrology is vital for the villagers to decide whether or not a date is auspicious (lucky) enough for someone to marry, to plant crops and so forth. Full moon days are very auspicious, eclipse days are not. Months and days of the week are similarly divided. Points of the compass have these attributes: east is auspicious, south is not. Aches and itches on the left side of the body are auspicious for men but not women; the opposite is true for the right side. Birds and animals are connected with good and bad omens: for example, it is seen as an absolute disaster for a vulture to land on the roof of a house.

The Hindu gods and goddesses, holy rivers

21.1 Shiva (Siva)

In his earliest form in the Indus valley civilization he is represented as a male figure seated with crossed legs. This figure has three faces and is surrounded by animals. This was the prototype of what was to become Shiva, Prince of the Yogins, Lord of the Beasts, whose faces look to the four quarters of the Earth.

In classical Hinduism he had many attributes.

- He is the god of love and grace.
- He has a dark side to his nature inherited from **Indra**, the Storm God and destroyer.
- His realm is the battlefield, cemetery and burning **ghat**, and he is often portrayed with a garland of skulls. He destroys the world at the end of the **kalpa** (era).
- He is the great ascetic whose yogic meditation keeps the world in existence.
- As the fertility god he is the patron of procreation, and his symbol became the *lingam*, symbol of the male sexual organ.

His following is strongest in Kashmir and southern India and is associated with a mother goddess who is his consort. This is *Shakti* (Sakti), who symbolises divine energy or power. She is also called Parvati, Kali and Durga.

Other aspects of Shiva include:

- *Pashupa*, the protector of cattle
- *Bhutapati*, the father of demons
- *Tryambaka*, accompanied by three mother goddesses
- *Digambara*, who is 'clothed in space' or 'sky-clad'
- *Nataraja*, the Lord of The Dance.

Shiva's appearance

He wears a tiger skin and snake collar. His hair is tied in the knot of the ascetic and he is adorned with the crescent moon and trident. He is usually shown with four arms and the third eye open. He rides the bull *Nandi*, which has become a god because Shiva is so holy. Sometimes he is shown with a blue throat because he drank the poison produced by the churning of the Sea of Milk, so saving the world. As Lord of the Dance he is shown dancing a joyful dance with which he fills the cosmos until it is on the point of annihilation, so that it has to be destroyed to be reformed again. Statues of him dancing show him crushing the dwarf (a symbol of ignorance) underfoot.

Vishnu appeared in the Vedic era but was not important at that time. In those days he was a sun god. It was in the immediate pre-Christian era that he was to become important, and it was towards the end of the pre-Christian era that the trinity of Brahman deities, the **Trimurti**, emerged. They are:

- **Brahma** – who created the world
- **Vishnu** – who preserves and protects the world
- **Shiva** – who destroys.

This proved to be short-lived and Brahma's importance waned, leaving Vishnu and Shiva as the most important gods.

The Avatara doctrine

This is set out in the Bhagavad Gita and literally means 'a descent'. It tells us that Vishnu takes on an earthly form to save the world when the forces of evil threaten its destruction. Vishnu has 10 avatars.

The avatars of Vishnu

(1) *The fish (Matsya)*, who saved **Manu** (the first man), the Sages (ancient wise ones) and the Veda from the Great Flood which engulfed the world.

(2) *The tortoise (Kurma)*: the gods put Mount Mandara on his back. They had used the mountain to churn the milk ocean to recover the ambrosia (food of the gods) they had lost in the Flood.

(3) *The boar (Varaha)* killed the demon Hiranyaksha and rescued the Earth from the cosmic ocean into which the demons had thrown her.

(4) *The man-lion (Narasimha)*: the demon Hiranyakashipu could not be killed indoors or out, day or night, by god, man or beast, so Vishnu appeared from a pillar in the demon's palace as a man-lion at twilight and killed the demon on his threshold.

(5) *The dwarf (Vamana)* appears before the demon Bali, who granted him as much space as he could cover in three strides. He covered Earth, air and sky in two strides but refused the third stride, leaving the nether region to Bali.

(6) *Rama of the axe (Parashu Rama)* cleared the Earth of *kshatriyas* 21 times to defend the Brahmans against royal misbehaviour.

(7) *Rama*, king of Ayodhya, hero of the **Ramayana**, who killed the demon Ravana of Sri Lanka.

(8) *Krishna* – see below, section 21.3.

(9) *The Buddha* was probably included to attract the heterodox into Vaishnavism. Certainly there was tolerance between the two traditions, and the divisions between them became blurred in a later period. Perhaps it is recognition of what the Vishnu cult had borrowed from Buddhism. Another theory claims that Vishnu became incarnate as The Buddha to end animal sacrifice.

(10) *Kalkin* is the incarnation of the future, who appears in various forms: a horse, a horse-headed man, a man on a white horse holding a flaming sword. It is he who will bring judgement to Earth and restore the Golden Age at the end of the present Dark Age. He will destroy evil so that goodness can flourish.

It is possible that the origin of the first three avatars stems from the cults of sacred animals. The seventh and eighth are the most popular, and today only Rama, Krishna and Buddha have followings. The cult of Rama only appeared at the time of the Muslim invasions.

21.3 Krishna

Krishna's name means 'dark' or 'black' so it is possible that he could have been a god of the dark aboriginals of India. When the Greeks invaded northern India in the fourth century BCE they equated him with their own Herakles or Hercules. Various stories have been added over the centuries. He first appears as a hero who kills Kamsa, his maternal uncle (or cousin) as foretold in a prophecy which had made Kamsa order a slaughter of the innocents at Krishna's birth. As a child he is constantly involved in naughty pranks and impresses adults by performing miracles. As an adolescent he gets involved in amorous adventures with the *gopis* or milkmaids, playing a flute and calling the wives and daughters of the place to come to him. Krishna ruled **Mathura** (the kingdom of Kamsa) for a while, but was forced to lead his followers to Dvaraka, on the west coast, where he married Rukmini and established his kingdom. Eventually, his kingdom broke up in a drunken feud and his son was killed. Krishna wandered into the forest and was killed when a hunter mistook him for a deer and shot him in the heel, which was his one vulnerable spot.

21.4 Hanuman

Hanuman is the monkey god. He has great strength and is a great devotee of Rama. In March and April there is the festival of *Hanuman Jayanti*, to celebrate the birth of Hanuman. A fair may be held near a Hanuman temple.

Legend tells us that he organised the building of a bridge from India to Sri Lanka. While riding in the sun his shadow fell on the sea and it was grabbed by a sea monster who used it to pull the god into the water. Hanuman increased his size to gigantic proportions so the monster did the same. Then Hanuman became tiny and entered the monster's body and escaped through its ear before it could recover from the surprise. Hanuman was caught by his shadow on another occasion, this time by the mother of the demon Rahu. Hanuman entered her body by becoming small and then swelled to enormous proportions to burst her apart.

21.5 Ganesha

Ganesha is the elephant-headed god. He may well have been a local god in western India who was absorbed into the Hindu tradition as a son of Shiva (Figure 21.1).

The *Shiva Purana* tells us how Shiva's wife Parvati asked her son to guard her room to prevent anyone entering, no matter who it was. When Shiva wanted to enter, Ganesha refused to allow it. Shiva enlisted the help of other Hindu gods. There was a fight and Ganesha was beheaded by Shiva's trident on the battlefield. Parvati said that Shiva would have to replace his head with that of the first living thing that he met. As it was an elephant, Ganesha duly received an elephant's head.

Hindus pray to Ganesha as the remover of obstacles before they marry, take exams, move house, or undertake anything else new or important.

Figure 21.1 The Hindu God Ganesha
(Carlos Reyes-Manzo Andes Press Agency)

Hindus tell stories of how Ganesha came to have only one tusk. One story tells how the gluttonous Ganesha went for a ride on a rat after a feast. A snake frightened the rat and Ganesha fell, his stomach bursting open. He gathered up his guts and used the snake as a belt to hold himself together. The moon had seen all this and was howling with laughter. This angered Ganesha, who tore off a tusk and threw it at the moon adding a curse that the moon would lose its power of giving light every so often. Another legend says that he used the tusk to write the **Mahabharata**, because he is also the god of literature.

21.6 Rama

Rama was born into a royal family but had to leave because of his step-mother's plotting. His wife **Sita** went with him, but she was kidnapped by Ravana, the demon king of the Rakshahas, who had tricked Rama into going off to hunt a phantom deer. An eagle revealed the place of her imprisonment in Sri Lanka. Hanuman, the king of the monkeys, was Rama's ally, and he discovered that she was still alive. Rama therefore took an army to rescue her, but the ocean refused to divide to let the army cross. Then Nala, the son of the blacksmith god, Visvakarma, taught the monkeys to build a bridge, and this was ready in five days. Rama's army fought the demons. His arrows shot off the ten heads of Ravana but they grew again, so he used a magic arrow which passed through Ravana's chest and returned to Rama, leaving Ravana dead. However, Rama would not have his wife back until her purity was proven because there were rumours that she had been ravished by the demon. Sita therefore built a funeral pyre and walked into the flames, which did not harm her, but took the shape of a divine being and lifted her up. This was the proof that Rama wanted, and they were reunited.

The legend of Rama never developed beyond the **Sanskrit** epic; see Ramayana section. Rama is an avatar of Vishnu; see section 21.2, above.

21.7 Hari Hara

This is a god who represents an attempt to join Vishnu and Shiva, love and terror. His left side is Vishnu, and his right side Shiva. Each side has the attributes appropriate to its god; the hair knot, trident and tigerskin of Shiva, and the tiara, disc and robe of Vishnu.

21.8 Durga

Her name means 'The Inaccessible' and she is another form or aspect of Jaganmatri, the Divine Mother and wife of Shiva. She forms a triad with the goddesses Uma and Parvati. This relates to aspects of Kali, because Kali is the basic form of all three members of the triad. This is the case with Durga Pratyangira, where Durga has vampire-like teeth and a flame-decked hat. She has four arms which carry the trident of Shiva, the sword, drum and bowl of blood.

Jaganmatri

This means 'World Mother', and is another name for Durga.

21.9 Ganga

Ganga is the goddess of purification of the River Ganges and her name means 'Swift-goer'. She is identified with Parvati and was depicted as a crowned mermaid whose forehead was marked with ashes or as a white queen enthroned with a lotus and a lute. When the faithful look at the Ganges and touch and drink its waters, they are cleansed from sin.

21.10 Kali

Shiva, like the other gods, has a female partner to whom he delegates power. Her different names are thought to reflect the different attributes of the 'Great Mother' who has been part of Indian thought since the earliest times. Kali or Durga is the most important. Her strength and dominance come from the pre-Aryan culture of India which was matriarchal (female-dominated).

The two aspects of Kali

There is a fierce aspect of death and judgement in which Kali is portrayed wearing a garland of skulls and a skirt of severed hands. The other aspect shows her as the night of rest and peace between the cycles of world creation. Even in the fierce aspect, Kali is said to bring peace by overcoming the fears of her faithful followers. Although Shiva is remote from time and creation, Kali touches him and brings him to the world of time and touch as the creator and animator of all things.

21.11 Lakshmi

Lakshmi, the goddess of love and beauty, was born from the churning of the Sea of Milk. She is the wife of Vishnu, and brings good fortune and prosperity. She is also known as *Sri*, and was reincarnated as Sita and as Rukmini, the consort of Krishna.

21.12 Holy rivers

The Ganges (**Ganga**) is the greatest of these. It is personified as a goddess that Hindus believe originally flowed only in Heaven, until brought to Earth by Bhagiratha to purify the ashes of his ancestors. She was reluctant to descend and broke her fall by cascading on Shiva's head. This was necessary to prevent the Earth from shattering. Confluences, or places where two rivers join are very holy places. The Ganges confluence with the Yamuna at Allahabad is the most sacred place in India. The Sarasvati is another important river and is personified as a goddess of learning and eloquence.

The scriptures and literature

22.1 The Rig Veda

Between 1500 and 1200 BCE **Aryan** tribes invaded India and settled in the Punjab. They composed hymns which make up the Rig Veda or 'Wisdom of the Verses', the oldest work of literature in an Indo-European language. It is also the oldest living religious literature of the world.

The Indians are unique in that they are the only Indo-European people who have a religion that is in direct descent from that of the parent culture.

There is a collection of 1028 hymns to the Vedic gods, and other collections called *Samhitas* were made for chanting. There is also a collection for the sacrifice, the **Yajur Veda**. These secondary collections reproduce a large proportion of the Rig Veda, but are reorganised for their special purposes.

There is a fourth collection called the **Atharva Veda** or 'wisdom of The Atharvan Priests', which is distinct in that it contains spells and chants for such purposes as magical aids to victory in battle, or medical healing and so forth.

The Brahmanas ('Discussions of The Ritual')

This series of works explain the hymns and deal with their ritual application, mythology, sacrifice and the universe. They date from 800 to 600 BCE.

The Aranyakas and Upanishads

These carry the meditations and ideas of the secondary collection further. The Upanishads are secret teachings concerning 'cosmic equations'.

The subordinate set of works

Most of these are now lost. They are concerned with sacrifice and its needs, and include astronomy, ritual and grammar.

Indo-European elements

These include worship of male sky gods, especially the god Dyaus, whose name is related to the Greek Zeus and Roman Jupiter or Jove. The Vedic 'World of The Fathers' is akin to the Nordic Valhalla or 'Hall of The Slain'.

Why the Vedas are important

Veda means 'knowledge'. It is the collective term for the holy scriptures of Hinduism which were directly revealed as eternal truths to be 'heard' or received by the **rishis** (seers). They in turn recorded it in Sanskrit, which they regarded as the most perfect human language. They are therefore not the creation of man or god; they are eternal.

Such is the veneration for the Vedas that even though their religion, which revolves around the fire sacrifice ritual, has been superseded by later Hindu doctrines, it has not relinquished its absolute authority and sacredness. It is still at the core of almost all the various forms of Hinduism. Even after thousands of years, devout Hindus learn and recite parts of the Veda because in religious terms this has great merit.

22.2 The Bhagavad Gita

- This is 'The Song of The Lord'.
- It is the most famous and popular Hindu scripture.
- It has 18 chapters and 700 verses.
- It is part of the great epic, the *Mahabharata*.
- It was probably composed in the fourth and third centuries BCE.
- It is a dialogue between the bewildered nobleman **Arjuna** and Krishna, who is disguised as his charioteer.

The story

Arjuna, on the eve of battle, was tempted to withdraw, because in doing his duty he would be killing his relatives and friends in the enemy army. It would be better to let them keep the kingdom that they held, even though it was not theirs by right. Krishna's advice makes up the substance of the book, and is an amalgam of almost every Hindu point of view.

Krishna's advice and the lesson for Hindus

His advice is that a man should do his duty according to his class and stage of life. Arjuna is a *kshatriya*, one of the warrior class whose sacred duty is to fight in defence of goodness. Man has a duty to support the stability and solidarity of society (*loka sangraha*). He must recognise the necessary part which every caste and occupation plays in the social system. The Gita encourages acceptance of the world and active participation in it. It is believed that one should engage in good actions without thought of personal reward. This should be done in devotion to the Lord Vishnu.

> The major strength of the Gita is that it emphasises the points of agreement between the various systems of thought instead of their disagreements. Not surprisingly, it is the best-known and most valued Hindu scripture.

22.3 The Ramayana

- This is a major epic poem, dating from the second century BCE to the second century CE.
- It is a quarter of the length of the *Mahabharata*, having 24 000 verses instead of 100 000.
- It is a close second to the Gita in popularity.
- It is the story of Rama the king, and his wife Sita, and the hatred of them by Ravana the demon king of Sri Lanka. (See section 21.6 for the full story of this.) Rama is virtuous and brave, the ideal ruler, and Sita is the Indian ideal of womanhood: faithful, devoted and chaste.
- The poem promotes three main virtues:
  - (1) patient endurance in adversity.
  - (2) ardent piety.
  - (3) the proper performance of duty.
- Public recitations and dramatic performance of it are an important way of spreading Hindu ethics.

22.4 The authority of Sruti

Sruti means 'what is heard'. It is a revealed scripture, and the name is applied to the Vedas and Upanishads, which were 'heard' by ancient seers. Originally these were handed down orally. The most sacred are the Veda, made up of four divisions:

- Rig Veda
- Sama Veda
- Yajur Veda
- Atharva Veda.

Acceptance of the authority of *Sruti* is one of the features of Hinduism. In ancient India those who accepted the Vedic revelation were **Astika** (orthodox). Jains and Buddhists did not, and so were **Nastika** (unorthodox).

22.5 The Puranas

These Hindu chronicles or epic poems celebrate the power and work of the gods. Tradition recognises 18 poems; six each for Vishnu, Shiva and Brahma. In a broader sense, all traditional Hindu narrative literature is covered by the term 'Puranas'. The myths, legends and genealogies of the gods are covered in great depth.

Important points to note

The Puranas and the epics with which they are closely linked in origin, became the scriptures of the common people, available to all regardless of sex or class. This contrasts with the Vedas, which were restricted to the men of the top three orders. The Puranas thus brought new non-Brahmanic influences into orthodox religion.

- Vedic and Puranic mythology are in part continuous, but the emphasis differs: in the Rig Veda Indra, for example, is a god of war, the monsoon, and the prototype of the warrior; but to the masses he was a rain god and still is today.
- Little is learned of goddesses in the Veda, whereas Puranic myth gives them fuller treatment.
- The importance of some gods rises in Puranic Hinduism. Vishnu and Shiva from being minor Vedic gods become the principle gods of the Purana. The different stages of their rise can be seen as they absorb the identities of the other popular gods.
- By 1000 CE sectarianism creeps into mythology. The main interest now is cosmology, the myths of the great ascetics, and sacred places such as rivers and fords.

Cosmogony

Puranic cosmogony (the study of the evolution of the universe) expands on the cosmogony of the Brahmanas, Upanishads and Epics. Hindus believe that in the beginning the god Narayana who is identified with Vishnu, floated on the snake Ananta ('Endless') on the primeval waters. A lotus grew out of his navel, and it was in this lotus that Brahma was born, reciting the four Vedas from his four mouths and creating the 'Egg of Brahma' which holds all the worlds. The Vedas do not see an end to the world but it is periodically destroyed by the Fire of Time. Some sources say that Shiva dances the *tandava* dance of doomsday and destroys the world. Then creation starts all over again.

Cosmology

Puranic cosmology (the structure of the universe) sees three levels: heaven, earth and the netherworld.

- Heaven has seven levels, at the top of which is the world of Brahma (or *brahma-loka*).
- Earth has seven circular continents. In the middle of the central one is Meru, the cosmic mountain. To the south is *Bharatavarsa*, which is the old name for India. The continent is surrounded by a salty ocean. The other continents are surrounded by oceans of other liquids.
- There are seven levels below the earth. These are the hells where demons and serpents live.

23 Ritual, worship and pilgrimage

23.1 Individual ritual

The following is a summary of the ritual acts carried out by a woman after a good harvest, to thank the minor god, and to ensure that he will help in future years. The services of a Brahman are not needed, nor that of any other specialist.

First
- She rises early and bathes.
- She puts on clean clothes.
- She fasts until the ritual is complete.

Second
- She replasters the kitchen floor and hearth with cowdung.
- On the freshly plastered hearth she prepares *karah*, which is a sweet pudding to be used as an offering.

Third
- She takes the image of the *devata* from the inner room where it is kept.
- She smears a small area of the verandah floor with the same plaster of cowdung used in the kitchen.
- A small wooden stool is placed in this area and the image is placed upon it.
- Anyone now approaching this area must first remove their shoes.

Fourth
- The woman removes her shoes and then bathes the statue in fresh water.

Fifth
- Now she bows before the image and offers flowers and incense.
- She applies a red powder to the forehead of the statue.
- She ties a sacred thread around its waist.

Sixth
- She offers some of the pudding to the *devata*, pressing a little bit of it to its mouth.

Seventh

- She gives the rest of this food offering to her family and close neighbours. This food offering is now known as *prashad*.
- The rest is put to one side for other friends and relatives who call at the house that day.
- No morsel of *prashad* must be dropped or left in a place where it might become polluted by contact with the impure – for example, with leather shoes.

Eighth

- The woman puts the image away later in the day.
- The worship area is cleared of debris from the ritual.
- The remains of the offerings are thrown into a nearby stream.

23.2 Priestly ritual and public worship

This involves a scriptural recital (*katha*). A Brahman priest recites a piece of scripture in Sanskrit and it is then explained in the local dialect. It must be a Brahman priest because only he has the training and knowledge. This is preceded by a formal act of worship in which the person who has asked for *katha* worships Ganesha and the nine planets to secure their blessings upon the recital.

First

- The man returns from the fields in the evening.
- He bathes and puts on clean clothes.
- The day and time were decided beforehand by a Brahman priest who used an almanac to make sure it was auspicious (at a favourable or lucky time).

Second

- His wife then replasters the kitchen hearth with cow dung.
- She does the same to the place in the main room where the worship is to take place.
- Then she prepares *prashad* for distribution after the *katha*.
- Her *prashad* is made from flour fried in **ghi** and sweetened with crude sugar.

Third

- The priest arrives and washes his hands.
- He will have bathed and put on clean clothes beforehand.
- Then he prepares the **mandala** (sacred diagram) on the area of the floor replastered for that purpose. The mandala is made up of symbolic representations of the nine planets and deities or sacred beings. It is traced on the floor in white flour.

Fourth

- Guests start to arrive.
- When it is time to begin, the priest blows the conch shell.
- The householder sits next to the priest in front of the mandala when invited to.
- Then the priest ties a length of red *moli* (thread) to the man's wrist and tufts of sacred *kusha* grass to the third finger of each hand.

Fifth

- The priest recites from the Sanskrit text.
- He also instructs the householder regarding worship of the symbols in the mandala.
- Offerings are made to each of these: water, rice, flowers and incense.
- Ritual gestures, bowing with folded hands, are made to each symbol in turn.

Sixth

- It is now that the reading begins. The priest chants the verses and then explains them.
- When this is concluded, the prashad is given to all present. None of the prashad must be trodden on.

Seventh

- When the guests go, the wife scrapes up the diagram and offerings and puts them on a tray. Her husband then throws them into a stream.

Features common to both rituals

- Participants must bathe first, and put on clean clothes. Shoes must be removed.
- The ritual site must be smeared with cow dung.
- Ritual equipment is disposed of afterwards by being thrown into running water, and precautions are taken over the disposal of the *prashad*.

23.3 Worship in the temple

The temple is not as important in Hinduism as the mosque in Islam, the synagogue in Judaism, or the church in Christianity. Even so, it is regarded as the centre of religious life. Orthodox Hinduism has no group worship or service for a congregation.

During worship, Hindus sit on the floor facing the shrine. Men and women may sit on different sides. The god's image is dressed in royal robes and flowers. Music is played and scriptures recited.

Worship can be performed individually in the temple, but in some reformed sects congregational worship has developed. During festivals, the faithful gather in crowds to see a professional **pujari**, or priest, conduct a ceremony.

Large temples have several shrine rooms and courts. A shrine will normally have a canopy or pyramid over it. Shrines are beautifully painted and contain many sculptures.

Temples also fill the roles of social centre and centres of pilgrimage. Some have schools and give religious instruction.

23.4 Havan: *the offering of fire*

This is based on the sacrificial worship of the Aryans. The priest and his helpers put pieces of wood and camphor into a portable fire-altar and light them. He then pours *ghi* (liquid butter) into the fire, while reciting the Vedas. The following prayers are offered.

(1) A prayer for purity – Purity is essential to approach the Holy One. The priest takes water in his left hand and dips one of his right-hand fingers into it. Then he touches his ears, nose, eyes, mouth, arms, body and legs. Then the worshippers do the same.
(2) A vedic prayer for the good of all.
(3) Prayers for the chief gods.

23.5 Arti: *the worship of light*

This is the ceremonial of love and devotion to the Lord. Symbols are used, representing the five elements from which Hindus believe that everything is made.

- *Fire* – a flat tray with five lights on it is passed before the shrine.
- *Earth* – this is represented by incense and flowers.
- *Air* – a fan is waved.
- *Ether* – a conch shell is blown.
- *Water* – is placed in a shell or other container.

The ceremony

This has five main points:

(1) The *arti* tray is moved slowly before the images of the gods.
(2) The lights are held before pictures of the gods.
(3) A spot of red paste is put on the foreheads of the images, pictures and worshippers.
(4) Each person puts money on the tray and then each passes his or her hands over the flames and over his or her forehead and hair. This is how they receive God's blessing and power.
(5) The congregation receive *prashad*, a mixture of dried fruit, nuts and sugar crystals. This is a token of God's love for the faithful.

The singing of Bhajans

Bhajans are hymns expressing devotion to God. This is very popular and Hindus sing them anywhere. They are especially sung in the temples of Vishnu and Shiva, and there is often dancing as well, because dance is a form of worship. The worshippers will press the palms of their hands together before they begin. Then they bow; these are gestures of worship. In the past there were temple dancers who dedicated the whole of their lives to worship.

23.6 Personal worship

Every Hindu starts the day by having a bath and reciting the *Gayatri Mantra*, which is the most sacred of all Vedic verses or prayers. It is recited three times a day by the *Brahmans*, *Kshatriyas* and *Vaishyas*, at dawn, noon and sunset.

Mala japa

A **mala** is a string of 108 beads rather like a rosary. It is fingered while repeating the name of God, and while saying the word 'OM'. This repetition is known as **japa**.

Private worship

There is great variety even within castes. Prayer takes place before shrines at home as well as in temples. Some people use **yoga** to refresh the soul in unity with God. Fasting and pilgrimages are also a vital part of private devotion.

23.7 Animal sacrifice

Vedic large-scale animal sacrifice died out long ago, but, in the Middle Ages it arose in another form, and still continues in some temples. The ritual involves beheading an animal, such as a goat, in front of the god; perhaps Durga or Shiva. This is done so that the blood splashes on to it. Then the worshipper offers the blood to the god, a piece of meat to the priest, and he himself can eat the rest. Note that Hindus are able to do this without breaking the non-violence rule, because the soul of the animal goes straight to Heaven, which is a great blessing for it.

Centuries ago there was human sacrifice. This was provided by volunteers who hoped to go to Heaven as a result, or those who wished to fulfil a vow, and by criminals donated by the king for that specific purpose.

23.8 Pilgrimage

Why pilgrimage?

Clearly there is immense satisfaction to be had from fulfilling a religious yearning to visit a holy place, and this is even more so when it involves much effort and sacrifice. Pilgrimage has a value in this life and the next because the pilgrim acquires merit and a good *karma*. It helps to build up the balance of good actions to weigh against bad deeds. Hindus believe in the continuity of life, so a pilgrimage may be undertaken to benefit ancestors. People take time off work and may use buses, trains or just walk to reach their chosen destination.

The value of pilgrimage

Value is determined by the following factors:

• the importance of the shrine
• the distance to be travelled

- the means of transport
- the purpose of the pilgrimage
- the time of year.

Some effects of pilgrimage

It has a levelling effect in that people of any caste or class may travel the same road. At the temple of Jagganath at Orissa all caste barriers vanish while people are there (Figure 23.1). At the holy city of Benares (Varanasi) all who bathe in the Ganges receive equal cleansing. Those who worship God in different forms such as Shiva or Krishna forget their differences, and if they should pass minor local shrines on the way to their destination, they will offer worship at them all.

Figure 23.1 Places of Hindu pilgrimage in India, showing the principal deity or form of worship: *V* Vaisnave; *S* Saiva; *D* Sakta (Mother Goddess or Devi). Shows a pilgrimage route *(tīrtha yātrā)*, mainly by train, a round tour of India taking about ten weeks

Figure 23.2 Hindu pilgrims in Kathmandu, Nepal
(Carlos Reyes-Manzo Andes Press Agency)

Centres of pilgrimage

Benares (Varanasi)

This is the most famous centre and is situated on the banks of the River Ganges, the holiest of rivers, at the point where it is joined by the Varuna, one of its tributaries. It is Varuna that gives it one of its other names, Varanasi. A third name is Kashi, which means 'resplendent', a name given because of its superb temples and religious importance. Famous centres are normally associated with stories of the gods, and in this case it is Shiva to whom the city is especially sacred because it is thought that he once lived there. Rama is also remembered every year at the Festival of **Dussehra** in October and November when there is a 30-day enactment of the Ramayana.

Those who die in Benares and have their ashes thrown into the Ganges are said to be freed from rebirth providing they have repented and died in faith. Pilgrims take home bottles of Ganges water because it is sacred.

Puri

Puri, in Orissa, is the site of one of the most famous Hindu temples dedicated to Jagganath, or Vishnu. An image of Krishna is taken in procession on a huge cart around the town. Local people and pilgrims join together to pull it through the streets.

Vrindavan

This city on the River Jumna is accepted as the site of Krishna's birth, and has been called the Bethlehem of India as a result. Pilgrims follow a special route around the city to see places associated with incidents in his youth. They may then proceed to Dwarka on the west coast of India because it was here that Krishna had his palace and finally left the world.

Rameshwaram

This is in southern India and is sacred to Vishnu and Shiva. The shrine is said to have been built by Rama and his wife Sita and was dedicated by them to Shiva. This was because Rama and Sita landed there when she had been saved from the demon Ravana. Rama had become impure by killing Ravana's soldiers, and the building of the shrine purified him, and enabled him to offer thanks to Shiva and worship him too.

24 Festivals and fairs

Hinduism has more festivals than any other religion. Only a small number are universally observed throughout India. Many are celebrated in a group of northern or southern states, or even in one state. Large numbers of festivals are found in just a few or even one village. Festivals of other religions such as Islam can and do take place alongside Hindu festivals.

The Anthropological Survey of India (1959–61) carried out research in 290 districts in 19 states and found that there were:

- 15 festivals in at least six states
- 50 regional festivals
- 300 local festivals.

One wonders what the figure would be for the entire country!

There are three main groups of festivals

- Festivals which follow the *lunar cycle*
- *Occasional* festivals which celebrate the birthday of a famous person
- *Seasonal/agricultural* festivals

Here are some notes on the most important festivals.

24.1 Divali

Divali is also known as *Deepavali*; both names mean a row or garland of lights. It is the most widely celebrated Hindu festival, lasting from two to five days and taking place at the same time throughout India.

Lamps are lit and are sometimes floated along the river because light symbolises the victory of goodness and virtue. The lamps or *divas* are small earthenware bowls filled with oil or *ghi* with a cotton wick. They can be placed in rows inside and outside houses and are lit when evening falls. These days, small electric lights may be used.

Lighting these lamps is associated with the welcoming home of Rama and Sita after their victory over Ravana. Other associations concern the defeat of King Mahabali by the dwarf avatar of Vishnu, the god Yama, or Lakshmi the goddess of wealth.

Lakshmi **puja** (worship of Lakshmi) is a common feature but takes place on different days, depending on the area. In some places the trading castes close accounts and at home or in the temples coins are heaped on to the ledgers. Then an image of the goddess is placed on top for worship. Lakshmi *puja* is the centre-piece of Divali in some areas where the *divas* are to help her to find the way to the worshippers' homes, to bring blessings and happiness.

Activities include gambling, the women drawing colourful designs on the floor near the threshold, sending cards and the distribution of food and sweets in front of the temple.

Remote villages have their own unique celebrations such as singing traditional songs and consulting mediums for problems such as illness, education and marital desertion.

24.2 Holi

This is a Spring festival in northern India, and is associated with tales of Holika, the demoness. Its main features are the relaxation of the normal social hierarchy and the building of a bonfire. In northern India Divali lasts for two or three days; it lasts five days elsewhere.

Food offerings are partly roasted on the fire before being eaten as holy food (*prashad*). The direction of the bonfire flames will reveal which land is to be the most fertile in the coming year.

Coloured dye, powder and paint are thrown in inter-caste and inter-sex rivalry, and mud is thrown, while women may give men a beating. In connection with fertility and the spring there is erotic dancing and the shouting of obscenities. In Gujarat, babies and young children are carried round the fire in a ritual to bring them protection.

The dye-throwing and child rituals are connected with Krishna, who disguised himself as a cowherd in order to misbehave with the milkmaids. Another story tells how the baby Krishna slew the demoness Putana. In yet another story Krishna is chased by King Kamasa until he killed the wicked king and took his kingdom.

24.3 Navarati/Durga Puja/Dassehra

This occurs in September to October and is one of the few genuinely all-Indian festivals. *Dussehra* ('the tenth') is the day after **Navaratri** (nine nights), but refers to the whole 10 days in some parts of India.

The main themes are the worship of the goddess in various forms, especially Durga who killed Mahishasura, the Buffalo Demon; and also the victory of Rama over Ravana the demon king on Dussehra, the tenth day.

The festival is called *Durga Puja* in West Bengal and surrounding states. Durga is a goddess and is one of the names of Devi, wife of Shiva. Images of her dressed for battle and riding a lion are worshipped for nine days. On the tenth (day) they are immersed in a river or pond, to celebrate the legend of when Mahishasura once defeated all the gods, who then sent Durga to kill him armed with a weapon from each god. She rode to the battle on a lion given by Himavan and wearing superb jewellery as well as armour provided by Vishnu.

The weapons donated by the gods included:

- Shiva's trident
- Vishnu's disc
- Yama's spear
- Agni's dart
- Vayu's magic bow
- Sutya's quiver of arrows
- Kala's sword and shield
- Kubera's club
- Indra's thunderbolt.

At the Minakshi temple at Madurai in Tamil Nadu, Minakshi is identified with Durga. The key stages of the festival are:

- *First night* – an image of Minakshi is placed on the special shrine of the goddess with an amulet tied around the left wrist to protect the goddess in battle.
- *Eighth night* – the shrine is decorated to show Minakshi beheading Mahishasura.
- *Ninth night* – she is shown worshipping Shiva.
- *Tenth day* – the ritual washing of Minakshi's hair, after which the goddess and Shiva are paraded around Shiva's part of the temple. The worshipping of Shiva and the ritual of hair washing are performed to make amends to Shiva for killing the demon who was one of his devotees

Other goddesses are honoured at Navaratri. A notable example is Saraswati, the goddess of learning, arts and beauty.

In northern India the festival celebrates great events in the story of Rama; and Delhi has a superb *Ram Lila* based on the Ramayana (*Lila* is a Sanskrit word for play or sport). The festival culminates when the actor playing Rama shoots an arrow which sets fire to an effigy of Ravana that has been filled with fireworks.

24.4 Raksha Bandhan/Shravani Purnima/Salono/ Rakhi Purnima

This festival occurs in July/August. *Raksha* means 'protection', and *Bandhan* means 'to tie'.

In northern India girls and married women tie an amulet called a *rakhi* on to the right wrist of their brothers as a protection against evil influences. (Amulets may be sent through the post.) They receive cash and gifts in return.

Family priests make visits to receive presents during the festival, and members of the 'twice-born' castes change their sacred threads.

The festival is called *Rakhi Purnima* in the Indian state of Andhra Pradesh, where workmen tie multi-coloured threads to their work tools. Work is also halted for the day.

24.5 Vasanta Panchami/Shri Panchami/ Saraswati Puja

Vasanta Panchami is widely celebrated in northern India as marking the coming of Spring (January/February). Some temples in southern India celebrate it, but it is not a public or household festival in the region.

Families wear yellow clothes because the name of the festival literally means 'yellow fifth' or 'spring fifth'. In addition to this, they have a ceremonial bath and the women may fast.

The festival is also called *Shri Panchami*, because long ago it was associated with Shri or Lakshmi, the goddess of wealth. Now it is linked with Saraswati, goddess of learning and the fine arts. In many places books and writing implements are not used on this day. Although it is called *Saraswati Puja* (*puja* means worship), this name is more normally used for one of the days in the Navaratri festival. In West Bengal clay statuettes of this goddess are paraded through the streets before immersion in a river or pond.

24.6   The Kumbha Mela festival

This huge gathering of pilgrims occurs every 12 years at four sacred places in northern India:

- Prayag (Allahabad)
- Hardwar
- Nasik
- Ujjain.

These places were chosen because legend tells of a battle between the gods and the demons over a pitcher (*kumbha*) of immortality-giving nectar which had been obtained from the ocean floor by churning it up. The gods won and became immortal, but four drops of the nectar fell during the battle, one at each of the four sites.

24.7   Fairs

Melas or religious fairs are held throughout the year and vary a great deal in size and importance. The smallest and most local are called *marhais*. The *Kumbha Mela* (see above) is an excellent example of a larger gathering.

The family and rites of passage

25.1 Initiation (Upanayana)

This was once confined to the three highest classes but is now practised by the Brahmans only. It makes a boy a full member of the Aryan community.

The three main elements of initiation

(1) The initiate receives the sacred thread at the Upanyan ceremony. The thread crosses the left shoulder and under the right arm. He will wear this thread all of his life, being careful to keep it free from defilement.
(2) Then he is entitled to hear, learn and recite the Vedas, though this will only be so in strictly orthodox families. In fact, printing has made the Vedas available to anyone irrespective of class or sex.
(3) He will be taught the Gayatri, which is a very sacred verse of the Rig Veda. This is his spiritual birth; he is now 'twice born' (**dvija**).

25.2 Marriage

Monogamy (one partner) is the rule in Hinduism. The marriage ceremony can take place in a temple or at home (Figure 25.1). The ceremony is elaborate and used to last for days, but modern practice is to limit it to one day. In traditional practice bride and groom did not see each other before the wedding and the bridal veil could not be removed until the bride was given away by her parents.

The ceremony

- The bride's father pays homage to the groom.
- Her mother and the other women perform the consecration ceremony.
- Then the priest reads their family trees.
- The bride's sari is tied to the groom's scarf to link them.
- The priest recites mantras and prayers while they make the fire offering.

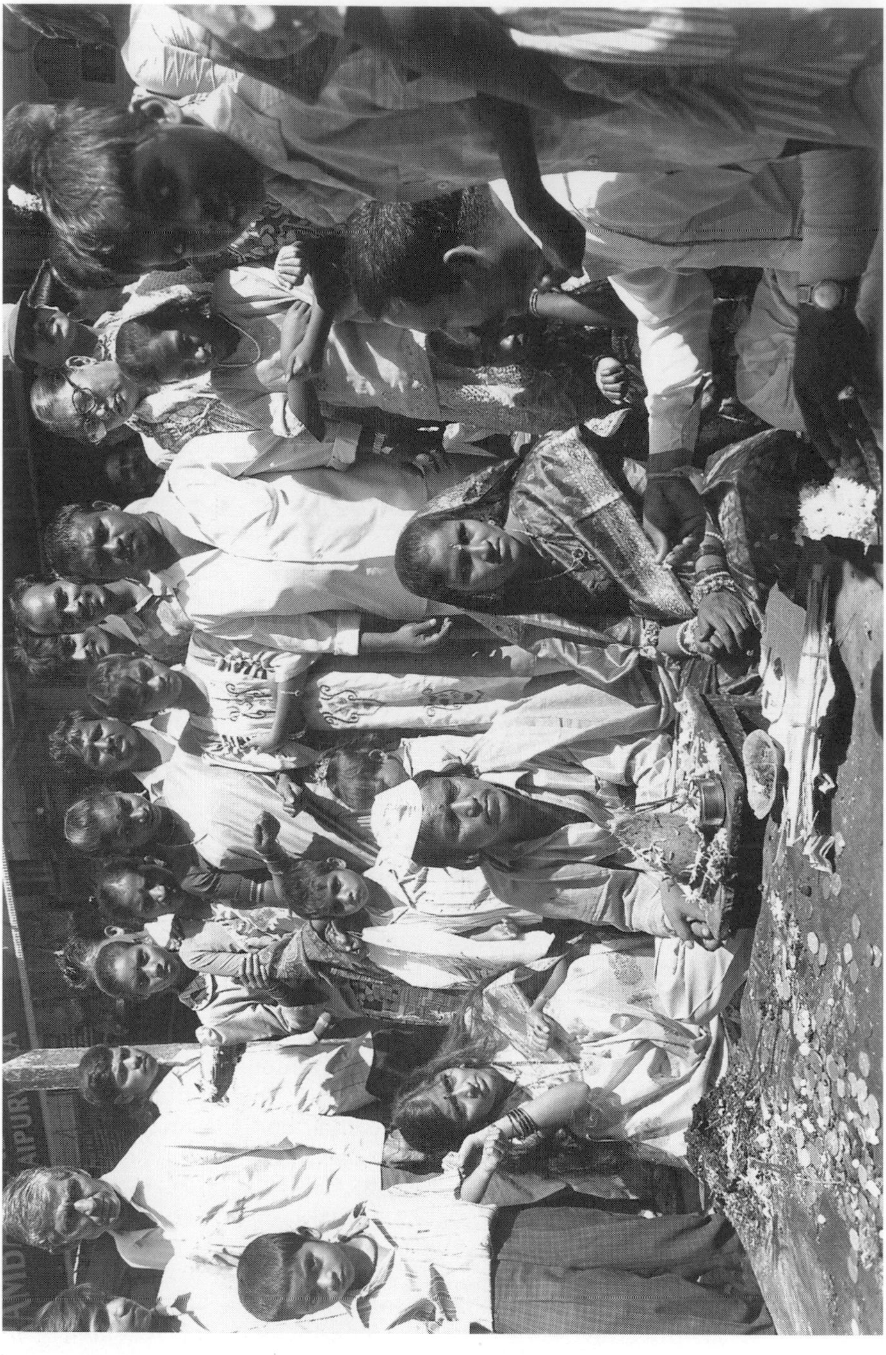

Figure 25.1 A Hindu wedding in Bombay, India
(Carlos Reyes-Manzo Andes Press Agency)

- Then the couple walk round the sacred fire. This is the focal point of the wedding. They take seven steps together as the groom recites:
  'This I am, that art thou; that art thou, this I am; I am the heavens, thou the earth. Come let us marry, let us beget offspring. Loving, bright, genial, may we live a hundred autumns.'
- Gifts are exchanged while guests toast the couple.
- The bride stands on a grinding stone and her husband says: 'Be firm as a rock'. This seen as a sign of permanence.

After the ceremony

After sunset on his wedding night a man should sit silent with his wife until the stars appear. When the Pole Star appears, he should point it out to her and say to the star: 'Firm art thou; I see thee the firm one. Firm be thou with me, O thriving one! 'Then he says to his wife: 'To me Brihaspati has given thee; obtaining offspring through me, thy husband, live with me a hundred autumns.' This ritual is laid down by the scriptures to guard against the unexpected in life, and the uncertainties of earthly bliss by the steadfast influence of the 'constant star'.

Divorce

The Hindu Code introduced by the Indian Government allows divorce, but, for the strictly orthodox this is not possible once the seven steps are taken. This ancient rite binds them not just on earth but in the next world too. In the west a marriage can be annulled if it has not been consummated, but this is not the case in Hinduism. This was a difficulty in the days of childhood marriage, because if a girl was widowed before she reached puberty, then she would have to spend her days as an ascetic praying for her husband's soul.

A Wife's status in marriage

Hindu society is strongly patriarchal or male-dominated, and a wife is subordinate to her husband. This is given scriptural authority in some texts which state that women can never be independent.

- She is subject to her father in childhood.
- She is subject to her sons in old age.
- The only property she can own is jewellery or other similar personal possessions.
- She must wait on her husband in all ways.
- She must get up in the morning before him, and must go to bed after him.
- She must completely obey him even if he is a bad husband.

Possibly because of Islamic influence in the north, the women of the higher classes were often kept in confinement. If they went out, they had to wear a veil and have an escort. Though this has declined as a social practice, it survives to some extent in the villages. In the south it has never been the case.

Although the law bans polygamy, it was once allowed in Hinduism. Men of the ruling families had harems of wives and concubines. Rich men did the same. However, Rama and Sita provide the ideal in their devotion to one another, and a man would not take a second wife unless his first wife was childless or produced only daughters. This is because it is his son's duty to continue the family and he must have a son to perform his funeral rites.

On the other hand, women must be treated with kindness and respect, and mothers are very much honoured. Interestingly, some classes and castes have inheritance through the female side and they practised polyandry (more than one husband) until recently.

25.3 Death, burial and cremation

As a rule, the dead are cremated, though small children, ascetics and some low castes are usually buried. For 10 days after a funeral, the mourners are secluded, because both they and the corpse are ritually impure. During this time ceremonies are carried out to give the deceased a new spiritual body so that his or her soul can pass on to the next life.

Great care is taken in the performance of these rites, to prevent the soul from remaining as a ghost and causing trouble for the relatives. This is why it is important for Hindus to have a son, as only he can perform the funeral rites. If there is no son, then an orthodox Hindu will have an adopted substitute, even though this is not as good.

At the ceremony, dirges are played on drums as the body is carried to cremation. The eldest son leads the procession and carries a lamp. He whispers the letters AUM or OM to attune the spirit to God. He also lights the funeral pyre to free the soul. Offerings of balls of rice and containers of milk are made.

After 10 days, if all is well, the soul passes on to a new life, and the mourners are no longer ritually impure, because they will have undergone the purificatory rites. Offerings are made periodically to feed the soul.

25.4 Suttee (or sati)

In times gone by, a high-class widow would be burnt alive on her husband's funeral pyre. This was never demanded of a mother with young children, and was supposed to be voluntary. In reality, family and social expectations meant the widow had little choice. In religious terms, the justification was that she would purge both her own and her husband's sins, and they could then enjoy millions of years in heavenly bliss. If she did not comply, then the following would happen:

- She would have to be an ascetic for the rest of her life.
- Her head would be shaved, and she would not be allowed to have jewellery, cosmetics or fine clothes.
- She would have to pray continually for her husband's spirit.
- She would become a household drudge, and would be neglected by all.
- She would be inauspicious (bad luck) to anyone who came into contact with her.
- In normal circumstances she could not remarry, though it was not impossible; she could marry the dead man's brother or next of kin.

25.5 Girls at puberty

There is a traditional rite for when a Hindu girl begins her menstrual cycle. She is kept in a dark room for four days and is forbidden to see the sun. She is regarded as unclean or ritually impure and no one may touch her. Her diet is boiled rice, milk, sugar, curd and tamarind without salt. On the fifth morning, she goes to a neighbouring tank escorted by five women whose husbands are alive. She is smeared with turmeric water, they all bathe and return home, throwing away the mat and other things that were in the room.

The Rarhi Brahmans of Bengal compel a girl at puberty to live alone and forbid her to see the face of any man or boy. She has to stay in a dark room for three days to undergo penance. She is not allowed to eat meat, fish or sweetmeats, only rice and ghee are allowed.

The Tiyans of Malabar believe that a girl is polluted for the first four days of her first menstrual period. She has to keep to the north side of the house where she sleeps on a special grass mat in a room hung with garlands of young coconut leaves. Another girl will stay with her at this time but she must not touch another person, tree or plant. She must not see the sky, crows or cats. Diet is vegetarian without salt, tamarinds, or chillies. To protect against evil spirits she is allowed a knife which is either carried on her person or is placed on the mat.

25.6 Pregnancy and childhood

- Three rites are performed during pregnancy.
- A short ceremony is performed as soon as a baby is born and before the umbilical cord is cut.
- The next ceremony is ten days later, when mother and child are no longer ritually impure. It is then that the baby is named.
- There is a ceremony when the baby is four months old and has his first sight of the sun.
- There is another ceremony when the baby is weaned.
- High-class boys receive their ritual tonsure during their third year.

Questions

1. Questions (a)–(d) can be answered in a single word, phrase or sentence. Question (e) requires a longer answer.

    (a) What name is given to the Ultimate Reality (Supreme Being) worshipped by all Hindus? *(1 mark)*

    (b) Which is the earliest of the Vedas? *(1 mark)*

    (c) What special name is given to the 'eternal self' by Hindus? *(1 mark)*

    (d) Name **two** avatars of Vishnu. *(2 marks)*

    (e) Explain, using examples, the importance of symbols in Hindu worship. *(5 marks)*

    (Total 10 marks)

    (SEG Paper 1480/1, Section A, 1998 Short Course Specimen Papers)

2. (a) What is a *samskar*? *(2 marks)*

    (b) What might a Hindu hope to gain by making a pilgrimage to Varanasi? *(6 marks)*

    (c) Explain why the final *samskar* (cremation) is important in the Hindu view of life. *(8 marks)*

    (d) 'When you're dead, you're dead, and that is the end of you.'

    Do you agree? Give reasons for your answer showing you have considered another point of view. *(4 marks)*

    (Total 20 marks)

    (London)

3. (a) What is meant by 'caste'? [2]

    (b) Describe the Hindu caste system. [6]

    (c) How might belief in *dharma* (religious duty) affect the life of a Hindu today? [7]

    (d) 'Hindus in Britain cannot continue to live by the rules of the caste system.'

    Do you agree? Give reasons to support your answer and show that you have thought about different points of view. [5]

    (MEG Sample Paper, Summer 1998)

4. (a) Describe how Hindus in India and in Britain celebrate the festival of

    either

    Divali,

    or

    Holi.   (*7 marks*)

    (b) What is the religious meaning of each of these festivals of Divali
         and Holi?   (*7 marks*)

    (c) 'Hindu festivals are social events rather than religious ones.'   (*6 marks*)

         Do you agree? Give reasons for your answer, showing that you
         have thought about more than one point of view.   (*Total 20 marks*)

    (*NEAB SYL 2, Paper 3, Short Course, 3 June 1997*)

5. 'My favourite god is Shiva because when we went to India my Mum bought me a
    necklace and Shiva was on it. I like him because at night when I have bad thoughts
    I think about him and they go away.' (Comment by a Hindu girl)

    (a) Describe the features and symbols which might show that the image on
         the necklace was Shiva.   (*7 marks*)

    (b) Explain the importance of Shiva in Hinduism.   (*8 marks*)

    (c) Do you think this girl's view of Shiva is childish? Give reasons in support
         of your view.   (*5 marks*)

                                                                          (*Total 20 marks*)

    (*SEG SYLA, Paper 2, June 1995*)

Hinduism: a glossary

Acharya (Acarya)
Sanskrit: 'One who teaches by example'; a special spiritual teacher of the *Vedas*
Advaita
A term for non-duality from '*a*' ('not'), and '*dvaita*' ('duality'); the unity of *Brahman* (ultimate reality) and *Atman* (human soul)
Agama
A collection of authoritative scriptures
Ahimsa (Ahinsa)
Respect for life; not killing, non-violence
Ananda
A Sanskrit term for bliss; with *sat* and *cit*, it is one of the three attributes of Brahman in the Vedanta philosophy
Anasakti
The doctrine of 'selfless action'
Anrta
The Vedic concept of chaos
Antaryamin
The soul within the soul, the inner controller
Aranyakas
Lit: 'belonging to the forests': Hindu texts, attached to the *Brahmanas*, composed or studied in the forests of India
Arjuna
An epic hero, his dialogue with *Krishna* on the eve of batle forms the subject matter of the *Bhagavad Gita*
Artha
Economic development; the second human aim
Arti (Arati)
A welcoming ceremony in which auspicious articles such as lamps and incense are offered to the god or to saintly people
Aryan
From Sanskrit '*arya*' meaning noble, applied to the Vedic Indians' tradition
Ashram (Asram)
A place set up for spiritual development
Ashrama (Asrama)
One of the four stages of life adopted according to material considerations, but ultimately as a means to attain spiritual realisation; also, a centre of religious teaching and spiritual living, a retreat for meditation and self-discipline
Astika
Orthodox Hindus who accept the Vedic revelation; they are divided into six schools of thought

Asuras
Lit: 'spiritual' or 'divine': originally used of the supreme gods of Hinduism; later applied to demons and anti-gods of the Vedic hymns, against whom the Aryan gods struggled
Atharya Veda
The fourth Veda
Atman (Atta)
Lit: 'self', the real self, the soul, the principle of life
Avatar (Avatara, Avtara)
Lit: 'a descent': the descent of a god/deity, usually *Vishnu*, who has 10 avataras
Avidya (Avijja)
Lit: 'not knowing' or 'ignorance': the condition of those involved in the cycle of rebirth
Bhabhut
The ashes from a fire offering, preserved by an Indian village worshipper
Bhagat
A devotee; one who practices *Bhakti*
Bhagavad Gita
'The Song of The Lord', spoken by *Krishna*; the most famous and popular scripture
Bhagvan
A name for the impersonal supreme Spirit, God
Bhajan (Bhajana)
A hymn
Bhakti
'Love' or 'devotion': loving adoration to God with ardent worship
Bhakti yoga
The path of loving devotion, aimed at developing pure love of God
Bhedabhedavada
The doctrine of identity-in-difference as found in the *Brahma Sutra*; *Brahman* seen as both identical with and different from *Atman*
Bheru
The ferocious aspect of the god *Shiva*
Bhopa (Bhuvo)
An Indian village priest, or servant of a local deity or god
Bhutapati
Shiva as father of demons
Bhut
Ghost
Brahma
The creator god, one of the *Trimurti* or triad with *Vishnu* and *Shiva*
Brahmacharya (Brahmacharin)
The first of the four *ashramas* or stages of life, the celibate student; this stage lasts for 12 years
Brahmachari
Someone in the first stage of life
Brahm
Brahman ghost
Brahman
The ultimate reality, the absolute or god, it has no attributes, and is indescribable
Brahmanas
Sacred texts of the Hindu priestly class, attached to the *Vedas*
Brahma Samaj
A reformed Hindu sect founded by Ram Mohan Roy in 1827
Brahma Sutra
A collection of statements about *Brahman* which, with the *Upanishads*, forms the basis of Vedanta philosophy
Brahmin (Brahman, Brahmana)
First of the four *varnas*, the priestly class
Buddha
In Hm an avatar of Vishnu

Caste
Divisions or groups within Indian society, they are not the same as the four classes or *varnas*
Chamar
A member of a 'scheduled class' (untouchable or outcaste) whose traditional occupation is connected with tanning leather
Chandala (Candala)
General term for an untouchable or outcaste
Chela
A disciple of a guru; also an Indian village practitioner who seeks to overcome the effects of sorcery by exorcism and the use of *mantras*
Chuhra
An outcaste or untouchable who works as a sweeper
Cit
Consciousness, one of the three essential properties of the eternal self, with *ananda* and *sat*
Curail
Female ghost
Darshanas
The 6 philosophical schools
Dakshina
The fee paid to an Indian family priest, for the performance of a religious ceremony
Devata
A minor god
Deva
Superhuman, spiritual beings; the shining ones
Dharma
Lit; 'the quality of the self', 'that which sustains one's existence', generally, religious duty
Dhatu
The six sense objects (five sense organs plus *manas*)
Dhoti
A cotton garment worn over the lower body and legs by men
Dhyana
Meditation
Digambara
Shiva 'clothed in space' or 'sky dad'
Divali (Diwali)
'Row of lights': the festival of Lights ending one year and starting the next (also Dipavali/ Deepavali)
Duhkha (Dukkha)
Suffering
Durga
A goddess; one of the names of Devi, wife of Shiva
Dussehra
'Ten Days': the festival celebrating the victory of Lord Rama over Ravana (also called Vijaya Dashami)
Dvija
One who is 'twice born'; applied to the three upper classes
Dwarka (Dvarka, Dvaraka, Dwaraka)
A pilgrimage site on the west coast of India
Gandhi
Twentieth century spiritual and political leader
Ganesha
Elephant-headed Hindu god
Ganga
The River Ganges, the most sacred river of India
Gayatri Mantra
The most sacred Vedic verse or prayer
Ghat
A flight of steps leading to a river landing place; burning ghats or cremation places

Ghi
Clarified butter used in sacrifices and cremation
Gram-devata
Godlings in villages with limited local powers
Grihastha (Gristhi, Grhastha)
The second of the four stages of life: the householder
Gunas
Lit: 'rope or qualities': the three forces or qualities, through the interplay of which the Universe evolved
Hari Hara
A god joining Vishnu and Shiva; love and terror
Harijans
Lit: 'Sons of Hari': Gandhi's term for the untouchables or outcastes: The Indian constitution calls them the 'Scheduled class'. They call themselves *Dalith (Dalit)*, meaning oppressed
Hanuman
The monkey god who serves Rama and Sita
Havan (Homa)
The Fire ritual at weddings and other ceremonial occasions
Havan kund
The container in which the havan fire is burned
Holi
The Spring festival of *Krishna*
Indra
The most important Vedic god
ISKON
The International Society for Krishna Consciousness, a religious group of the Vaishnava tradtion
Isvara
Sanskrit: Lord, Master, King, God: most often refers to *Shiva* as the Supreme being. In the Bhagavad Gita it is applied to *Krishna* as the Lord of Beings
Jagat
The cosmos of moving beings; that which can be felt, heard and smelt
Japa
The repetition of the name of God as a devotional exercise
Jati
Lit: 'birth': Occupational kinship group, another term for caste, also, family, lineage or rank
Jenoi (Janeu)
Sacred thread worn by males of the 'twice-born' castes
Jnana
Knowledge or wisdom coming from direct insight into the nature of ultimate reality; one of the ways to salvation
Jnana-yoga
The path of knowledge to liberation
Kali
Lit: 'black': she is Shiva's consort
Kali Yuga
The fourth of the ages; the iron age or age of quarrel or hypocrisy
Kalkin
Avatar of Vishnu as incarnation of the future appearing as a horse, horse-headed man, or a man on a white horse with a flaming sword
Kalpas
Alternate ages of activity and rest, through which the Universe has evolved
Karah
Sweet pudding used as an offering
Kama
The third of the four aims of life-regulated sense enjoyment
Karma (Kamma)
Lit: deeds, doing or action: these determine a person's destiny in a future life

Karma-marga
The path of action leading to salvation
Karma-yoga
The path of pious work aiming at enjoying this world, in this life and the next
Katha
The reading of scriptures by a *Brahman* priest, sponsored by a worshipper
Khota
The anger of an Indian village godling, seen as the cause of suffering among the community
Kirtan
'Glorification'; usually performed with musical instruments
Krishna
Popular god, an *avatar* or incarnation of *Vishnu*
Kshatriya (Khetri, Khatri)
Second of the four *varnas* or divisions of Hindu society; the ruling or warrior division
Kurma
Tortoise avatar of Vishnu
Lakshmi
The goddess of fortune
Lingam
The symbol of the male sexual organ
Mahabharata
The longer of two Indian epic poems; the other is the *Ramayana*. It includes the *Bhagavad Gita*
Mahatma
'Great soul', a title given to leaders such as Gandhi
Mahavakyas
Great sayings in the Vedic scriptures
Mala
A circle of stringed beads used in meditation
Manas
A sixth sense which co-ordinates the perceptions of the other five
Mandala (mandal)
A circular sacred diagram, also an area or community/group
Mandir
Temple
Mantra
Lit: 'that which delivers the mind': a sacred prayer repeated often (In Vedic literature, a hymn or verse which aids meditation)
Manu
The ancestor of the human race who outlined the rules of conduct for Hinduism. Each age has its own manu: the present one is the seventh of fourteen
Marg
A path leading to salvation
Marhais
The smallest, local religious fairs
Mata
An independent female *devata*: *Matas* have specialist functions – for example, Sitalamata is the smallpox goddess, Hadakaimata, the goddess of rabies
Mathura
The birthplace of *Krishna*, a holy place
Matsya
Fish avatar of Vishnu
Maya
From the human point of view, it is the power to create illusions, and then illusion itself; from the divine point of view it is the power which creates the world
Mayin
A title for God as the wielder of **Maya**

Mela
A religious fair
Metempsychosis
The transfer of the soul from one body to another
Mimamsa
One of the six schools of philosophy
Moksha (Moksa, Mukti)
Liberation from the cycle of rebirth
Mundan
Head-shaving ceremony
Murti
'Form', the image used as a focus of worship
Nandi
Bull ridden by Shiva
Narasimha
Man-lion avatar of Vishnu
Natavaja
Shiva as Lord of the Dance
Navaratri (Navaratra)
Nine nights festival before *Dussehra*
Nazar
The Evil Eye
Nastika
Unorthodox schools of philosophy that do not accept the Vedic revelation
Nirgunam Brahman
Term for *Brahman* without *gunas* or qualities
Nyaya
One of the six orthodox schools of philosophy
Om (Aum)
The sacred symbol and sound representing the ultimate; the most sacred Hindu words
Pancayat
The caste assembly which enforces caste rules, and settles disputes between fellow caste members
Pancgavya
A mixture of the five products of the cow, consumed as a purifying agent. includes milk, curds, *ghi*, cow dung and urine
Panchatantra
Part of the supplementary Vedic scriptures (animal stories with a moral)
Pap
Sin
Parashu Rama
Rama of the Axe; an avatar of Vishnu
Paratantra
The doctrine that all worldly things depend for their activity on God
Parvati
The goddess of the Himalayas; one of the names of the consort of *Shiva*
Pashupa
Shiva as protector of cattle
Prahlada
A devotee of *Vishnu* connected with the *Holi* festival
Prakrti
Sanskrit: 'making before', used in the *sankhya* school of philosophy for Nature or Primordial Matter, eternal and self-existing
Pranam
Greeting involving bowing with hands together before the deity, or bowing down to touch the feet of the deity or a guru
Prashad
Sanctified food at a sacrifice, eaten by those present at the end of worship

Prasada
'Grace', the gift of *Krishna*, used in the Gita
Pravachan
A lecture based on scripture
Pret
'Lingering shade' the state of the soul between death and the completion of funeral ceremonies
Puja
'Worship': usually the raising of hands, palms together
Pujari
Village priest
Punya
A meritorious act that brings a reward in this life or the next – for example, meditation and generosity
Puranas
'Ancient', part of the *smrti* scriptures
Purohit
A family priest
Purusha
The soul as distinct from material nature: in the *Rig Veda* it is used for Cosmic Man
Rajas
One of the *gunas* or qualities, translated as 'energy', 'passion', or 'force'
Raksha Bandhan
The festival when women tie a decorative bracelet on their brothers' wrists
Rama
One of the ten *avatars* of *Vishnu*, as king of Ayodhya, hero of the *Ramayana*
Ramayana
The story of *Rama*, an epic poem in *Sanskrit*
Rig Veda
Lit: 'verse knowledge' or 'word knowledge', the Royal Veda, the first and most sacred scripture
Rishi (Rsi, risi)
The seven seers who received the *Vedas* from the gods
Rta
The Vedic concept of cosmic law by which all things are maintained in existence
Sadhana
Regulated spiritual practices or discipline
Sadharan dharma
General code of ethics
Sadhu (Saddhu)
Holy man, ascetic (Sanskrit)
Sagunam Brahman
A term in the *Upanishads* for the Divine with *gunas* (qualities); this came about because of the difficulty of understanding *Brahman* without qualities or attributes
Saiva
A follower of the god *Shiva*
Salagram
An ammonite stone with spiral markings, one of the symbols of the god *Vishnu*
Sama Veda
The *Veda* of chanting; material mainly from the *Rig Veda* arranged for ritual chanting in sacrificial worship
Samsara (Sangsara)
'Going through' or transmigration or rebirth of the soul in different species
Samskaras
Rites of passage initiating new stages of life
Sanatan Dharma
The eternal, imperishable religion, preferred by some of the faithful to the word Hinduism
Sangha
An assembly of sages

Sankhya
One of the orthodox schools of philosophy
Sannyasin (Samyasin, Samnyasin)
Someone in the last of the four stages of life, having renounced worldly matters
Sanskrit
Sacred language of the scriptures
Sarana
A description of *Krishna*, as a refuge for his followers, used in the *Gita*
Sat
'Being' or 'existence' and hence 'the good' or 'the true'; one of the three attributes of the divine principle, *Brahman*, with *ananda* and *cit*
Sattva (Sattwa)
One of the three *gunas* or qualities; 'goodness', sustaining and nourishing
Satyagraha
'truth-force' or non-violent action; Gandhi's policy of non-co-operation with the British
Seva (Sewa)
Service, to the divine or to humanity
Shaivism (Saivism)
The religion of those who are the devotees of the god *Shiva*
Shakti (Sakti)
Energy and power, especially of a god
Shiva (Siva)
A god; the name means 'kindly' or 'auspicious'
Shivaratri (Sivaratri)
Annual festival in honour of *Shiva* (also *Mahashivarti*)
Shraddha (Sraddha)
Ceremony in which sanctified food is offered to departed ancestors
Shri (Sri)
'Fortune': a title of respect; fem. *Shrimati*
Shudra
The fourth varna: artisans; they are of higher status than the outcastes or *untouchables*
Sita (Seeta)
Rama's consort
Smrti (Smirti, Smiriti)
'That which is remembered': scriptures other than the *Vedas* and *Upanishads* (which are revealed) for example, the *Gita*
Sruti (Srti, Shruti)
'What is heard': the four *Vedas* and the *Upanishads which were 'heard' by ancient seers*
Sudra
The lowest of the four division of society
Suttee
When a wife was burned alive on her husband's funeral pyre
Svatantra
A doctrine that God alone is autonomous; his activity and existence do not depend on anything else, but all other beings are dependent
Svayambhu
A descriptive name for God found in the *Upanishads*; from the root 'sva' self, literally meaning self-existent
Swami (Svami)
Lit: 'controller': one who can control his senses, this is an honorary title for religious teachers and holy men
Swastika
Sanskrit 'well being': a mark of good fortune
Tamas
Ignorance, dullness or denseness; the lowest of the three *gunas*
Tantra
Texts containing dialogues between *Shiva* and his spouse

Totka
A magic ritual carried out by a village priest
Transcendental Complex
The quest for liberation and salvation from *samsara*, the cycle of rebirth and continued existence
Transmigration
Belief that soul inhabits many bodies in successive rebirths
Trinurti
The three gods: *Brahma*, *Vishnu* and *Shiva*
Tryambaka
Shiva accompanied by 3 mother goddesses
Tuna (Tona)
Sorcery practiced by a villager to cause suffering or disaster
Untouchable
Those outside the caste system (outcastes)
Upanaya
Sacred thread-tying ceremony
Upanishad (Upanisad)
'To sit down near': a sacred text
Vaikuntha
The heavenly realm of *Vishnu*, where liberated souls live
Vaiseshika
One of the six schools of philosophy
Vaishnavism (Vainavism)
The religion of those who are devotees of *Vishnu*
Vaishya (Vaisya)
The third of the four *varnas* or social divisions (merchants and farmers)
Vamana
Dwarf avatar of Vishnu
Vanaprasthi
The third of the four stages of life (Lit: 'forest dweller')
Varaha
Boar avatar of Vishnu
Varna
'Colour': the four divisions of Hindu society
Varnashrama dharma
The system dividing society into four *varnas* (divisions) and life into four *ashramas* (stages)
Varuna
Vedic sky god
Vayu
Vedic god of wind or spirit
Veda
'Knowledge': the earliest Hindu scriptures
Vedanta
Lit: 'end of the Veda'; one of the six philosophical schools
Vidya
'Knowledge', especially spiritual wisdom
Vishnu (Visnu)
One of the three gods of the *Trimurti*
Vrat
Vow
Vrindavan (Brindavan, Vrindavana)
The village connected with *Krishna* and the *gopis*
Yajna
A sacrifice to get extra merit
Yajur Veda
The sacrificial Veda: texts from the Veda with instructions for use in sacrificial worship

Yama
The god of death who punishes the wicked
Yantra
A mystical diagram, such as a mandala, used in ceremonies
Yatra (Jatra)
Pilgrimage
Yoga
'Communion'; the union of the soul with the Supreme; a method of discipline leading to salvation; one of the six philosophical schools
Yogi
A person who practices yoga (fem. *yogusi*)
Yuga
Age, or extended period of time; there are four

PART V

Buddhism

Buddhism: origins

26.1 Introduction

Buddhism began in India around 500 years BCE. Many people at that time had become disillusioned with some of the beliefs of Hinduism, especially the caste system and the endless cycle of birth, death and rebirth. People turned to other beliefs and many new sects arose. It was in this climate that Buddhism appeared.

26.2 Historical background

Around 1000 BCE India was conquered by a race of people called the Aryans, who came through the north-west mountain passes. They brought with them a religious treasury called the *Veda*, the earliest body of Hindu scriptures. This was a period when original thinkers were to search for new religious paths.

The Aryan invaders dominated the native population. They had two classes: the **Brahmins**, the religious class, who administered rites, and the **kshatriya** or noble class, who held political power.

The Buddha's family lands were in north-east India in the foothills of the Himalayas. There was fertile farmland and large areas of forest where those looking for spiritual enlightenment would go to meditate.

26.3 The early life of the Buddha

He was the son of King Suddhodana and Queen Mahamaya, and was born in 563 BCE near Kapilavatthu in the foothills of the Himalayas in what is now Nepal. Seven days after his birth, the queen died and the baby was reared by her sister, Mahapajapati Gotami, who was the king's second wife.

His name was Siddhartha, which means 'One whose aim is accomplished', and his family name was Gautama. The family traced their descent from the sun, and were part of the Sakya clan, so he was later also known as 'Sage of the Sakyans' or 'Sakyamuni' and 'Kinsman of the Sun'.

The name 'Buddha', taken by him in 531 BCE, means 'Enlightened One'.

As he belonged to the Kshatriyas – the second of the four classes of Hindu society – his youth was comfortable, and he enjoyed all the pleasures that would be expected for someone of his background.

He was married at the age of 16 to his cousin Yasodharo, who was also 16. They had a son named Rahula, which means 'fetter' or 'bond'.

26.4   Mahamaya's dream

This happened the night before the future Buddha was born. A silvery white elephant danced three times before her while holding a lotus flower in its trunk. It then entered her womb through her side. The priests interpreted the dream as foretelling the birth of a son who would become either a universal monarch or a buddha.

Ten lunar months after conceiving, the queen went to visit her parents. On the full moon day of *Vesakha* (May) she gave birth as she clutched the branch of a sala tree. This took place in the curtained enclosure set up for her in Lumbini, a garden or park. This place, now called Rummindei, is in Nepal.

Siddhartha was immediately acclaimed by Brahma and other Hindu gods, and a choir of angels sang in the brilliantly lit heavens. To show that his message would have a vital influence in the world he took seven steps to north, south, east and west. Then he announced that this was to be his last incarnation and that he was chief of the world.

The sage Asita or Kala Devala, the king's religious adviser, went to examine the baby. He said that prophetic signs on his body revealed that he was to become a buddha. Although this delighted him, he was very sad, because he knew that he was too old to see the fulfilment of his prophecy. The king was alarmed by the sage's conflicting emotions, but Asita explained his smiles and tears and restored the king's confidence in Siddhartha's future. The king and Asita then worshipped the child.

26.5   The judgement of the Brahmans

- 108 brahmans were invited for the name-giving ceremony.
- Eight of them were specialists in bodily marks.
- Seven of them predicted two possibilities:
    (1)   if Siddhartha remained at home, he would become a universal monarch;
    (2)   if he left home, he would become a buddha.
- Kondanna, the youngest of the eight, said that he would definitely become a buddha.
- Kondanna was to become one of the Buddha's companions and one of the first five disciples.

26.6   The Buddha's first jhana *under the jambu* tree

The boy was taken to a ploughing festival, where he and his nurses waited in a tent under a jambu tree. The nurses left him on his own while they went to enjoy the festivities. On their return they found him sitting cross-legged, absorbed in a trance (*jhana*). When the king saw this, he worshipped him for a second time.

26.7 Gautama's transformation

At the age of 29 he had a spiritual crisis. He left his family, property and class privileges to become a wandering holy man wearing only rags. He had come into contact with old age, illness and death and was shaken by the impermanence and uncertainty of life on earth.

He was out driving one day with his charioteer when he saw an old man tottering along. Gautama asked the charioteer what was wrong with the man. He explained that the man was old and that everyone had to face the problem of aging. Then they saw a sick man fallen and lying in his own excreta. As before, the charioteer explained that this was a sick man and that all men are subject to sickness. In a third incident, they saw a funeral and Gautama was touched by the sorrow of the mourners. The charioteer explained that death comes to everyone. Then he saw a man with a shaven head and yellow robe. His calmness impressed Gautama, who decided to discover the reason for such serenity in the midst of such wretchedness. It was on the way home from seeing the yellow-robed man that he heard of the birth of his son.

26.8 The Great Renunciation or Retirement

Gautama decided to abandon his privileged life. This has become known as 'The Great Renunciation'. He went to find teachers to show him the truth. A sage called Alara Kalama taught him until he had to admit that Gautama was his equal. He invited him to help teach the community of his disciples. He then went to another teacher called Uddaka and made further progress.

Then he moved on to a woodland grove at Uruvela where five ascetics joined him (ascetics are people who give up the pleasures of this world). One of them was Kondanna, the brahman who had predicted that he would become a buddha one day. For six years he practiced extreme asceticism, but realised that it would not achieve enlightenment so he began to eat proper amounts of food again. His companions were outraged by this and left him. He remained at Uruvela and pursued enlightenment alone.

26.9 The Great Enlightenment and the struggle with Mara

Gautama sat under a banyan tree considering the meaning of life and the causes of suffering. He spent the day in a grove of sal trees, and in the evening sat beneath a pipal tree (now called a bodhi or bo tree). He would not move again until he had reached enlightenment.

Mara, the evil Tempter, tried to prevent his enlightenment, but Gautama sat in meditation, supported by the ten Great Virtues (**paramitas**) that he had achieved in his past lives as a **bodhisattva** (buddha-to-be). These ten virtues are essential to attain enlightenment and become a buddha.

The ten virtues

- charity
- morality
- renunciation

- wisdom
- effort
- patience
- truth
- determination
- universal love
- equanimity.

Mara tried to persuade him to abandon his quest but Gautama made it clear that he intended to defeat Mara's ten 'armies'.

Mara's ten 'armies'

(1)   lust
(2)   dislike for higher existence
(3)   hunger and thirst
(4)   craving
(5)   torpor and sloth (laziness)
(6)   fear (cowardice)
(7)   doubt
(8)   hypocrisy and obduracy
(9)   gains, praise, honour, false glory
(10) exalting oneself while despising others.

The result

Mara was defeated and disappeared. Gautama spent the rest of the night in meditation to gain knowledge of his former lives and to gain the super-human divine eye or 'third eye', which would give him the power to see the passing away and rebirth of all things. Then he realised the Four Noble Truths.

So, at the age of 35 he had achieved enlightenment; he had become the Buddha.

26.10   The death of Buddha

At the age of 80, with his life's work done, the Buddha set out with a group of monks from Rajagaha. They went north and reached Vesali, the capital of the Licchavis. The rainy season was spent in the village of Beluva, where Buddha became very ill. However, he overcame the illness because he wished to prepare his disciples before he died. Ananda, his most devoted disciple, asked for instructions for the order of the Sangha. Buddha replied: 'dwell by making yourselves your island, making yourselves, not anyone else, your refuge; making the **dhamma** your refuge, nothing else your refuge.' Then he announced that he had decided to die in three months, and told his followers to live by what he had taught them. They were told to spread this abroad for the benefit of mankind and out of compassion for the world.

They then moved on to Pava where the Buddha ate his last meal, after which he became very sick. Then they set out for Kusinara (Kusinagara) now called Kasia. Ananda wept because he knew that Buddha was about to die, but Buddha told him not to weep because 'separation is inevitable from all near and dear to us. Whatever is born, produced, conditioned, contains within itself the nature of its own dissolution. It cannot be otherwise.' A wandering ascetic named Subhadda came to see Buddha, and after talking he joined the order that night, and so was the last direct disciple.

Buddha said: 'What I have taught and laid down, Ananda, is *dhamma* and as **vinaya**, this will be your master when I am gone...'. To the monks he said: 'transient are all conditioned things. Try to accomplish your aim with diligence.' These were his last words.

After cremation, his relics were divided into eight portions for various kingdoms. **Stupas** were built over these relics and commemorative feasts held.

26.11 Buddha and doctrine

Buddha said 'After me your master will be the doctrine itself.' No one has ever attempted to become universal spiritual leader in the same way that the Pope is for Roman Catholicism; it has never been thought necessary. That is why diversity and opposition have developed within Buddhism over various doctrines, practical devotions, and the large number of schools and observances. There are local groupings of monasteries who appoint leaders. There is a widespread wish to be true to the basic doctrine which now takes the Buddha's place.

27 The spread of Buddhism

27.1 The spread of Buddhism in India

In India, Buddhism continued for over a thousand years before it almost disappeared. During Buddha's time (520–480 BCE) it was most successful in the north-east of the country and was one of the many sects flourishing at that time. What was special about it was that it appealed to all castes. Buddha said that virtue, not birth, makes a man 'spiritual' or '*brahman*'. Buddha's second caste of nobles or *kshatriyas* were enthusiastic converts.

There were three influences in the distinctive nature of Indian Buddhism:

(1)   the internal influence of the **Theravada** and **Mahasanghikas**
(2)   the establishment of councils
(3)   the conversion of Emperor **Ashoka**.

27.2 The internal influence

There were two main types of believer.

The Ancients – Theravada

- This is the Southern School found in South East Asia.
- These were very conservative and the traditions kept by them can be found in the canon of scriptures.
- Their name is *Sthavira* (*Thera* in the Pali language; hence Theravada).
- Followers see their way as purer and more authentic.
- This school was to be called the Theravada or '**Hinayana**', a term of contempt used by followers of the **Mahayana**. It means the 'Lesser Vehicle' or lower way.

Theravada – basic views

- It demands loyalty to the *dhamma* and *vinaya* (teaching and discipline)
- The Three Refuges (see Chapter 29) must be performed.
- There must be loyalty to the **Tripitaka** or 'Three Baskets' (see below, section 27.5)

- There is support for spiritual leaders and emphasis on the **sangha** ('assembly' or monastery).
- Theravadins are enthusiastic about spreading the faith and in being an example to others.

Mahayana – basic views

- Followers believe that all Buddhists are working their way towards enlightenment and that Buddha is the ideal to follow in this respect.
- It is believed that *bodhisattvas* remain in the world to help others in their quest. They have achieved enlightenment but renounce full **nibbana** to do this. They show love and compassion to everyone and this helps to spread the message.
- Mahayana emphasises scriptures not in the *Tripitaka*, and the **Three Bodies** of Buddha, which are:
  (1) The Body of Truth
  (2) The Body of Bliss
  (3) The Body of Appearance.
- There will be a future Buddha (*metteya*) who will restore the teaching where necessary.

Great Assembly (Mahasanghikas)

- This is the Northern School found in North Asian countries.
- This was the less traditional school.
- Their doctrine was more open to development and was written in Sanskrit, a more scholarly language than Pali.
- Here the influence of the Buddhist laity was significant.
- It is from this second type that a form of Buddhism called the Mahayana or 'Greater Vehicle' emerged.

Summary

Each school came to be dominant and formative in its own area. The growing gap between the two vehicles led to moves to re-establish pure doctrine, which led to the setting up of councils to confirm discipline and rules and decide the basic content of the scriptures. These councils were the second influence.

27.3 The establishment of Councils

The First Council, at Ragjir or Rajagaha

The problem was that the Buddha did not nominate a successor and he wrote nothing down. His view had always been that the *dhamma* would show the way. The difficulty arose over interpretation, especially when training monks.

500 **arhats** (those who had fully trained themselves in the development of their mental powers), met to debate the problem. Two monks with astonishing power of memory were called on to lead the monks in reciting the *vinaya* (discipline) and the *dhamma* (law). The monk Upali was the authority on *vinaya*, and Ananda knew the *dhamma*.

After some discussion, agreement was reached. Then 500 more monks arrived. Their leader explained that they wished to preserve the *dhamma* as he had personally heard it from Buddha. So the council was divided between the liberals who followed Kasyapa, and the more traditional party.

The Second Council of Vesali

700 monks from the Vajji territory met. Some wanted a relaxation in the 10 points of discipline. Their movement, known as the Great Assembly (Mahasangha), separated itself from the First Council of Rajgir.

They believed that a man who had become enlightened could still fall into error, ignorance and doubt. This caused a split.

Yasa, an elder monk, called a council made up of monks from the 'Western Country, the Southern Country, and the Eastern Country'. Discussion achieved nothing so a committee was formed and ruled that the Vajjians were unlawful on all 10 points. This was confirmed by the full council. The defeated group refused to accept the judgement and held their own council. They came to be known as *Mahasanghikas*.

From these events emerged the two major schools: the *Theravada* or *Hinayana*, the Lesser Vehicle; and the *Mahayana* or Great Vehicle. The term 'vehicle' is used because the *dhamma* or doctrine is seen as a raft or boat that carries the follower across the ocean of this world to salvation on the far shore. It was accepted that differences of opinion were likely to develop, but that the *sangha* had to be undivided by controversy. If it should arise then the dissenting group should leave and set up their own *sangha*.

This 'Law of Schism', as it was called, preserved unity of the *sangha* and allowed for honest differences of opinion.

27.4   The conversion of Ashoka

The third factor in the development of Buddhism emerged at this time. It was the conversion of the Emperor Ashoka to Buddhism. He ruled the Magadhan Empire, covering north and central India, from 272 to 232 BCE.

Buddhism was a growing social and intellectual movement, and it was clear that he would have to take it into account. Ashoka's rule is outstanding for his adoption of the social principles of Buddhism.

He took the role of a pious layman, which was to help other religious groups as well as Buddhism. The Third Council was held at the Imperial capital, Pataliputra (Patna). Ashoka supported opposition to the doctrine of the Pan-realists (**Sarvastivadins**) which was contradictory to orthodox Buddhism.

As a result, the Pan-realists migrated westwards, eventually settling in Kashmir and Gandhara. At this conference the monks agreed on the contents of the Pali canon of scripture or **Tripitaka**.

27.5   The Three Baskets, or Tripitaka

They are:

(1)   **Vinaya Pitaka** (discipline)
(2)   **Sutta Pitaka** (themes)
(3)   **Abhidhamma Pitaka** (analysis).

Vinaya Pitaka (Discipline)

This is the oldest part and holds the purest collection of Buddha's teaching. It derives from the questions put to the monk Upali by Kassapa regarding discipline for monks and nuns in monastic life.

The main points

- It deals with the need to live peacefully.
- There must be care for those who are ill.
- There must be the giving of charity.
- There must be instructions for teachers and pupils.
- There is a detailed explanation of various points of the Public Confession (**uposatha**) used in the *sangha*.
- There are rules governing ceremonies.

Sutta Pitaka (Themes)

This contains the **Dhammapada**, which is a vital part of the Pali Canon and is made up of 423 verses of sayings of the Buddha in 26 chapters, in which there are five collections of teachings (*nikaya*):

- long expositions or commentaries (*digha nikaya*)
- medium expositions (*majjima nikaya*)
- joined together expositions (*samyutta nikaya*)
- expositions classified by a numerical system (*anguttara nikaya*)
- minor expositions (*khuddaka nikaya*).

(*Note*: exposition includes explanation, discussion and clarification.)

Abhidhamma Pitaka

This explains the teachings of the *Sutta Pitaka*. It is an analysis of psychic and mental phenomena, the essence of life and the source of higher knowledge. It was added last as an explanation to accompany earlier teachings. Some of it is set out in question and answer form. The most important parts are those of the two ancient schools of the *Theravadin* and the *Sarvastivadin*.

27.6 The expansion of Buddhism outside India

There were two possible routes for Buddhism to expand. It could go north and east over the mountains, or south and east by sea. Westward expansion was limited to border regions between India and Afghanistan and the countries beyond, which had experienced Hellenism from Alexander the Great and his successors. A good example was King Milinda's dialogues with Buddhists in his lands.

Northern expansion

- **China**

This was mainly by the *Mahayana* and it spread along the silk road to China and over the high desert plateaux. Central Asian towns were important in the spread of Buddhist ideas. In the first century CE it had reached Kiangsu. In the second century CE Emperor Han became a Buddhist. This was important because it led to the setting up of an office of translations, for texts, mostly in Sanskrit and Chinese. Buddhism adapted to the Chinese way of thinking, which was practical, moralistic and tolerant of diverse opinion. Two important religious groups developed:

(1) the T'ien T'ai sect
(2) the Amida cult and the Pure Land cult.

(1) *The T'ien T'ai sect* This practised transcendental meditation. The chief focus is on Sakyamuni (the historical Buddha) who is transcendental (or beyond normal human experience). The movement was founded by Chih I (538–97). Its chief scripture is the *Lotus Sutra*, and it has a system of meditative exercises consisting of:

  (1) correct posture
  (2) correct breathing
  (3) contemplation of the breathing
  (4) compassionate, friendly, joyful and detached thoughts
  (5) Buddha contemplation
  (6) contemplation of sentences from the *Lotus Sutra*.

(2) *The Amida cult and the Pure Land cult* In *Mahayana* this is the transcendent Buddha of Infinite Light. It is believed that faith gives a measure of enlightenment through Amitabha's grace.* This is known as the 'Easy Road' through 'other-power' as opposed to the 'Saintly Road' through 'self-power' (normal in traditional Buddhism). Sometimes it is called the Lotus School. Mahayana taught that those unable to achieve enlightenment alone could do so through faith that *buddhas* and *bodhisattvas* could help them. Some buddhas had created Buddhalands, that of Amida being the Pure Land in the West. By calling the name of Amitabha, and having faith in him, a person is assured of rebirth in the Pure Land. This captured people's imagination and provided a simple faith for those who had to work daily and were too poor to study and carry out elaborate rituals.
* Transcendent Buddha, i.e. when he left this earthly life.

- ## Development in China

In the sixth and seventh centuries CE the Chinese began to show interest in philosophical and religious questions, so more religious texts from India were translated. Buddhism became one of the three religions of China, with Confucianism and Taoism. There was a saying: 'The three religions are one religion'. Other features of Buddhism in China included new rites and observances. There were statues of Buddhas in the temples everywhere because each age has its Buddhas. People went on pilgrimages to sacred mountains, monks guarded the ashes of ancestors in cemeteries, and there were rosaries with 108 beads for reciting praises to the name of Amida.

- ## Korea

Chinese Buddhism spread into Korea and merged with the local religion, holding a very important position under the protection of a number of rulers. Korea acted as a bridge for the spread of Buddhism to Japan.

- ## Japan

Buddhism was taken to Japan by Korean scholars in the sixth century CE. In 600 CE Prince Shotoku, the regent, was converted and Buddhism became the official religion of Japan. Japan was divided into feudal clans and was backward at this time. The progressives used Buddhism, which they regarded as the modern doctrine, as a weapon against Shinto, which was the traditional religion favoured by the conservative feudal leaders. Shotoku took the side of the progressive Soga clan, which was Buddhist.

Twelve sects developed, with further internal divisions and interaction between the various sects. Alliances and compromises were made with Shinto, and they shared temples. Shinto gods were represented as *avatars* (other forms) of the Buddha. In the following centuries important people became monks as in India and China, and monks influenced the conscience and policies of the rulers. Monasteries owned estates employing thousands of people. They became such a problem that the shogun (regent of the Empire) had to break their power by war. Monasteries also held poets, artists, builders, administrators and military tacticians!!

Buddhism was the state religion until 1860, when Shinto became the national religion again, as a sense of national identity grew in Japan. Some of the important sects include:

(1) Pure Land (*Jodo*), a pietist or devotional sect
(2) Zen (from the Chinese *Ch'an*), a meditational sect
(3) Tendai (from *T'ien Tai*), a philosophical sect
(4) Chen-yen
(5) Shingon
(6) Hosso
(7) Soka Gakkai
(8) Nichiren.

- **Tibet**

Here Buddhism developed in a quite unique way, merging with old beliefs and traditions. It has a mixture of *Theravada* and *Mahayana*. **Tantras** (sacred texts) are used for their magical powers and to reveal the path to *nibbana*. *Tantras* are taught to Tibetan children, and monks have to recite them daily. Monks have played an important role in national and political life. Their leader is the chief monk, the **Dalai Lama**, who ruled Tibet until Red China took over. He is the traditional ruler of Tibet and the highest Buddhist monk in Tibet and Mongolia. This is not a hereditary or elected position because it is believed that is held by the same individual in successive incarnations. He is sometimes called the 'Grand Lama'. The name Dalai Lama is from Tibetan: Mongolian '*dalai*', or ocean, plus Tibetan '*bla-ma*', superior one; a Buddhist monk, **lama**.

Southern expansion

- **Sri Lanka**

In the third century CE, Buddhism was taken to Ceylon (Sri Lanka) by Ashoka's son Mahinda, who had become a Buddhist monk and achieved *Nibbana*. He converted King Anuradhapura. It was here that the Pali canon of the Ancients were preserved by reciting the scriptures. Ancient chronicles reveal the increasing influence of Buddhism on all aspects of life for all classes of society. Older rituals were accommodated; for example, **pirit**, the chanting of holy texts against demons. Local Buddhist councils were held and large temples built; the most impressive being at Kandy and Anuradhapura. The *sangha* has thrived as shown in monasteries, universities and festivals such as the great procession from the temple of the Buddha's Tooth. This is a *Theravadan* country.

- **Burma**

In 250 BCE the Emperor Ashoka sent the first missionaries Sona and Uttara to 'Suvanna-bhumi' the Golden Land. Again, Buddhism existed alongside Hinduism and older beliefs, but eventually became the official religion. *Theravada* is followed here, and there is a strong monastic tradition. Most notable is the emphasis on **Abhidhamma** of the canon of scripture. Throughout the period up to 1000 CE, Buddhists made their way from India to Burma.

- **Thailand**

Thailand lies on the western side of the Indo-China peninsula and was open to Indian influences. Archaeologists have shown that Buddhism was practised in the area west of Bangkok from the first century CE. Discoveries have included fine pieces of sculpture, sancturies, **Buddha-rupas** and the typical symbol of the *Dharma-cakra* or 'wheel of the law'. Thai Buddhism has basically the same characteristics as Burmese Buddhism.

- **Indo China**

This consists of Laos, Cambodia and Vietnam. Because of its position, its Buddhism has become a mixture of *Mahayana* from the north and *Theravada* from the south and west. Other influences include the developments in China and the animism of the mountain peoples of the area. (Animism believes that spiritual beings live in mountains, trees and other natural objects.)

- **Indonesia**

The influence of Buddhism was great for 1000 years until the arrival of Islam. Probably the greatest centres of Buddhist learning and culture in South East Asia between the seventh and eleventh centuries CE were the islands of Sumatra and Java, where the influence of eastern India, especially Bengal, was strong. The Chinese pilgrim I Tsing travelled throughout India and Indonesia in the late seventh century, and wrote that the rulers supported Hinayana Buddhism. Later, the Sailendra Dynasty that ruled Malaya and most of Indonesia promoted Mahayana. They also had close contacts with eastern India, especially the great centre at Nalanda. From North East India the Tantric form arrived and became predominant until Buddhism gradually disappeared within a form of religion dominated by *Brahman* priests and Hindu cults.

27.7   Buddhism in the West

It is only in the last hundred years or so that Buddhism has really become known in the West (Figure 27.1). In the early 1960s there were a number of scriptures in translation plus a few scholarly works, but few serious practitioners. Then in 1967 Sangharakshita, and Englishman born in London in 1925, founded the Friends of the Western Buddhist Order. The FWBO, as it is known, has taken a different approach to the other attempts to establish Buddhism in the West.

Adapting Buddhism to modern conditions

Before the FWBO, Buddhism was taught on traditional lines, with teachers from the East conveying their own form of Buddhism, say from Japan or Thailand. FWBO presents its faith in a way that is relevant to the modern West without losing its essence.

Figure 27.1 A shrine in a Buddhist Vihara, Chiswick, London
(Carlos Reyes-Manzo Andes Press Agency)

They also draw freely from the whole of the Buddhist tradition for development and inspiration, unlike the other Buddhist groups in the West – nearly all of which are devoted to the study and practice of just one school. At the same time they draw on sources of inspiration outside Buddhism if they are helpful.

This means that Westerners do not have to abandon their cultural roots to become Buddhists. So artists and poets from the West whose work reflects some aspect of the *dharma* act as a bridge between the two cultures. This approach has proved popular outside the West, including the slums and villages of India. There are 18 main centres in the UK, with others throughout Europe, America, Australasia, and Asia.

28 Buddhist teachings

28.7 The Truth

This can be simplified as follows:

- Buddha realized that Mankind cannot see the Truth that he could now see. Because of this problem, he was unsure whether or not to teach his findings to the rest of the world.
- The *brahman* Sahampati persuaded him to accept the challenge of teaching the world. He did this by presenting the Buddha with an image of a lotus pond, which naturally will have some lotuses still under water because they are still un-developed; others will be at the surface; and there are those which are above the water and quite untouched by it. This analogy also applies to the human world.
- The Buddha understood the point and took up the challenge (Figure 28.1). He decided to teach his five former companions first. He sent to see them and told them that he was now an arhat ('perfected one') and wished to teach them the *dhamma*.
- They would not accept this at first, because when he had given up extreme ascet-icism they assumed that he had given up the quest for enlightenment. Then they realised that his transformation had taken place, and so he preached his first sermon; the Benares Sermon, known as the 'Sermon on Setting in Motion the Wheel of Truth'.

28.2 The Benares Sermon

This is Buddha's analysis of the problem of human life and how it can be solved. The sermon is traditionally presented as the first preaching of the Buddha, in the Deer Park. It contains the basis of the doctrine (*dhamma*) in two parts.

(1) The *dhamma* is the middle between two extremes, being based on reason.
(2) The reality of life is diagnosed as a doctor diagnoses illness with a cure or prescription for it.

28.3 The Four Noble Truths

The first two are the problem; the last two are the answer to the problem.

(1) Suffering is universal.
(2) The cause of suffering is universal.
(3) The remedy for suffering is universal.
(4) The path of release from suffering is universal.

From The Four Noble Truths Buddha formulated the *Law of Dependent Origination*: by this law, each condition that we find ourselves in arises out of another, which in turn depends on the conditions which come before; in a methodical chain.

Suffering

Buddha said that the noble truth of suffering is:

(1) birth
(2) decay
(3) illness
(4) death
(5) the presence of objects we hate
(6) separation from objects we love
(7) not to obtain what we desire.

'Briefly, the fivefold clinging to existence is suffering.'

The fivefold clinging to existence

The five clingings are :

(1) material existence
(2) feeling
(3) perception
(4) mental formation
(5) consciousness.

Everything that we accept as making up solid realities is impermanent, insubstantial and a source of sorrow. These are the three characteristics of human life.

The cause of suffering

Buddha defines this as the 'thirst that leads to rebirth, accompanied by pleasure and lust, finding its delight here and there.' Thirst has three aspects:

(1) thirst for pleasure
(2) thirst for existence
(3) thirst for prosperity.

Desire (Tanha)

• The cause of suffering is desire.
• It is caused by selfishness and attachment to this life and everything associated with it.
• There is nothing permanent in this existence, and our desires change continually.

- Everything is subject to natural law or, to put it another way, the only certainty in this life is that none of us will get out of it alive. We came into this world with nothing and just as surely as we will go out with nothing.

The ending of suffering

Buddha said that this comes about with the complete ending of 'thirst', which consists of:

(1) the absence of every passion
(2) abandoning this thirst
(3) doing away with it
(4) deliverance from it
(5) the destruction of desire (*tanha*).

Extremes to avoid

The Buddha warned that there are two extremes to be avoided:

(1) *Passions and luxury* – which is low, unworthy, vulgar and useless; and
(2) *self-mortification* – which is painful, unworthy and useless.

The 'Lotus of the True Law'

This is Buddha's prescription; a middle way between the extremes of selfish desire and self denial. This is the way to personal enlightenment and *Nibbana*. It leads to wisdom and knowledge giving true insight and inward calm.

28.4 The Eightfold Path which ends suffering

(1) Right understanding

- This requires an understanding of the meaning of the Four Noble Truths, and the true nature of the self.
- This means seeing the world the way it really is, and looking at life from the right viewpoint.

(2) Right intention

This means to follow the middle way and for the right reasons.

(3) Right speech

- This means not to lie, slander or boast.
- Base and disgusting speech should be avoided.

(4) Right conduct or behaviour

- This comes from right thoughts.
- It involves acting morally, and being kind and considerate to all people and creatures.
- No stealing and wrong doing amid the senses.
- Buddha said 'let a man overcome evil by good'.

(5)   Right occupation or living

- Do not choose a livelihood that will cause bloodshed.
- Do not sell alcohol.
- There must be no trafficking of slaves or women.
- People should work to the best of their ability in a useful occupation.

(6)   Right endeavour or effort

- Know yourself and pursue the noble eightfold path at your own pace.
- Seek the truth and reject lies.
- Seek the good and avoid evil.
- Pursue that which gives merit, such as concentrating on good things, love, and tranquility.

(7)   Right contemplation or mindfulness

- Work for freedom from unnecessary wants.
- Avoid extremes of self denial or self indulgence.
- There are *five hindrances* to get rid of:

  (1)   sense-desires or covetousness
  (2)   malevolence
  (3)   sloth and torpor
  (4)   restlessness and worry
  (5)   doubts and questionings.

(8)   Right concentration or contemplation

- Concentrate the mind completely on the achievement of *Nibbana*.
- There are *seven limbs of awakening*:

  (1)   mindfulness, investigation of *dhamma*, or of things
  (2)   mental states
  (3)   energy
  (4)   rapture of mind
  (5)   impassibility of body
  (6)   concentration and
  (7)   even-mindedness.

28.5   The self

There are five points to remember:

- Buddha said that there is no eternal or permanent self.
- The self (**atta**) changes continually; our thoughts, feelings and ideas continuously change.
- He taught the concept of **anatta** or 'no self'.
- This is because the five elements (**skandhas**) of the self change constantly and can dissolve at any time, so they create only illusion. The five elements are :

  (1)   the physical body (**rupa**)
  (2)   feelings (**vedana**)

(3)   sight or perception (**samina**)
(4)   consciousness (**samskara**)
(5)   thought (**vijnana**).

- So, any individual is only a collection of these illusory elements, and therefore there can be no permanent self.

Rebirth

When a person dies these five elements, the self, are reborn in another body. This is a state of 'impermanence' (**anicca**). As long as a person is bound by desire, the cycle of rebirth will continue by the Law of **karma** (or **kamma**). It is cause and effect. To escape, end desire and follow the middle way.

28.6   Karma

Karma and salvation

There are three points to note.

(1)   No state of being is final, because all things age, die and suffer rebirth. This is an endless process because all existence has consequences. Some are experienced in the life in which they come into existence, others in the very next life; some in more remote future lives.

This 'wheel' of rebirths is set to turn endlessly. What Buddha offered was a method to enable people to break the circle and stop this process for themselves.

(2)   No death is final. Sooner or later every living creature is born again, and, sooner or later, will die yet again.

(3)   Any being may not necessarily be reborn as the same life form. For example, a demon could become human; or a man could become a **deva** or an animal.

Karma and the mechanism of destiny

Whether a human being is reborn in a higher or lower form is determined by merits or demerits collected during the particular incarnation just ended.

Each action has consequences carrying a future of happiness or unhappiness. The wise man Nagasena explained this to King Milinda, who asked him the meaning of transmigration or rebirth.

The sage told him that a being that is born here, dies here, springs up elsewhere and repeats the process endlessly. When the king asked the reason for human inequalities such as wealth, power, health and intelligence, the sage explained by asking the king why some vegetables are salty, some bitter, some sweet and so on. The king realised that it was because they came from different kinds of seed. Nagasena explained that the differences in men could be explained the same way.

In other words, we all have our own *karma*, which we have inherited from previous lives; that is, the seed we sowed then has grown and borne fruit in this life, and the seed we sow now will do the same in a future life.

The nature of humankind

Human beings have two parts.

A three-dimensional physical body

- This has six senses: the five normally accepted, and a sixth sense called **manas**, which groups the other five to give a complete picture of anything that is being perceived.
- In Buddhism the body, especially sexual activity, is seen as a danger that drags people down to the material sphere.
- This body has no real substance, as can be seen by how quickly it decomposes after death.

A mental component

- In this is found all activities not limited to the senses; for example, intellectual faculties. Buddhism puts them into groups of main activities.
- In the west we would assume that because there are mental activities, there must be a mind, an 'I', as a permanent reality. Buddhism believes this to be an illusion, a group of accidental, disconnected acts.
- Humans are dominated by illusions, infatuation and stupidity. They think that things are real and belong to them.
- People believe that they are a permanent and substantial reality, but they are really an accidental assembly of elements. When people realise this, they will lose their desire for possessions – including personal experience, their own body or spiritual elements.

28.7 General behaviour

The cornerstones of Buddhist conduct are right thinking, effort and action. Buddhists must not harm other people or living creatures. They must avoid jobs involving danger or harm to others, such as alcohol, drugs, tobacco and weapons. They must be considerate and help those in need. Injustices such as stealing, fighting, wars and telling lies are forbidden.

Employers and employees

Workers have to be respected and not exploited, being paid a fair wage. The worker must be honest, respectful and work willingly.

29 The three jewels or refuges

Every meeting of Buddhists opens with the recitation of the Three Refuges, which are:

(1) I go to the Buddha for my refuge
(2) I go to the teaching as my refuge
(3) I go to the order for my refuge.

29.1 The first refuge: the Buddha

Buddha's authority

There are six points to note.

- Buddhism developed from the experience of Buddha's life journey.
- He was given the status of an infallible and authoritative master.
- He earned this status through the confidence he inspired in his disciples.
- His teachings are preserved in texts universally accepted as authentic.
- They appear in several languages, especially in Pali Canon of the monks of Sri Lanka and southern Buddhism generally.
- The literal interpretation of the canon (sacred books) rests on the acceptance of Buddha as infallible.

29.2 The second refuge: the teaching, life's quest and personal achievement

Buddha said that the seeker of enlightenment should verify the teaching through personal experience. The approach should be to respect the findings of one who 'having succeeded thus' (**Tathagata**) speaks of his experiences so decisively, but not with unquestioning faith.

The seeker should accept:

(1) the basic principles set out in the Benares Sermon and the first three Noble Truths; and
(2) the practical Path with its eight parts; and the practical precepts ordered by Buddha which are binding for monks.

The message is proven if it leads the seeker to what was promised, that is the ending of desire and the attainment of *Nibbana*. The seeker must be the one who makes the effort; no one can do it for him or her. He did not want others to submit unconditionally to his teaching.

29.3 Discipleship

This is vital in the pursuit of enlightenment. The person who wishes to be a Buddhist states that (s)he is committing him/herself to Buddhism, the Buddha, the *dhamma* and the *sangha*. It is essential that (s)he commit him/herself to the exercises which lead to *Nibbana*.

These fall into two groups:

(1)   abandon all passions and
(2)   strive for final concentration.

29.4   The third refuge: the order (sangha)

This was the assembly of five monks (**bhikkus**) who were Buddha's first disciples and who formed a community or order. Buddhists say that they go to the order for refuge, because for anyone in a position to devote their life to the search for enlightenment, it offers ideal conditions. Discipleship could take several forms.

Not everyone could, or would want to, abandon the life of the world completely, so they would become lay disciples obeying the five moral precepts:

(1)   No violence or taking life
(2)   No stealing
(3)   No sexual activity outside marriage
(4)   No lying
(5)   No alcohol.

They make offerings of food, clothes and other basic needs to the monks, so that desire and worry would not distract them from the pursuit of spiritual liberation. There are devotional activities such as meditating in the temples, listening to monks read scripture, and veneration of the Buddha's relics.

Becoming a monk

The outward symbol is a yellow robe, which stands for wisdom, knowledge, concentration and morality. It shows that the wearer has recognised the way to escape desire and pursue *Nibbana*.

Monks in the *sangha* have no property, they renounce worldly goods. They are celibate and even give up their own individuality in order to end desire. A strict self-discipline is adopted, helped by meditation.

The alms bowl and the shaven head are other outward signs of the monastic life (Figure 29.1). Apart from the five precepts already mentioned, there are five more which bind monks and which can be followed by lay people. The last two only apply to monks.

• Not eating at forbidden times – they should take only a very light breakfast and the main meal before noon.
• No dancing, singing or watching shows.

Figure 29.1 The London Peace Pagoda, Battersea, London
(Carlos Reyes-Manzo Andes Press Agency)

- Abstaining from garlands, scents, and ornaments.
- No high or broad beds.
- No acceptance of gold or silver (money)

Such a retreat from the world could start as early as the age of eight. Full acceptance into the *sangha* could not occur until the age of 20.

Monastic life can be temporary. Many still seek a spiritual period to help them to reach enlightenment or to make spiritual progress. Monasteries are centres of organised study as well. A person might spend weeks, months or even years in a monastery to receive education, plus other refinements and merit for himself and his family. Those making a permanent commitment face a long hard road. The quest for liberation may take several lifetimes. It is only in another life that present disciplined effort can be rewarded by escape from the endless wheel of rebirth.

The procedure

- *The applicant (known as a* naag) *joins for a trial period* before what is called the 'period of study'. This is before the rainy season, when the monks do not travel outside their monastery. At the end of this time he can leave if he wants to. Should he wish to continue, then he will prepare for ordination.
- All debts must be cleared and he must show that he can live in poverty. He visits his family and the friends who will support him when he has become a monk, and they gain merit by supporting him.
- *On the eve of ordination*, the *naag* and his friends process through the streets, and a bell is rung to show that he is about to become a monk. He wears a white robe which symbolises purity, and the music played creates a joyous atmosphere. Family and friends will give him gifts.
- *On the day of the ceremony*, his head and beard are shaved, and he sets out for the monastery dressed in expensive clothes because Gautama was dressed this way when he set off from home to pursue enlightenment.
- *On the way to the monastery*, the *naag* carries a wax candle, a joss stick and a flower. He removes his fine clothes at the monastery door and enters in poverty.
- Then his father presents him to the seated elders and monks. Holding a yellow robe, he sits and asks for ordination.
- *When approval is given*, he goes out, puts on his monk's garb and then returns to request instruction in the ways of the monastery. If he answers the monks' questions satisfactorily, then he is admitted to the *sangha*.
- *Then his training begins* under a tutor whose quarters he shares. He also becomes the pupil of a spiritual master (*acarya*).
- He is now a novice (*shramanera*) and spends his time in the study of religion, some secular studies, and instruction for life in the sangha.

Questions asked of applicants to join the sangha

The Buddha had simply said '*Ehi*' (Come!) in the early days, but as numbers and diversity of applicants increased, so it came about that a selection process had to be established. A group of five to ten monks ask the following questions:

- 'Are you afflicted with the following diseases: leprosy, boils, dry leprosy, consumption, fits?'
- 'Are you a human being?' (There were stories of non-human beings which had taken human form to be admitted, trained and liberated.)

- 'Are you a man?' (Buddha agreed to the foundation of a monastic set up for women, but insisted on complete separation between monks and nuns.)
- 'Are you a free man?' (A slave needed his master's permission.)
- 'Have you debts?' (A person could not enter the sangha to escape debt or other financial obligations.)
- 'Are you in the royal service?' (If too many people left military or civil service it would disrupt the running and safety of the kingdom.)
- 'Have your parents given consent?' (Parental authority, even over adult sons was great.)
- 'Are you 20 years old?' (This was the minimum age, not to enter, but to take vows. Even so, Buddha himself had taken younger candidates from time to time.)
- 'Are your alms bowl and robes in due state?' (They had to be offered by the candidate, or by his parents or other proposer.)
- 'What is your name?'
- 'What is your *upajjhaya*'s name?' (The name of this teacher and spiritual instructor was a guarantee of the right preparation of the candidate.)

Then the chief monk asks the examining monks three times if they think that the candidate should be accepted. If they agree they remain silent. Once accepted, the candidate can don his monastic robes again. The time and the day are recorded, because this will dictate his position in the order of precedence in the *sangha*.

The monk's life

The *bhikkhu* is a mendicant monk. This means that he lives solely on alms, the gifts of others. He is allowed three articles of clothing: an inner and outer garment and a cloak. He has a bowl for collecting food, a water filter, a fan, a stick, a tooth pick, a needle and a razor. These are returned to his *sangha* if he leaves or if he dies. His food, mostly balls of rice, is sought as alms every morning and has to be eaten by noon. Butter, *ghi* (melted butter), oil, sugar and honey are only given to the sick as a curative treatment. Meat and fish are rarely eaten and only if it is certain that the animal or fish was not killed specially to provide food for the monk. (This would be against the first precept.)

The monastery

In the early days, shelter was improvised and temporary. Monks lived in caves, leaf shelters, or just sheltered under the branches of a tree.

Then, permanent structures of wood stone and brick were erected. These eventually became large complexes.

Whether to stay in one place or to become an itinerant or wanderer was originally down to personal preference and the practical consideration of climate. Travel is easy in the dry months, but during the monsoon it is quite impossible.

Routine

As the number of monks and monasteries grew, there developed the need for a proper structure to regulate communal life. A set order to the day was organised. A typical day is as follows.

(1) Rise early and wash before meditation.
(2) Dress before going out to seek food each morning from lay people.
(3) Return to the monastery to wash before eating.
(4) Masters give spiritual instruction.

(5) Spiritual and physical rest in the hot part of the day which lasts till about 4pm.
(6) Those monks qualified for the task now go out and take part in discussions and confer with the laity.
(7) Return to the monastery at nightfall and bathe.
(8) Final discussion of the day between masters and disciples.

The ceremony of Uposatha

All monks in an area met every two weeks; at every full moon and every new moon. At these times they confessed to each other privately any failure to obey the code of behaviour. This is now neglected but lay people use these days for stricter religious observance. To a lesser extent the same applies to the other two quarter days of the month (the days halfway through the lunar fortnight). The full moon day is the most important day of them all. *Uposatha* days are similar to the Christian Sunday or the Jewish Sabbath.

Authority, discipline and harmony

The monastery is a community of 'solitary monks who live together'. Discipline is voluntary and based on long tradition. Authority is applied by a Superior who is helped by a Council. The entire community will be consulted if necessary.

30 Worship, pilgrimage and festivals

30.1 Pagodas and stupas

These are called *Cho-ten* in Tibet. They are mounds of stone built over relics of Buddha taken from India to countries where his teaching spread. A collar bone was taken to Sri Lanka, for example. If no relic was available, then a sacred text was buried under the *stupa*.

Some of the most superb examples are in Burma. The Shwe Dagon in Rangoon has a circular central mass of masonry covered in pure gold leaf. It has four shrines, each with a golden image of Buddha. It is about the same height as the dome of St Paul's Cathedral in London. This is turn is surrounded by a circular open marble pavement, and beyond this are monastic buildings and shrines. People visit from all over South East Asia. Two other famous pagodas are in Mandalay and Moulmein.

30.2 Worship at home

There is a shrine room with a Buddha statuette, incense burner, candles and trays of food offerings. In Japan, ancestral tablets, in which the spirits of ancestors are believed to live, are found on the family *butsudan* shrine or altar with copies of the sutras. This practice dates back to the thirteenth century. Homage is paid to Buddha; the Three Refuges and Five Precepts are intoned. A rosary or *seikbadi* may be used.

In Japan, there are great similarities with Shinto. Offerings may be made for easy pregnancy. A ladle can be offered in prayer for a child, but if the bottom is knocked out, then an abortion is wanted. A model breast is offered in prayer to ensure that a mother has enough milk for her baby.

30.3 Temples

- Their structure symbolises the five elements: fire, air, earth, water and wisdom. There is a square base to symbolise the earth, and the structure has a pinnacle to represent wisdom.
- The image of Buddha resides in the main part, which is a shrine to him. The faithful sit barefoot facing it, while chanting a vow of loyalty to Buddha, *dharma* and *sangha*.

- Offerings are left and they raise their hands to their foreheads and then upward, before bowing three times in homage. They listen to monks chanting sacred texts and then take tea and socialise.
- Drums, bells and incense are used while *sutras* and prayers are offered.
- In Japan the temple is always built inside an enclosure, which may contain a number of temples.
- The entrance has fierce-looking statues to ward off evil. They are normally covered with paper because the faithful write petitions on scraps of paper, chew them and throw them at the figures. If they stick, the prayer will be answered.
- The temple will have a pagoda, three to five stories high, with intricate ornamentation.
- The main sanctuary has an altar with boxes of *sutras*, lighted candles and images of *buddhas*, *bodhisattvas* and *devas*.

30.4 Pilgrimage

There are four places which the devoted person should visit. They are:

(1) Where Buddha was born, at Kapilavastu, where Ashoka erected a pillar
(2) Where he achieved enlightenment, at Bodh Gaya
(3) Where the Wheel of the Dharma was set in motion by Buddha when he preached his first sermon under the Bodi tree
(4) His place of death, Kusinara, where the Nirvana Temple marks the place.

To visit them brings merit, blessings, helps towards a good rebirth, and deepens spiritual power. Gifts are offered and meditation takes place. There is a bodhi tree under which Gotama sat as he achieved enlightenment. The Mahabodhi temple is nearby. Also there is a statue of Buddha preaching the Benares sermon. Other sacred places are those where relics of the Buddha are buried:

(1) the Temple of the Sacred Tooth at Kandy in Sri Lanka
(2) the Shwe Dagon or Golden Pagoda on the northern outskirts of Rangoon, which has a hair relic
(3) the branch of the bodhi tree planted at Boroburdur in Java

There are souvenirs with the names of those who have given money to the temple. These are placed on the shrine (*butsudan*) at home.

30.5 Festivals

These tend to be associated with events in the life of the Buddha. Buddhist calendars tend to combine lunar and solar elements and naturally chronology varies from country to country according to tradition. Theravada and Mahayana have their own distinct festivals.

Asala Puja or 'Day of Proclamation'

This is held at full moon in July to celebrate Buddha's first sermon. This is a national festival in Sri Lanka and in Kandy, the relic of the Buddha's tooth is carried through the streets.

Hana Matsuri: 'The Festival of Flowers'

This is a Japanese Mahayana festival celebrating Buddha's birth. His statue is washed with sweet tea and hydrangea leaves in memory of the time when as a child he was bathed in a sweet scented lake in the Park of Lumbini. His image is garlanded with flowers and paraded through the streets, and its path is strewn with paper lotus flowers.

Higan

This is held every Spring and Autumn in Japan to remember the dead. Prayers and gifts are offered. People go to the temples to hear sermons and give thanks for the dead.

Hungry ghosts

This is held in China and is also known as 'All Souls' Day', though it lasts for seven days. It ends on the fifteenth day of the seventh month.

Mu-lien, one of Buddha's chief disciples, visited his mother in the lowest hell and saved her by giving all buddhas and monks a feast.

On the full moon day, monks performed the 'release of the burning mouths'. This tantric ritual lasts five hours and takes place in the evening when it is easier for hungry ghosts to move about.

In the first half of the ceremony the monks invoke the help of the Three Jewels to break through the gates of hell to open the throats of the sufferers and feed them holy water in the second half. Sins are purged, and the Three Refuges administered. They take the *bodhisattva* resolve. Finally the *dharma* is preached to them, and the ghosts can be reborn immediately as humans or in the Western Paradise.

New Year

This is in April. The various Buddhist countries have their own traditions: for example, the Thais buy birds and fish to set free as a mark of compassion to all living things. In Sri Lanka there is a water festival on the first two days, when people sprinkle each other with water as a symbol of purification. In the next three days they visit monasteries and give gifts to the monks. There are processions in the streets and in temples, statues of Buddha are bathed, and the dead receive prayers and offerings. In Tibet there is a spectacular display of sculpted scenes from the Buddha's life, all made out of butter, coloured with various dyes. Some scenes are enacted in puppet shows.

Obon

This is on 13–15 July. During this time the Japanese light lanterns to guide their ancestors' spirits back home. Small fires may be lit for the same purpose, and freshly gathered herbs and flowers are placed before the family altar. The spirits go away again on the third day. In Hiroshima, the small fires take the form of small lights in tiny receptacles which are floated down the river. Dancers form a circle and priests go round to recite a short scriptural passage before the family altar.

Magha Puja

This Thai festival is at the time of full moon in February. It is also known as All Saints' Day or Dharma Day. It commemorates the time when, three months before his death,

Buddha received 1250 of his enlightened disciples who turned up spontaneously. This is when he gave them the code of discipline which, ever since, monks have recited every two weeks. In big temples, 1250 lights are lit to represent each of the disciples.

Parinibbana or 'The Great Death'

This is a *Mahayana* festival to celebrate Buddha's achievement of *Nibbana*. As he approached death, Ananda, his favourite disciple, asked for final instructions. He replied that they had all their instructions in the rules he had already given, and if followed, this would lead to enlightenment.

Poson

This celebrates the arrival of Emperor Ashoka's son Mahinda as a missionary to Sri Lanka. He first visited Mihintale, and it is that town that is the centre for the festivities. Some temples organise religious processions called *perahara*. Holy objects are paraded through the streets, accompanied by as much noise as possible. A cardboard image of Mahinda is carted through the streets while children let off firecrackers.

Wesak

Wesak is the Sinhalese name derived from the Indian name Vaishaka, and is the most important religious festival, because it commemorates Buddha's birth, enlightenment and death all of which occurred on the same day of the year.

Lights and decorations are put up in homes and temples and offerings are made. Wesak lanterns are made of thin paper stuck on to a light wooden frame. People send Wesak cards to their friends. People abstain from farming and any other occupation that could harm living creatures. They also visit the temple, feed the monks and listen to sermons (on radio and television as well these days). Some people will observe the eight precepts.

Rites of passage and the family

31.1 Birth

- Parents name their child at the local temple.
- A monk sprinkles it with water while blessing it for a happy life.
- A pure wax candle is lit and the molten wax allowed to fall into a bowl of water to symbolise the union of the four elements. This symbolises the harmony the child will aim for during this life.

31.2 Marriage

Arranged marriages were once the rule, but this is not so much the case now.

In the ceremony in *Theravada* lands, a cotton thread is placed round the buddha-rupa and then links everyone together. Monks read out the scriptures and bless the marriage couple. Then two pieces of cotton thread are cut. The leading monk ties one thread round the bridegroom's wrist, and the groom ties the other thread round his bride's wrist. They wear these threads until they fall off.

In Thailand, the ceremony takes place in the home, where monks sprinkle holy water as a sign of purity. Scriptures are read and the monks are given food. This ensures a happy future for the newly-weds. They pay homage before Buddha's image, candles are lit and incense burnt. Then they bow to receive the gift of a coral crown and salutations from the groom's friend.

As he does this, he makes a sign with his thumb on their foreheads. Any married people at the ceremony must then place a drop of water on the couple's heads as a blessing. The bride's friend gives everyone a flower before they sign a book to express their good wishes. Everyone then feasts and dances.

31.3 Death

A true Buddhist refers to death as 'blissful rest'. There is no hard and fast rule regarding the body. Tibetans cremate the Dalai Lama's body, but others are left in remote places for birds and animals to eat.

In Sri Lanka burial is normal, but cremation is common, and a monk's ashes are deposited in a *stupa* or mound. As death approaches, care is taken to prepare the mind which must be tranquil and filled with pure thoughts.

Scriptures are read; in China and Tibet this will normally be the Book of The Dead. It is believed that consciousness continues for three days after the physical body dies, so sacred texts are read during this time too. The Chinese and Japanese believe that the *bodhisattva* prepares the way to the Pure Land or that Amida comes to meet the dying person.

Theravadin monks recite sacred texts for 12 days after a death.

At the burial, those present pour water into bowls placed one inside the other to symbolise their desire to transfer their merit to the dead person, to improve the quality of their rebirth.

Monks do not conduct burials or funerals. This is because Buddha was not cremated by his disciples but by the Mallas in Kusinara. Monks are present, though, and will remind people about impermanence and the ever changing nature of existence.

31.4 Family

Husbands must look after wives, be kind, faithful and affectionate. Wives must love their husbands and be good at running the home. There are five basic rules for bringing up a son.

(1) Protect him.
(2) Give him instruction.
(3) Guide him in the right way.
(4) See that he gets a good wife.
(5) Give him his inheritance.

He is expected to support his parents because they have supported him. He must uphold the family's good name, look after the family inheritance, and be respectful to dead relatives.

Questions

1. 'I take refuge in the *Dharma* (*Dhamma*).'

   (a) Outline the contents of the *Tripitaka* and state why it is called the three baskets *(8 marks)*

   (b) Explain the effect on a Buddhist's daily life of taking refuge in the *Dhamma*. *(7 marks)*

   (c) Which of the Three Refuges do you think is the most important for upholding Buddhist attitudes to life? Give reasons in support of your choice. *(5 marks)*

   (Total 20 marks)

   (SEG SYL A Paper 2167/2 June 1995)

2. Questions (a)–(d) can be answered in a single word, phrase or sentence. Question (e) requires a longer answer.

   (a) What does the title *Buddha* mean? *(1 mark)*

   (b) What is *Anicca*? *(1 mark)*

   (c) Which section of the *Tripitaka* gives rules for monks? *(1 mark)*

   (d) List two of the Three Jewels in which a Buddhist promises to take refuge. *(2 marks)*

   (e) Explain the main features of **one** method of meditation. *(5 marks)*

   (Total 10 marks)

   (SEG Paper 1480/1, Section A, 1998 Short Course Specimen Questions)

3. (a) How would you recognise a Buddhist monk? *(2 marks)*

   (b) Choose **one** of the five precepts.

   How do Buddhists try to put this precept into practice? *(6 marks)*

   (c) Explain why special rules are observed by monks and nuns. *(8 marks)*

   (d) 'Everyone needs rules to live by.'

   Do you agree? Give reasons for your answer, showing you have considered another point of view. *(4 marks)*

   (Total 20 marks)

   (London (1479) Specimen Papers for May/June 1999)

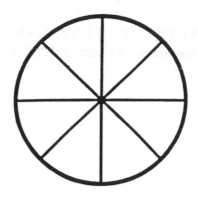

4. (a) What does this symbol represent? [2]

   (b) How did the life of Siddharta Gautama (the Buddha) reflect his teachings. [6]

   (c) Explain the importance of the Three Universal Truths in the life of a Buddhist. [7]

   (d) 'Buddhism is a more a way of life than a religion.'

   Do you agree? Give reasons to support your answer and show that you have thought about different points of view. [5]

   (*MEG Sample paper, Summer 1998*)

5. (a) Explain the meaning of **two** of the following parts of the eightfold path:

   (i) Right Livelihood,
   (ii) Right Mindfulness,
   (iii) Right Intention. [4]

   (b) What is the purpose of meditation within the eightfold path? [6]

   (c) 'The practice of meditation is essential in following the Buddhist path.' [10]

   Do you agree? Give reasons for your answer, showing that you have thought about more than one point of view.

   (*NEAB SYL A Short Course Paper 1, 21 May 1997*)

Buddhism: a glossary

Abhidhamma (Abhidharma)
'Further or Higher Teaching'; the philosophy and psychology of Buddhism in the abstract
Abhidhamma Pitaka (Abhidharma Pitaka)
The third section of the Canon of scripture of the *Theravada* Buddhists, it is abstract and imper-
sonal, concerned with analysis of psychical and mental phenomena. It is a systematic philosophical
and psychological treatment of the teachings of the first two sections, the *Sutta* and *Vinaya Pitakas*
Acanja
Spiritual master in monastic life
Agama
In *Mahayama* Buddhism, a collection of scripture regarded as authoritative, originally written in
Sanskrit. Also Chinese translations of the *Sutras* or Sermons as collected by the *Sarvastavadin*
school of *Hinayana* Buddhism
Ahara
In a material sense it is nourishment; in a logical sense it is the condition for an object's existence
Ahimsa
The doctrine of non-violence, harmlessness, respect for life; part of the *Eightfold Path* that forbids
the taking of life, including the killing of animals for food
Akusala
Pali: 'unwholesome', evil, brings about bad *karma*, and bad reincarnation; the urge towards
greed, hate or delusion
Amida
The Buddha of immeasurable light (see Amitabha)
Amitabha/Amitayus
In *Mahayana* Buddhism, the transcendent Buddha of Infinite Light (*Amida* in Japanese)
Anusmrti (Anapanasati)
Mindfulness of the breath, associated with the development of concentration and calm, and in
the training of insight
Anatta (Anatman)
'No self' or 'no soul'; denial of permanent personal self
Anguttara nikaya
Expositions classified by a numerical system (in the Sutta Pitaka)
Annica (Anitya)
The doctrine of the impermanence of all things
Arhat (Arahat, Arahant, Arhant)
'Enlightened disciple': the fourth and highest stage of realisation in *Theravada* tradition, when the
mind is free of hate, greed and delusions
Ariyatthangikamagga
The Noble *Eightfold Path*
Arupa-dhatu
The world of formless, superhuman activity, the highest meditative world

Ashoka (Asoka)
Emperor of India (273–232 BCE); disliked war, became a Buddhist and called a council to regulate monastic order and lay piety
Atta (Atman)
Self, soul, the illusory ego
Avalokitesvara
One of the greatest *boddhisattvas*, he is 'the Lord who is seen', or 'the Lord who lowers his gaze towards humanity in compassion and the wish to help'; worshipped as the feminine kwan Yin in China, or K(w) annon in Japan
Bhikkhu (Bhikshu)
Buddhist monk of the *Theravada* school (from a word meaning 'beggar', emphasizing the poverty of *sangha* members)
Bhikshuni (Bhikkhuni)
Buddhist nun
Bo
The tree under which the Buddha was meditating when he found Enlightenment
Bodhi
Enlightenment; the spiritual condition of a *buddha*, *bodhisattva* or an *arhat*
Bodhidharma
The 28th Patriarch in line from the Buddha, he took Zen from India to China around 520 CE; he was the first Patriarch of Zen in China
Bodhisattva (Bodhisatta)
In *Mahayana* Buddhism, one who has attained Enlightenment, but renounces entry into full *Nibbana* to help others; also, a 'Buddha to be' or one on the way to Enlightenment
Bompu Zen
'Ordinary' *Zen*, the first of the five types of Zen
Brahmacariya
Lit: 'holy living' term for chastity, sexual abstinence, a life of discipline
Brahma Viharas
The four spiritual abodes, states of mind or sublime states: love or loving kindness (*metta*), compassion (*karuna*), sympathetic joy (*mudita*), serenity or evenness of mind (*upeksa*) Brahmim – highest or religious/priestly caste
Buddha
'Enlightened One' or 'Awakened One'; *Mahayana* Buddhism recognizes more than one Buddha
Butsudan
Japanese altar to the Buddha which is set up in the family home. Ancestral memorial tables are kept there and it is the focus of prayers and offerings
Ch'an
See *Zen*
Cittamatra
The aspect of *Nibbana* as Nothing but Thought
Dai jo Zen
The fourth of the five types of *Zen*; *Mahayana Zen*
Dalai Lama
'Great Ocean'; the head of Tibetan Buddhism, leader of the Yellow Hat monks, he is seen as the reincarnation of the *bodhisattva* Chenresi
Dana
'Generosity', 'giving'
Deva
The shining ones, superhuman, spiritual beings
Dhammakaya
One of the 3 different aspects of Buddha's nature in Mahayana doctrine 'eternal teaching or essence'
Dharma (Dhamma, Dharam)
'Path', 'Truth', 'Right'; teachings of the Buddha
Dhammapada
A scripture of the Pali Canon with 423 verses in 26 chapters

Dharana
The beginning of meditation, fixing thought on a single object
Dharma-cakra
Wheel of the law
Dharmavinaya
The Doctrine or Discipline which was the basis for community religious life in early Buddhism
Dhyana (Jhana)
More advanced meditation; intense or ecstatic concentration
Digha nikaya
Long commentaries in the Sutta Pitaka
Duhkha (Dukkha)
The first of the Four Noble truths; suffering
Gatha
Hymn or set of verses composed by Buddhist monks who are in a state of spiritual insight
Gautama (Gotama)
Family name of the Buddha
Gedo Zen
The second of the five types of Zen (Lit: 'the outside way')
Gompa
Monastery, place of meditation
Hinayana
'Lesser Vehicle' or 'Small Vehicle': in *Mahayana* Buddhism this is the doctrine of the Elders or *Theravada* Buddhists of Sri Lanka and South East Asia; The conservative interpretation of Buddhism
Jataka
'Birth story': accounts of the previous lives of Buddha
Jhana
Buddha's trance
Jiriki
Lit: 'self' or 'own power': how the Pure Land sects describe *Zen*; the way of salvation by self effort
Kama
Pleasure or desire, the chief obstacle to spiritual progress
Kama-dhatu
The plain of material desire or passion
Kapilavastu
The birthplace of Buddha
Karma (Kamma)
'Action': actions that affect circumstances in this and future lives; Buddha said that the effect depends on deliberate intention in actions
Karuna
Compassion: one of the two pillars of *Mahayana* Buddhism (the other is Wisdom [*Prajna*]; the second of the *Brahma Viharas*.
Kashaya (Kesa)
The robe of a monk, nun, or priest
Kattandiya
Leaders of Buddhist ritual in Sri Lankan villages
Kaya
The material body; it can also mean the 'body of the Law'
Khandha
See Skandha
Khuddaka nikaya
Minor expositions in the Sutta Pitaka
Klesa (Kilesa)
Emotional defilement or 'fire': greed, hatred and delusion
Koan
Lit: 'a problem' or 'a riddle': in Zen it is a riddle or paradoxical question which cannot be solved by the intellect, and which is used to develop intuition

Kshanti
Patience, forebearance
Kshatriya
Second or warrior class
Kusala
Personal liberation
Kwan Yin (Kwannon)
The name of the Mahayana Bodhisattva of great mercy, represented by a woman with a child; The protector of women and children
Lama
Tibetan Buddhist priest; teacher or one who is revered
Lotus sutra
Chief scripture of the T'ien T'ai sect
Madhyamika
School of philosophy founded by Nagarjuna in 2nd century BCE, it holds a middle position between realism and idealism
Magadhi
The language of the community into which the Buddha was born
Mahapara-nibbanasutra
Lit: 'the sutra of the great final appearance', an account of the passing of the Buddha
Mahasanghika
The followers of the Great Sangha party of Buddhism; these accepted the findings of the Second Council
Mahayana
The Great Vehicle, or major part of Buddhism, its main features are the *Bodhisattva* Ideal, the 'wisdom' of the *Theravada* school, and compassion; it is universalist in appeal
Maitreya
The Buddha who is to come; the friendly, benevolent one
Mala
String of 108 beads (Japanese: *Juzu*)
Manas
A sixth sense which co-ordinates the perceptions of the other five senses
Mantra
A sacred formula or chant
Marga (Magga)
'Path' leading to the end of suffering; fourth Noble Truth
Mara
The Evil one who tried to tempt Buddha away from Enlightenment
Metempsychosis
Lit: 'the transfer of the soul from one body to another'; the doctrine of the cycle of rebirth
Metta (Maitri)
The subject of the *Metta Sutta*: the doctrine of good will towards all; also 'loving kindness', a pure love in which there is neither grasping nor attachment
Metteya
A future Buddha
Miccha
That which is false
Middle Way
Buddha's recommended path between extreme materialism, and sensual indulgence on the one hand, and severe asceticism on the other
Mudita
The third of the *Brahma Viharas*: 'sympathetic joy', delighting in the good fortune of others
Mudra
Ritual gesture, as with the hands of Buddha images
Naag
An applicant to become a monk

Nagarjuna
The founder of the *Madhyamika* school of philosophy
Naga
Serpents which can change themselves into men, and protect Buddhas and Buddhists
Nama
Lit: 'name', it is used for Spirit, a collective term four four of the five *Khandas*, excluding *rupa* (the first)
Nikaya
Collections of teachings
Nibbana (Nirvana)
'Blowing out', the extinction of the self, the goal of Enlightenment and religious life
Nirmanakaya
One of the 3 different aspects of the Buddha nature in Mahayana doctrine – the historical Buddha
Nirodha
'Cessation' of suffering and desire, the third Noble Truth
Om Mani Padme Hum
A *mantra* meaning 'Hail to the Jewel in the Lotus'
Padmasana
The Lotus or basic position in meditation
Pali
The language of the *Theravada* scriptures
Pancasila
The five rules for all Buddhists: no killing, theft, luxury, lies and alcohol
Panchen Lama
The Lama who ranks second to the *Dalai Lama*
Paramita (Parami)
'Perfection, cultivated on the path
Parinnirvana (Parinibbana)
Final and complete *Nibbana* at the passing away of a Buddha
Parisad
The four categories of Buddhists: monks, nuns, laymen, laywomen
Patimokkha
The 227 rules followed by a Bhikkhu, and recited in confession
Pirit
Charm, or ceremony of protection from evil in Sri Lanka
Pitaka
'Basket' (collection) of scriptures
Posan
Festival commemorating the introduction of Buddhism into Sri Lanka
Prajna (Panna)
Insight, wisdom
Pratimoksha (Patimokkha)
The training rules for monks and nuns
Pravrajaya (Pabbajja)
The renunciation of the world before training to be a monk
Prayer beads
Buddhists use 108 in two parts, each representing the 54 stages of becoming a *Bodhisattva*
Preta
The shades of the dead, the 'hungry ghosts'
Puja
A gesture of worship or reverence paid to gods, normally the raising of the hands, palms together; includes general worship too
Punya
A meritorious act which brings reward in this life or the next
Pure Land
4th century CE school of Buddhism

Rajas
One of the three fires, *dosa* and *moha* are the others
Rinzai
One of the larger sects of *Zen*
Rupa
Bodily form; one of the five elements which make up the nature of dwellers on the lowest plane
Rupa-dhatu
The plane of forms
Saddha
Confidence or faith
Saddharmapundarika Sutra
The Lotus of the Good Law Sutra in *Mahayana* Buddhism, which believes it to be the teaching of the transcendent Buddha
Saijojo zen
The fifth and highest type of *Zen*
Samadhi
Intense concentration in meditation, the last stage in the Eightfold Path
Samatha
'Calm abiding' meditation
Sambhogakaya
In Mahayana doctrine one of the 3 different aspects of the Buddha nature: the transcendental Buddha
Samjna (Sanna)
Perception, third of the five *skandhas*
Samma
That which is true, just or exact: this applied to the Buddha, the Eightfold Path and Enlightenment
Samsara
Transmigration, the continual round of birth, death and rebirth
Samskara (Sankhara)
Fourth of the five *skandhas*, mental/karmic formation
Samudaya
The second Noble truth: the origin of suffering
Samyutta nikaya
Joined together expositions in the Sutta Pika
Sangha
'Assembly', monastic life founded by the Buddha. In *Theravadin* countries it is used for the order of *bhikkhus*; in *Mahayana* countries there are lay people as well; in Japan, it includes priests
Sankhara
Intellectural faculties, one of the five elements which are part of the nature of dwellers on the lowest plane
Sarana
Refuge or entry into the *Sangha*
Sarvastivadins
Early Buddhist school which split from the *Hinayana* school
Satori
'Awakening', Enlightenment in *Zen*
Sattva
'Being', living beings who live at various levels of this world, and in underworld and heavenly regions
Satya (Sacca)
Truth
Seikbadi
A rosany
Sesshin
An intensive period of *Zen* practice in a monastery or temple

Shakyamuni
Buddha's historical title: 'Sage of the Shakyas' (his tribe)
Shikan taza
'only sitting', pure concentration of thought in *Zen*
Shojo Zen
Third of the five types of Zen; small vehicle, *Hinayana Zen*
Shramanera
Novice monk
Siddhartha (Sidhatta) (Siddattha)
'Wish-fulfilled', Buddha's personal name
Sila
'Discipline', 'Morality'
Sramanera
A novice in a monastery
Sunya (Sunna)
The emptiness of the Absolute; the denial of all conceptual constructions in relation to ultimate reality
Stupa (Thupa/Cetiya)
Mound containing relics
Sutra (Sutta)
Text, the word of the Buddha
Sutta Pitaka
The second of the three collections, mainly of teachings that make up the canon of basic scripture; dialogues of the Buddha
Tanha (Trsna)
Desire or thirst, the cause of suffering (second Noble Truth)
Tantra
Texts revealed by the Buddha: magic spells, descriptions of divinities and instructions for worship
Tariki
In Pure Land Buddhism this means reliance on powers outside oneself, salvation by outside powers
Tatha
'Suchness': the Ultimate and Unconditioned nature of all things
Tathagata
Lit: 'He who has arrived at Enlightenment', a title of the Buddha
Theravada (Sthaviravada)
'Way (or doctrine) of the Elders', the southern school of Buddhism, found in South East Asia; Sometimes called *Hinayana*
Three Bodies
The *Mahayana* Buddhist doctrine of three different aspects of the Buddha nature: *dhammakaya* or the eternal teaching or essence; *nirmanakaya* or the historical Buddha; *sambhogakaya* or the transcendental Buddha
Three Jewels
Buddha, the Dhamma and the Sangha
Trikaya
See 'Three Bodies'
Tripitaka (Tipitaka)
'Three Baskets': the Pali canon of scriptures acknowledged by *Theravadins*
Triratna (Trisharana)
The Three Jewels (see above)
Trishna (Tanha)
The cause of suffering (thirst, craving, attachment, desire)
Tulku
Reincarnated Lama
Upasaka (male)/Upasika (female)
Buddhist disciples who practice their religion in the world without retiring to a monastery or convent

Upaya
'Skilful means': different ways the Buddha uses to teach
Upeksa (Uppekha)
The fourth of the *Brahma Viharas*, the ability to overcome feelings of pleasure or pain; 'Evenness of mind'
Uposatha
Fasting, or it can be public confession, undertaken twice a month by monks
Uppajjhaya
Teacher and spiritual instructor
Vaisakha (Vesakha, Wesak, Vesak)
Buddha Day: the name of a festival and a month
Vajrayana
'Thunderbolt' or 'Diamond Way': teachings that came later, mainly in India and Tibet
Vedana
The second of the five *skandhas* or elements that make up the nature of dwellers on the lowest plane; it is feeling
Vihara
A dwelling place, monastery, also a stage in spiritual life
Vijnana (Vinnana)
The fifth of the five *skandhas* or elements of the nature of dwellers on the lower plane: consciousness
Vinaya
Monastic disciplinary rules
Vinaya Pitaka
The first of the *Three Baskets* of scripture containing the *Vinaya*
Vipashayana (Vipassana)
'Insight', meditation
Viraya
'Energy', 'Exertion'
Yogacara
A school of philosophy
Zazan
Sitting meditation in *Zen*
Zen (Ch'an, dhyana)
A school of *Mahayana* Buddhism which developed in China and Japan

PART VI

Sikhism

32 Origins: the Khalsa

32.1 Introduction

- The word 'Sikh' is a Hindi word deriving from Sanskrit and means 'disciple'.
- Sikhism was founded in the Punjab region of India in the late fifteenth and early sixteenth centuries CE by Nanak.
- Nanak was born in a Kshatriya (warrior class) family.
- He was brought up as an orthodox Hindu in the village of Talwandi where he was born.
- From an early age, he was interested in religion and devoted himself to the service of God.
- As a young man, he became a spiritual teacher or guru.
- He bathed in the river before dawn and then meditated. Then he and his followers would sing hymns before returning for breakfast and the day's work.
- One day he went to bathe but fell into a trance, remaining in the water for three days.
- He did not speak for a day, and then said: 'there is no Hindu nor Muslim'.
- He felt that both religions contained some of the truth about God, but that their rituals were clouding the truth that they were both trying to teach.
- Nanak believed that the only way to find God was to look into one's heart and meditate.
- He went on a number of journeys, his followers being made up of both Hindus and Muslims, visiting the main religious centres of India, Sri Lanka and Tibet, and later visiting Makkah.
- Before he died he appointed one of his followers to become guru of the Sikh community. This was Bhai Lehna whom he renamed Angad which comes from ang, meaning 'limb'. It was a pun meaning 'part of me'.
- This is important because each succession was a continuation of the Guru Nanak; the succession was spiritual not physical. That was why he did not name one of his sons as his successor, but the person most suited.

32.2 The Khalsa

For a century some **Sikhs** had fought for independence against the Mughal Emperors, and the **Guru** now decided to unite the effort. So it was that Guru Gobind Singh (see section 33.4) called the Sikhs to meet him at Anandpur on Baisakhi day, 1699 CE. He stood in front of his tent with a sword in his hand and asked if any of them would lay down their life for their guru. A man stepped forward and was taken into the tent from which the Guru returned alone, his sword covered in blood. This happened five times until the Guru came out of the tent with all of them unharmed; the blood was that of a goat.

This episode was to show the Sikhs that they must be loyal and willing to die for the faith. Those that had stepped forward had proved themselves and were told to cry: 'To God be the victory'. The Guru now made a mixture of sugar crystals and water and sprinkled it on them, gave them some of it to drink, and got them to do the same for him. That day, most people present had been initiated like this. (Some refused because there were men and women of inferior castes present and/or they disapproved of the use of force.) The initiates were called the **Khalsa** (the pure or dedicated). The men were given the common name **Singh** (lion) and women were called **Kaur** (princess). The men were to have a common uniform based on five elements known as the five 'Ks'.

32.3 The five Ks

- These get their name from the first letter of the Punjabi words for them.
- They are a symbol of unity, loyalty, devotion, purity and enthusiasm for God and the Sikh community.
- Members have to be self-disciplined and uphold the glory of the Khalsa.
- The strict code of conduct bans the eating of meat from animals killed in a Muslim ritual, having sex with Muslim women, and smoking.
- The Five Ks are as follows:

    (1) **Kara**: the steel bracelet, worn on the right wrists, which shows bondage to God and the Khalsa
    (2) **Kirpan**: the small sword, which symbolises the courage to defend the faith and the poor
    (3) **Kesh**: the long hair, which is the symbol of strength, virility and saintliness
    (4) **Kangha**: a comb, which symbolises cleanliness and inner purity
    (5) **Kach**: trousers, which represent alertness, agility and chastity.

Some important points

- The turban was added to the above and is the most important distinguishing feature of a Sikh (Figure 32.1).
- Women adopted the five Ks as well.
- All decisions are made in the presence of the **Adi Granth** (see section 35.2).
- Within months, 80 000 had been initiated.
- The Khalsa is the focus of unity in Sikhism.
- Guru Gobind Singh said 'Where there are five there am I, when the five meet they are the holiest of the holy'.

32.4 Community and brotherhood

Every Sikh must give service to, and be loyal to, the community and its beliefs.

Figure 32.1 A Sikh member of Khalsa, wearing some of the 5Ks, London (Carlos Reyes-Manzo Andes Press Agency)

Its main features

(1) Guru Nanak's teaching as a guide

These ideas can be found in the Guru Granth Sahib (see section 35.2). They are the Word of God spoken through Guru Nanak (see section 33.3).

(2) Unity

If decisions are going to affect the community, then they must be made by the whole community. When the decision is made then everyone obeys. Most decisions are made by the community of the local **gurdwara** (see section 36.1).

(3) Equality

Status is man-made and not decreed by God, so there is no caste system in Sikhism. Everyone is born equal in the sight of God and so has a right to be free.

(4) High morality

This means to be truthful, tolerant, humble and fair. Everyone must work for and maintain the good of the community. Adultery, stealing, gambling and other forms of immorality are banned. Everyone should behave honourably towards others.

(5) Good works

God expects this and it brings the community closer to Him. Good works are the natural expression of sincere religious belief. They bring justice and moral order. Sikhs must be hospitable. The langar or communal kitchen is open to all.

(6) Work

Service is the key word; self-interest, idleness and immoral livelihoods are wrong. Work is for the benefit of others and is righteous in the eyes of God, whose name is repeated while Sikhs work.

- All Sikhs must earn an honest living.
- All work is a vocation no matter what it is.
- Prayers are said after work.
- A tenth of earnings is donated to support the community.

33 Sikh gurus

33.1 Introduction

The Gurus were the men who revealed the Sikh faith. They lived in northern India between 1469 and 1708 CE. They came from the *kshatriya* or warrior caste of Hinduism, and they said that their revelation came straight from God. This gave them the authority to preach it, even though their caste could study the *Vedas* but not teach them.

The basis of their teaching

(1) There is only one God.
(2) He has created and sustains all life.
(3) *All* people, no matter what their caste or class, are cared for equally by God.
(4) Anyone can receive enlightenment and spiritual liberation in this life.
(5) It is God who takes the initiative in bringing a person to spiritual liberation.
(6) All that person has to do is respond with faithful obedience.
(7) The person concerned must:

- serve God through worship
- live a useful existence as a householder
- be honest and hardworking
- be generous to the poor and needy.

33.2 The ten gurus

(1) Guru Nanak (1469–1539)
(2) Guru Angad (1539–52)
(3) Guru Amar Das (1552–74)
(4) Guru Ram Das (1574–81)
(5) Guru Arjan (1581–1606)
(6) Guru Har Gobind (1606–44)
(7) Guru Har Rai (1644–61)
(8) Guru Har Krishan (1661–4)
(9) Guru Tegh Bahadur (1664–75)
(10) Guru Gobind Singh (1675–1708)

See Figure 33.1.

Figure 33.1 The ten Gurus: *D* daughter; *S* son
(Source: K. Singh, *The Sikhs* (London: Allen & Unwin, 1953). Reproduced by permission of the publishers.

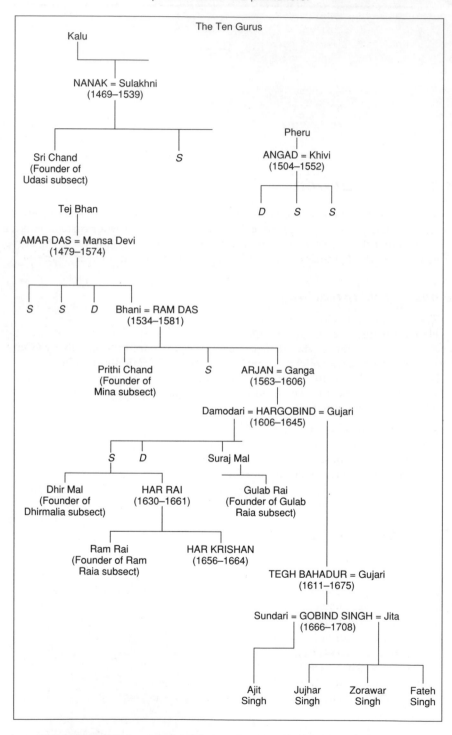

33.3 Guru Nanak (1469–1539)

Nanak was the first Guru. He was born in Talwandi (now part of Pakistan), and was brought up as a Hindu and learned Sanskrit. He was living in an area ruled by Muslims and learned about Islam while working as a local government official, but he was unable to find spiritual peace, and at the age of thirty faced the crisis that was to make him a Guru, a spiritual guide to others.

Nanak's religious calling

Nanak disappeared while bathing, as usual, one morning. He reappeared three days later, stating that he had been taken to God's court and had been given nectar to drink. While there he was told to rejoice in God's name and teach others to do the same. He now became a full-time preacher, helping others to learn to know God.

Nanak's missionary journeys

These occupied the next twenty years (until 1521). Then he established the first Sikh community in the village of Kartarpur. His disciples were called Sikhs, getting their name from the Punjabi verb *sikhna*, 'to learn'.

The choosing of the second guru

There was a need for someone to take over the leadership when Nanak died, so he chose Lehna to succeed him. Nanak changed Lehna's name to Angad, meaning 'my limb'. This signified that the new Guru was an extension of himself.

33.4 The other nine gurus

Guru Angad

- He collected the hymns of Guru Nanak.
- He consolidated the Sikh community.
- He had the faith taught to children.

Guru Amar Das

- He assembled the Sikhs at Goindwal three times a year when Hindu festivals were on. This forced the Sikhs to choose between their Sikh guru or Hinduism.
- He opposed all divisions based on caste.
- He disliked the custom of *purdah* (keeping women apart).

Guru Ram Das

- He started to build Amritsar, the future centre of Sikhism.
- He broke the remaining links with Hinduism and Islam to secure the independence of the Sikh religion.

Guru Arjan

- He is revered as the first Guru martyr of the Sikhs, having died in captivity after his arrest by the Mughal Emperor Jehangir.
- He produced the first version of the Sikh scriptures which became known as the Adi Granth.
- He completed Amritsar and built other towns.
- He built the Harimandir (House of the Lord) in Amritsar.

Guru Har Gobind

- Under his leadership, the Sikhs armed themselves to rebel against Mughal rule.
- He carried two swords; one the symbol of battle, the other of the spirit.

Guru Har Rai

- His 17 year rule was largely uneventful.
- He is remembered for being a man of peace and for being kind and generous.

Guru Har Krishan

- Most of his reign was spent under house arrest where he died of smallpox.
- Before his death, he announced that his successor would come from the village of Baba Bakala.
- His wisdom, for one who was very young, was astounding.

Guru Tegh Bahadur

- He was the youngest son of Guru Hargobind.
- He was a pious soldier who fought against Mughal rule.

Guru Gobind Singh

- He brought the line of gurus to an end.
- He founded the Khalsa.
- He introduced the rite of initiation and gave men the surname *Singh* (lion), and women the surname *Kaur* (princess). They also adopted a uniform, part of which is the turban.
- He installed the scripture which Guru Arjan had put together and which he had revised.
- He enthroned the Adi Granth as the sole Guru.

33.5   The importance of the gurus to Sikhism

They were the messengers through whom God revealed himself. They belong to a special group of men and women whose birth is regarded as non-Karmic. They were perfect men who did not have to be reborn under the law of *karma* but came back because God wanted them as his messengers.

For this reason Gurus had nothing to learn when they were born, which is why they are described as being able to speak at birth and were cleverer than the priests assigned to educate them.

Gurus are revered but not worshipped: only God is worshipped. Sikhs recognise that Christ, Buddha, Muhammad, Moses and Gandhi are similar men, sent into the world to reveal the message of God. They do not accept that God can be born, which is what Christians and Hindus believe.

34 Life and the path to God: Sikh beliefs

34.1 Introduction

- God created all life.
- Everyone is born equal, and everyone has a spark of God in them.
- Every living thing is subject to reincarnation or rebirth after death, in what is called transmigration. The main aim of humanity is to escape from this. This is impossible without the help of God.
- Every human being has a body, mind and soul which have unity. All three must be developed in harmony. This is achieved by finding harmony with God.
- The consequences of actions in this world follow us into the next. All actions are important.
- God gave humankind free will to choose his course. He also gave people the power of reason and the ability to know right from wrong. He had endowed humanity with the wisdom to make the right decisions.
- The laws of good health and proper work keep the body healthy.
- True religion affects every aspect of life. It also shows the way for right living.

34.2 God

There are three main aspects of God.

(1) He is One.
(2) He is the Truth.
(3) He is Eternal and Self Existent.

- His symbol is the number one and the letter O.
- He is the **Waheguru** (Lord of Wonder).
- He is the 'True Name' and 'There is no corner without His Name'. The True Name is the **Sat Guru** or the True God, God Himself. **Nam** (Name) is another name for God.
- God is the Creator and is everywhere in all things.
- He reveals Himself to humankind, but He has no incarnations (earthly forms).
- He cannot be described in any way. Even so, He is referred to by Sikhs in personal terms.
- God hates no one.
- He has no fear.

- The **Mool Mantar**, composed by Guru Nanak (see section 33.3), conveys all the basic beliefs about God.
- Sikhism teaches that because there is only one God there cannot be different gods for different religions.

34.3 The three Hs

(1) knowledge of the *Hand* – the dignity of labour
(2) knowledge of the *Head* – the search for truth
(3) knowledge of the *Heart* – the higher self

Guru Nanak set these out so that harmony can be achieved in human life. This leads to perfect freedom.

34.4 The five virtues

They are:

(1) truth
(2) contentment
(3) service
(4) patience and
(5) humility.

To follow these virtues means obeying God's Will and achieving union with Him.

34.5 The five cardinal vices

They are:

(1) lust
(2) anger
(3) greed
(4) worldliness and
(5) pride.

Combined with egoism they exclude God. Vice makes people selfish and deforms their existence. It is a wall or barrier preventing knowledge of God. Egoism (**haumai**) is the fruit of self-love and owes loyalty to no one; personal glory is all that matters. Vice causes self-delusion and exerts an endless pressure on anyone in its grip. Constant spiritual warfare is needed to remain free of it.

34.6 Grace

This is the gracious gift of God. Personal effort cannot achieve it. Grace (**nadar**) allows us to achieve personal inner harmony. With God's grace, salvation can be achieved. There are five stages on the road to union with God.

34.7 The five stages

(1) **Dharam Khand** (religious duty) – living by God's Law and providence, which are the symbols of His grace and mercy

(2) **Saram Khand** (effort) – maintaining a right relationship with God through self-discipline and personal effort; it is vital to respond to the will of God and rely on Him for guidance.

(3) **Karam Khand** (grace) – This is a state of bliss from developing divine virtues and achieving the spiritual graces.

(4) **Gian Khand** (knowledge) – Obedience to God's law leads to the wisdom that reveals knowledge of the world.

(5) **Sach Khand** (truth) – Becoming one with God through knowledge of the truth; it is a state of bliss from being in harmony with God.

35 Sikh scriptures

35.1 Some basic beliefs

- The scriptures are the Word of God (the Guru) (**gurbani**).
- The words of God (the Guru) come to Sikhs through the Guru Granth Sahib.
- These are the scriptures of the Lord God.
- God's Word is enshrined in them but the Guru is the Word.
- God revealed His Word and it will lead to Him.
- The revealed Word leads to the revealer, who is God.
- The Guru **Granth** Sahib inspired by God is the Guru.

There are two books of scriptures:

(1)   the **Adi Granth** (or Guru Granth Sahib)
(2)   the **Dasam Granth**.

35.2 The Adi Granth (or Guru Granth Sahib)

Adi Granth is the earliest title of the first book. It means 'first collection or compilation'.

Guru Gobind Singh gave the scriptures guruship just before he died. It became known as the Guru Granth Sahib.

The Adi Granth originates from the poetic compositions or hymns of Guru Nanak; there are 974. They were put into writing towards the end of his life and shortly after.

These were then added to by his successors and included some by Hindu and Muslim holy men. In 1604 Guru Arjan had an authoritative collection put together and kept in a new building in Amritsar called the Harimandir or 'God's House'.

Development continued in the following years until 1708, when the scripture was declared to be the Guru of the Sikhs. It contained the writings of:

(1)   six Gurus
(2)   twelve non-Sikhs
(3)   several bards from the court of Guru Arjan
(4)   three other Sikhs; Satta, Balwand and Mardana.

Composition

In the Guru Granth Sahib there are 13 divisions made according to musical regulations.

They cover the whole range of human experience. Some can be used for the morning, others for evening. Subjects covered include theology, philosophy, ethics, advice on personal and social matters, and mysticism.

The authority of the Guru Granth Sahib

Its content has been unaltered since 1708. There is a copy in every gurdwara (Figure 35.1). Every copy has the same number of pages – 1430. It is written in **gurmukthi** (or written Punjabi). The hymns are set music which is kept simple because it is only an aid to worship and should not distract from the words. It must be seen by everyone in the gurdwara because it is a visible sign of God's presence. It must be opened every day, and is closed when it is not read. Before it is taken from the dais in the gurdwara a prayer is said; everyone must stand when it is carried.

The book is not worshipped, although the faithful bow before it. Only God can be worshipped and the Word conveys who is God. When it is read, God is present. It is the source of knowledge, truth and wisdom.

It is read at rites of passage such as the naming of a child, initiation, weddings and burials.

All the knowledge and guidance necessary to be a disciple is contained in the Guru Granth Sahib.

35.3   The Dasam Granth

This is the collection of the tenth Guru, Gobind Singh ('das' means ten in Punjabi), who wrote enough poems to fill a 1428-page book. It was put together in 1734 (almost 30 years after his death). Gobind Singh did not allow any of his verses to be included in the Adi Granth.

The script is in gurmukthi or written Punjabi but the language of the poems varies, because he was fluent in Sanskrit, Persian or the kind of Punjabi used by the other Gurus, thus making it difficult to read.

Few Sikhs and not all gurdwaras have a copy. It is never installed in the gurdwara. It is not given the honour and respect accorded to the Adi Granth.

35.4   Mohan Pothi

This is the earliest collection of Sikh writing. It was produced by Guru Amar Das. This was at the time when Sikhism was spreading and guidance and instruction were needed for new members, so it was necessary to pass on the teaching of the first three Gurus. As a new religion, Sikhism had to be protected from attack by those who opposed it. The *Mohan Pothi* was made up of hymns composed by Guru Nanak and his two successors, plus warnings against useless practices and false teaching.

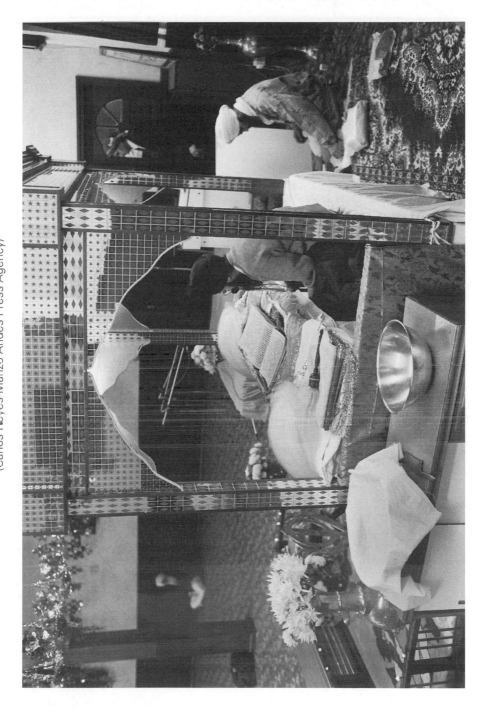

Figure 35.1 Reading Guru Granth Sahib Gurdwara, Shepherd's Bush, London
(Carlos Reyes-Manzo Andes Press Agency)

36 The gurdwara and worship

36.1 The gurdwara

In simplest terms, a gurdwara is any place – a room, a converted house, or a large purpose-built building in which a copy of the Sikh scriptures is installed (Figure 36.1). 'Gurdwara' means 'The Guru's door' or simply 'God's house'. In 1604 Guru Arjan installed a book he had compiled (containing hymns and other compositions) in a specially constructed building in Amritsar, the Harimandir or 'house of God'. Copies of the book were given to Sikh communities for use in their places of worship, and these places came to be known as gurdwaras. The last of the 10 Gurus died in 1708, having installed the book of scriptures as Guru (God is the true Guru and He speaks through the scriptures). The internal details of the gurdwara emphasise this.

36.2 The appearance of the gurdwara

- External appearance are of no importance.
- All gurdwaras have one common feature, the Sikh flag showing the Sikh emblem (Figure 36.2). This contains the following:
  (1) a *khanda* or two-edged sword, which symbolises that Sikhs are prepared to fight for the truth with the spirit as a weapon and if necessary, physical force;
  (2) two *kirpans* or scimitar-like cutting swords to represent the spiritual and earthly powers that the Gurus had;
  (3) a *chakra* or circle to remind that God is one and that Sikhs are inseparably united with Him through the faith.
- Another symbol to be seen outside gurdwaras is formed by two Punjabi letters, **ik onkar** which means that 'God is the one being or eternal reality'.

36.3 Inside the gurdwara

- Here can be found the Guru Granth Sahib under a canopy. Sixteenth and seventeenth-century Gurus sat in a special place to teach, while one of the faithful held a parasol over their head as a mark of respect. Now the scripture itself is a Guru and has the special canopy for the same reason.

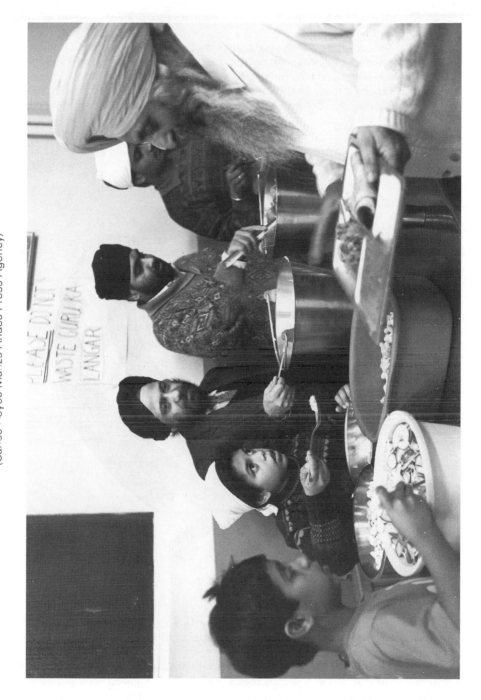

Figure 36.1 Serving Langar food at a Sikh Gurdwara, Shepherd's Bush, London (Carlos Reyes-Manzo Andes Press Agency)

Figure 36.2 The Sikh emblem: the whole emblem is called the Khanda, after the double-edged sword in its centre; it is composed of 3 symbols which represent Sikh beliefs about God:

1 The Khanda – the doubled-edged sword that represents the Supreme Truth who is the One God.
2 The Chakra – the circle which represents the infiniteness of God because both have no beginning and no end; a circle marks the limit within it and this reminds Sikhs that they must live within God's rule.
3 The Kirpans – these two swords symbolise *peeri*, or spiritual power, and *meeri*, or political power; this tells Sikhs that they have to defend the truth.

- The Guru Granth Sahib can occupy any position in the gurdwara but it tends to be opposite the entrance set a little way from the wall so that the reader and marriage parties can walk round the back.
- When the scripture is not in use, it is covered with a silk cloth called a **romalla**.
- The book may be put in a special room at night and replaced on the dais in a special ceremony every morning. In Amritsar the scripture is placed on a palanquin and is carried in procession by its bearers from the Golden Temple to its nightly resting place, it having been read throughout the day.

- The Sikhs have two names for the dais:

  (1) *palki*, meaning palanquin (a covered litter on poles carried by four men).
  (2) *takht*, meaning throne.

- There are no seats and the worshippers sit on the floor. There are two reasons for this:

  (1) the scripture has unique status raised up on its throne
  (2) the worshippers sitting before it are all equal.

36.4 The function of the gurdwara

It is a place where Sikhs gather to praise God and meditate on the words of the Guru Granth. Travellers can get accommodation there. The poor can get a free meal. There can be clinics and dispensaries in its precincts.

The gurdwara in Britain

It is the Sikhs' social centre. Sikh children are sent there to learn Punjabi, receive religious education, and learn how to read the Guru Granth Sahib properly. Weddings are held there, often during Sunday service; this is because of the unpredictable nature of British weather compared with that of the Punjab, where weddings are often held in the open air. Funeral services are held here before going to the crematorium (in the Punjab they are held at the cremation ground the day after the death).

36.5 Sikh worship

In the days of the 10 gurus worship took place in their presence and with them leading. They would teach and hymns composed by them were sung. Today the same principles are followed with hymns, lectures on their meaning and scriptural readings.

36.6 Worship at home

- If a family has a copy of the Guru Granth Sahib, it effectively has a gurdwara in the house, and can therefore offer worship there.
- For morning worship, the Sikh rises early to bathe and then meditate on God.
- Guidance about which hymns to use is taken from the **Rehat Maryada** ('The Sikh Way of Life'):

  (1) **Japji** Sahib (composed by Guru Nanak for personal use) and Ten Swayyas (poems) of Guru Gobind Singh (morning)
  (2) **Sodar Rahiras** (a prayer to focus the mind on the 'holy path') in the evening
  (3) **Sohilla** (a vesper prayer) before sleep.

- Worship can take place at any time, and a family may invite others to join in.

- Services are informal and can last from one to five hours. There is no specified time to begin.
- The hymns of Guru Nanak are sung and there are lectures and sermons to explain them. Prayers are offered at any time of day.
- The Guru Granth Sahib is installed on the **manji** (stool) in the morning and a verse read from it at random.
- Musicians sit near the scripture and sing verses from it. The congregation join in, and someone will explain the significance of the passage (anyone may do this).
- Throughout worship, members of the congregation will continue to enter and leave. Anyone entering must bow and kneel in front of the Guru Granth Sahib until the head touches the floor; they make an offering of money, a *romalla* (square of silk cloth) or food for the gurdwara's kitchen.
- After duly paying respect, the person sits on the floor with the rest of the congregation. Men sit on side, women the other, with a gap between them.
- The head is covered; women wear a muslin scarf and men and boys not wearing a turban tie a handkerchief on their heads. No one wear shoes, because to come into the presence of the Guru Granth Sahib is to come into the presence of God.
- Worship finishes with a set prayer called **Ardas**.

Ardas

The congregation stands and one of them steps forward to address God on their behalf. There are three parts:

(1)   the prayer to remember God and the ten Gurus
(2)   the prayer for faithfulness to the scriptures
(3)   the prayer for the blessing of God on the Sikh community and all humankind.

There are specific prayers after this – for example for the sick, the dead, newly-weds, thanksgiving for success and so on. The scriptures are covered with a silk cloth and removed from the dais. During *Ardas*, one of those present puts the blade of his *kirpan* (sword) into a container containing **karah parshad**, which is made of flour or semolina, water, sugar and butter. The *khara parshad* is given to everyone while notices are read by the secretary. This food is eaten with the right hand and is important because:

(1)   eating together shows that everyone is equal before God
(2)   no one leaves His presence hungry
(3)   it shows that God blesses mankind (sweet food is chosen to emphasise this).

Langar

After worship a full meal is served in the dining room of the gurdwara. This *langar* ('free kitchen') has been an important part of the Sikh way of life since the time of Guru Nanak. Sometimes it spreads to the street outside. It has the same meaning as the sharing of *karah prashad*. Passers-by are invited to join in.

Sikhism teaches that God is present in every human being. Faith and meditation bring the discovery of God within the soul. This is called **Nam simran** (calling God to mind). In simple terms, the more a person thinks about God, the more that person will be filled by His presence. This allows God-centredness to replace self-centredness.

Procedure

- A person should rise before dawn and bathe to symbolise washing the soul in God.
- At sunrise the 38 verses of the *Japji*, composed by Guru Nanak, the Jap (the 10th Guru's hymn) plus some other verses by Guru Gobind Singh, the Swayyas.
- In the evening two other hymns should be meditated on:

  (1) *Rahiras* (the Holy Path) at dusk
  (2) *Sohilla* (the vesper hymn) before bed.

- A *mala* or rosary with 108 knots is used to help meditation.
- The knots are passed through the fingers as the person repeats the word *Waheguru*, which means 'Wonderful Lord'.

36.9 Sikh worship in the UK

The family gets together in the evening to listen to passages of scripture and to pray (morning worship is difficult because of the pressure of work and school). It also serves the purpose of passing on the Sikh way of life to Sikh children born in Britain. Sikhism has no fixed holy day so most Sikhs go to the gurdwara on Sunday which is a public holiday. Gurdwaras train the young to sing the *gurbani* (scripture).

37 Sikh festivals and pilgrimage

37.1 Introduction

The Sikhs share the same calendar as the Hindus, but their religious new year falls on the first day of **Baisakhi**. This is the only fixed festival in Sikhism, and it takes place on 13 April. There was no interest in special holy days until the leadership of Guru Amar Das. He ordered the Sikhs to assemble before him at *Baisakhi* and **Diwali**, which are the two most important festivals in the north Indian Hindu calendar. The consequence was that the Sikhs had to choose where their allegiance lay; with the ways of the village or in the service of the Guru.

Guru Gobind Singh added a third gathering, *Hola Mohalla*, which coincides with the Hindu festival of *Holi*. These three celebrations, known as **melas**, are still observed by the Sikhs.

37.2 Baisakhi mela

Baisakhi marks the Sikh new year and is first in importance of all the *melas*. It is held on the Sunday nearest to the date of the initiation of the first members of the *Khalsa*. At that time, on 30 March 1699 CE, Guru Gobind Singh, the tenth leader, ordered the Sikhs to meet him at Anandpur. It was there that he introduced them to his new concept of loyalty and initiation as seen in the *Khalsa* code. Baisakhi has three aspects.

(1) Baisakhi is a religious occasion

- The day starts with bathing in a river, in the *sarowar* which is a pool found at most *gurdwaras* or temples in India, or by having a shower at home.
- Then there is private meditation, individual or family.
- Sikhs next go to the *gurdwara*, where there is a service and talks about the events in question.
- The cloth around the flag pole and the flag itself (**nishan sahib**) are ceremonially renewed.
- New members of the *Khalsa* are initiated.
- Any newly elected *gurdwara* committees take office.

(2) *Baisakhi is a memorial festival*

- In 1762 CE, after consulting the *Guru Granth Sahib*, the Sikhs responded to the plea of a Hindu *brahmin* whose wife was abducted by Usman Khan, an Afghan. The Sikhs took up arms to help him.
- The Amritsar massacre of Jallianwala Bagh took place in 1919 CE during the *Baisakhi mela*.

So the speeches at *Baisakhi* are not only spiritual in content but political as well.

(3) *Baisakhi has an Animal Fair*

- A large animal fair is held at Amritsar where the main *Baisakhi* festival has been held since the eighteenth century. This has been despite being banned by both Mughal and British rulers.
- Sikhs visit the Golden Temple to enjoy the fair and attend political rallies as well as selling animals.

37.3 Divali

This is held at the end of October and early November to coincide with the new moon. Houses are Autumn cleaned to remove mosquitoes and other insects before moving the beds indoors after the Summer. This is a festival of light so candles and *devas* (lamps) light the *gurdwaras* to signify the coming of light to the natural world and of inner light to direct Sikhs to union with God. Children enjoy sweetmeats and fireworks and are given gifts, and are told stories from Sikh history. Both friends and families exchange gifts as well. Three events in particular are associated with this festival

(1) *The foundation of Amritsar*

In 1577 CE Guru Ram Das laid the foundations of the city of Amritsar. Its Golden Temple is lit up by hundreds of electric lights.

(2) *The release of Guru Har Gobind*

Har Gobind was the sixth guru, and was released from prison on the orders of the Mughal emperor, Jehangir. He had been put there because his father, Guru Arjan, had been fined for rebellion, but the fine remained unpaid. Har Gobind refused freedom unless the 52 Hindu princes, innocent of any crime, and also held in the Gwalior Fort, were released with him. The emperor said that as many prisoners as could hold on to the guru's cloak while passing through the narrow passage on the way out would be allowed to go. This was clearly impossible so the guru sent for a cloak with long tassles for them to hold on to. Thus, they were able to pass to freedom.

(3) *The martyrdom of Bhai Mani Singh*

Bhai Mani Singh, the custodian of the Golden Temple, was martyred at Divalitide in 1738 CE. He had asked permission for Sikhs to celebrate the festival at the temple, but this would only be allowed if a large sum of money was paid to the authorities. It was hoped that the sum could be met from the offerings of pilgrims but they were frightened off by the presence of a Mughal army in the vicinity. Bhai Mani Singh was unable to pay the sum but was offered his life if he became a Muslim. He refused and was tortured and executed as a result.

37.4 Hola Mohalla

This festival is held in February and March.

- It dates from the time of Guru Gobind Singh.
- It was first celebrated in the year after the formation of the Khalsa (1700 CE). In that year the Khalsa assembled at Anandpur, divided into two armies and engaged in mock battles.
- It is thought that the Hindu festival of *Holi* was chosen for the time of the gathering because assembly would be easier in a holiday, and it would keep the Sikhs from joining in a Hindu festival.
- Today Anandpur is still the centre of the main festivities.
- There are wrestling and fencing tournaments, and fairground sideshows.
- An important event is the gathering of the *Nihangs*, the order of Sikhs set up by Guru Gobind Singh and who were the greatest warriors of the Sikh armies in the eighteenth century.
- Not surprisingly, the literal meaning of '*Hola Mohalla*' is 'attack and place of attack'.

37.5 Minor festivals

Sangrand

This is when the Sun leaves one sign of the Zodiac and enters another.

Puranmashi

This is the full moon day which ends every Hindu month, celebrated because Guru Nanak was born on a full moon. There are all-night vigils and hymns are sung.

Lohri

This takes place in January at the time of the sugar cane harvest in northern India. The homes of children born in the last year are visited by friends and neighbours, though there is no religious significance to this festival.

37.6 Gurpurbs

This is the other form of Sikh festival.

- They celebrate the birth or death anniversary of a guru. There can therefore be 20 of them.
- The main feature of a *gurpurb* is the continuous unbroken reading of the Guru Granth Sahib, known as an *akhand path*. A relay of readers begins at page 1 and times the recital to reach page 1430 at the time the festival is to start. This takes about 48 hours.

- Near the end, the *bhog* ceremony takes place, involving reading the Guru Granth Sahib from page 1426 to the end, followed by the first verse of the *Japji*, six verses of the *Anand Sahib*, the saying of the prayer *Ardas*, and the sharing of *karah parshad*.
- A service is held next.
- There is also a meal shared by anyone while the proceedings take place.

37.7 Pilgrimage in Sikhism

Sikhs are sceptical about suggestions that something is gained from visiting a holy place, although they do believe that any journey taken with devotion can become a pilgrimage. The Sikh gurus condemned much of what they saw at Indian places of pilgrimage as mere superstition. They believed that a renewed approach was needed and therefore recommended meditation on the inner presence of God.

In fact, Guru Nanak said that God's name is the real pilgrimage place. He said that it consists of the contemplation of the word of God, and the cultivation of inner knowledge.

Amar Das, the third guru, made his headquarters at Goindwal and ordered his followers to assemble there at three festival times of the Hindu calendar: *Magha*, *Divali* and *Baisakhi*. A pool was made there with 64 steps leading down to the water. Visitors bathed there, but Sikhs say this is for cleanliness, not purification. Even so, it would help any half-hearted Sikh who still had some belief in the value of bathing at holy sites.

Amritsar

This is the centre of the Sikhism and its Golden Temple is visited by the faithful. Some regard it as a pilgrimage and bathe there, and then cross the causeway to the Temple itself. Inside, they file past the Guru Granth Sahib, which is taken early in the morning from the building where it is kept for the night into the Temple, and listen to the readings which continue from before dawn until late at night. Whether or not this is seen as a pilgrimage depends on the individual.

38 Rites of passage

38.1 Introduction

Children's first lessons about Sikhism are taught at home. Guru Nanak and the gurus that followed called upon parents to pass on the beliefs and practices of Sikhism to their children. Guru Gobind Singh said that parents should educate children in the faith and baptise them. This would give society a moral foundation and ennoble people's lives. Education begins by learning the name for God (*Waheguru*) and the first hymn of the *Adi Granth*.

38.2 Birth and naming

- Children are named in the presence of the Adi Granth soon after birth.
- The first letter of the child's name is decided by opening the book and taking the first letter of the first word on the left-hand page.
- Water and sugar (**amrit**) are placed on the child's lips.
- Prayers are offered from the *Japji* and *Ardas* to:

    (1) commit the child to God's Grace
    (2) pray that he/she lives as a true Sikh
    (3) hope that the child will serve other people
    (4) be loyal to the Sikh homeland.

- The sharing of *prashad* signals the end of the ceremony and marks the entry of the child into the the Sikh community.

38.3 Initiation into the Khalsa

This ceremony dates from the time of Guru Gobind Singh. It is simpler today than in times gone by. Some Sikhs would prefer the full ceremony to be revived as a way of keeping the faith alive and ensuring devotion. It takes place in front of five members of the Khalsa.

The main points

- The five assemble before the Adi Granth and explain the faith.
- Then the initiate makes acceptance of the principles set forth.
- One of the five now says a prayer for God's protection.
- Then the five sit round an iron container full of fresh water.
- The initiate is then given five handfuls of holy water (*amrit*), which are placed on the eyes and ears.
- The five members recite the *Mool Mantra* five times.
- This is repeated by the initiate.
- Greeting are given and then the initiate is received as a son/daughter of Guru Gobind Singh.
- They are now called *singh* (lion) or *kaur* (princess).
- Lastly, everyone shares *prashad* from the same container.

38.4 Marriage

Sikh weddings are simple and must be public. They can be held anywhere. There is no formal betrothal. There is no child marriage. Marriage can only take place between members of the community. A Sikh man can have only one wife.

The ceremony

- Friends gather round the Adi Granth and pray.
- Because the marriage is witnessed by a guru it is a sacrament.
- The couple bow to the Adi Granth and then make their vows.
- The person in charge speaks to them separately about the duties of marriage.
- The groom promises to protect his bride; she promises to accept her role.
- The groom's scarf (*palla*) is handed to the bride.
- They hold the scarf and walk clockwise round the Adi Granth four times, pausing while four verses of a hymn are sung to music.
- Everyone is given *prashad* and prayers are said.
- Then there are presents and greetings.

38.5 Death

The soul (*jiva*) leaves the body at death for eternal life. It ends the cycle of rebirth or transmigration. The soul lives for ever as part of God through His grace. It is God's reward for the good deeds which have brought merit in this life.

- The body is washed and dressed in clean clothes before being put in the coffin.
- For members of the Khalsa, the five Ks are left on the body and there are no lamps or candles.
- Hymns are sung as the body goes for cremation.
- A relative lights the funeral pyre.
- Relatives go home and hear readings from the Adi Granth for the next 10 days.
- The period of mourning ends with the reading of the four final passages, after which the Adi Granth is covered with a silk cloth.
- All present then share *prashad*.

Questions

1. (a) Divali is an annual Indian festival.
Explain the event which Sikhs remember on this day. *(8 marks)*

   (b) During Divali, Sikhs are reminded of their responsibility to all people.
Explain Sikh teaching on wealth and poverty. *(4 marks)*

   (c) 'Someday the Sikh goal of a world without poverty will come true.'
Do you agree? Give reasons for your answer, showing that you have
thought about more than one point of view. *(8 marks)*

   (NEAB SYL A Paper 6, 16 June 1997)

2. (a) Name **two** things from Islam which Sikhism rejected. *(2 marks)*

   (b) Describe Sikh beliefs about the nature and attributes of God. *(6 marks)*

   (c) Explain what Sikhs believe about the original destiny of human beings. *(8 marks)*

   (d) 'Men and women are equal in Sikhism.'
Do you agree? Give reasons for your answer showing that you have
considered another point of view. *(4 marks)*

   (Total 20 marks)

   (London (1479) Specimen Paper May/June 1999)

3.

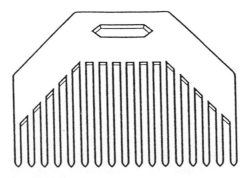

   (a) This picture shows a Kangha (comb). Name another three of the
Five Ks. [3]

   (b) How did the Khalsa come into being? [5]

   (c) Explain why the Five Ks are still important for Sikhs today. [7]

(b) 'Sikhism is a peace-loving religion.'
Do you agree? Give reasons to support your answer and show that you have though about different points of view. [5]

(MEG sample paper for Summer 1998)

4. (a) Describe the Amrit ceremony when Sikhs are initiated into the religion *(7 marks)*

   (b) Explain the extent to which the Sikh marriage ceremony is similar to and different from an ordinary Sikh service of worship. *(8 marks)*

   (c) 'Couples will have a better chance of a happy married life if they come from the same religion.'

   How far do you agree? Give reasons to support your answer *(5 marks)*

   (Total 20 marks)

(SEG SYL A Paper 2 June 1997)

5. Questions (a)–(d) can be answered in a single word, phrase or sentence. Question (e) requires a longer answer.

   (a) Who is the founder of Sikhism? *(1 mark)*

   (b) Which guru set up the Khalsa? *(1 mark)*

   (c) Give **one** belief contained in the Mool Mantar. *(1 mark)*

   (d) Name **one** of the 5 Ks **and** explain its symbolic meaning *(2 marks)*

   (e) Explain how and why the Guru Granth Sahib is given respect during worship. *(5 marks)*

   (Total 10 marks)

(SEG Paper 1480/1, Section A, 1998 Short Course Specimen Questions)

Sikhism: a glossary

Adi Granth
Lit: 'first book', or 'primal collection', or 'primal book', it is the Sikh scripture compiled by Guru Arjan, 1604 CE. It comprises the work of six Gurus and other non-Sikh *bhagats* (also known as the *Guru Granth Sahib*)

Akal Purakh
A name used for God by Guru Nanak, it means 'The Eternal One'

Akal Takht (Akal Takhat)
Throne of the Eternal or 'Throne of the Timeless One', it is a building facing the Golden Temple of Amritsar where the Sikhs have political gatherings

Akhand Path
The continuous reading of the *Adi Granth* holy book from start to finish; it takes 48 hours

Amrit
Sanctified sugared water used in the infant-naming ceremony. Also used at the initiation into the *Khalsa*

Amrit ceremony
This is known by a variety of names: *Amrit sanchar*, *Amrit sanskar*, *Amrit pahul*, *Khande di pahul*. It celebrates the founding of the Khalsa each April

Anand karaj
Anand is the Bliss of Marriage; this is the 'Ceremony of bliss'

Ardas
Formal prayer at a religious service

Baisakhi
See *Vaisakhi*

Bani (Vani)
Speech, hymn, it describes the compositions of the gurus in the *Adi Granth*

Bhagat
Used by Sikhs and Hindus for a devotee, a person who practices *Bhakti*

Bhog
Ceremony involving reading from scriptures and sharing the karah parshad, held near end of a gurpurb

Chakra
Circle to signify that God is one

Chanani (Chandni)
The canopy over the scriptures used as a mark of respect

Chauri (Chaur, Chowri)
The symbol of the authority of the *Adi Granth*, it is a fan waved over the scriptures, and is made of yak hairs or nylon

Darbar Sahib
The Golden Temple of Amritsar, the chief centre of Sikh pilgrimage

Dasam Granth
Lit: 'book of the Tenth'; the collected hymns of Guru Gobind Singh, the tenth guru **Devas** lamps
Dharam Khand
Guru Nanak taught that this is the first of five stages towards human liberation, being the stage of religious duty, the acknowledgement of God's law and providence
Divali
Hindu festival important to Sikhs because it was when the sixth Guru, Hargobind, was released from Gwalior Fort
Diwan
Lit: 'a royal court', Sikhs use this term for an act of public worship
Gian Khand
Guru Nanak taught that this is the second of five stages towards liberation. It is the attainment of knowledge, the understanding of the hidden qualities of Creation
Granth
The accepted scriptures, especially the *Adi Granth* or *Guru Granth Sahib*
Granthi
This is the 'reader of the *Adi Granth*' who officiates at ceremonies
Grihastha
For Hindus, the second of the four stages of life (being a householder, and having a family), Sikhs use it because they believe that salvation can be achieved within the context of everyday life
Gun
An attribute or virtue; it is a gift from God which people do not possess in themselves
Gurbani
The total expression of the word of God revealed by the *gurus*, and to be found in the *Adi Granth*
Gurdwara
Lit: 'the doorway to the Guru', it is the Guru's or God's house. It is a place of worship, a temple
Gurmat
Living according to the will of God as revealed through the *gurus*
Gurmukh
A person who has heard the word of the Guru (God) and obeys
Gurmukhi
The name given to the script in which the scriptures and the Punjabi language are written (Lit: 'from the Guru's mouth')
Gurpurb
The anniversary of a *guru*'s birth or death, can be used for other anniversaries
Guru
A holy man, a spiritual instructor; sikhs also use it as another name for God (Lit: 'the venerable one')
Gyani
A religious teacher attached to a Sikh *gurdwara*
Haumai
Egoism or self-centredness, the cause of doubt, violence and sorrow: it is the major spiritual defect and must be defeated for there to be hope of salvation
Hola Mohalla
A gathering that coincides with the Hindu festival of Holi
Hukam
God's will, the cause of the creation of the world
Hukam (Vak)
A random reading from the *Adi Granth*, taken for guidance
Ikonkar
'God is One', this is the affirmation with which the *Adi Granth* opens
Jamadut
The angels of death
Jamapuri
The 'city of the dead'
Janam Sakhi
Lit: 'birth evidences' these are the life stories of the *gurus*

Japji
The long hymn with which the *Adi Granth* begins
Jiania
The soul (from Punjabi) *Jiva* – human soul
Jivan Mukt
A spiritually enlightened person who has achieved this state while in this life
Kabir
One of the leading exponents of *bhakti*; some of his hymns are in the *Adi Granth*. It is possible that he influenced Guru Nanak
Kach (Kaccha, Kachhahira, Kachh, Kachera)
Undergarments or breeches which are one of the five Ks
Kakkar (Kakka)
See *panj kakkar*
Kam
Lust, one of the five weaknesses that attack the human soul
Kangha
Symbolic wooden comb worn in the hair; one of the five Ks
Kara
Steel bangle worn on the right wrist; one of the five Ks
Karam Khand
This is the stage of grace, the fourth of the five stages towards liberation in Guru Nanak's teaching
Kaur
The name given to all Sikh women and girls, it means 'princess'
Kesdharis
Lit: 'those who keep their hair uncut', referring to members of the Sikh community, one of the five Ks
Kesh (Kes)
The uncut hair, one of the five Ks; it is tied in a special knot
Khalsa
Lit: 'the community of the pure', it is the Sikh brotherhood, founded by Guru Gobind Singh in 1699
Khanda
Two-edged sword representing power and divinity, it is used in the *amrit* initiation ceremony and is on the Sikh flag
Khara parshad (Karah prasad)
Sanctified food distributed at Sikh ceremonies
Kirpan
A sword, one of the five Ks, it is a symbol of the active resistance to evil
Kirtan
Devotional singing of the hymns found in the *Adi Granth*
Krodh
Wrath, one of the five weaknesses that attack the human soul
Langar
The gurdwara dining hall and the food served there. (also *Guru ka langar*: 'the Guru's kitchen')
Lobha
Avarice, one of the five weaknesses that attack the human soul
Manji
The small platform on which the scripture is placed
Manmukh
A person who has failed to see the nature of the divine order, and who listens to his or her own wayward impulses instead of the Guru
Mela
A fair; this is used of Sikh festivals which are not *gurpurbs*
Moha
Worldly love, one of the five weaknesses that attack the human soul

Mul Mantar (Mool mantar)
Lit: 'Basic teaching' or 'essential teaching', it is the statement of belief found at the beginning of the *Adi Granth*
Nadar
Lit: 'The favoured glance or look', hence 'God's gracious glance' or 'grace'
Nam
For Sanskrit, it means 'name': Sikhism uses it as another name for God
Nam japan
A term meaning meditating on the Name, repeating the Name, as a way of achieving knowledge of God
Nam simran (Nam simaran)
To meditate on the name of God using passages of scripture
Nihangs
Order of warrior Sikhs set up by Guru Gobind Singh
Nishan sahib
The Sikh flag flown at *gurdwaras*
Nit nem
Reciting specified daily prayers
Pac Khanda
The five stages leading to spiritual liberation
Pagri (Padri)
Sikh headdress
Palki
A palanquin or covered litter on poles carried by 4 men
Palla
A scarf given during the wedding ceremony as an essential element in the ritual
Panj kakkar
The five Ks, the symbolic marks of an initiated Sikh
Panj piare
Lit: 'the five beloved ones', they were the five companions of Guru Gobind Singh, who with him founded the *Khalsa*. They are symbolically represented at every *amrit* ceremony
Panth
The Sikh community
Parmesha
A title of God as the Supreme Being
Patashas
Sugar bubbles or crystals used to prepare *amrit*
Pattit
Lit: 'fallen ones or apostates'. These are Sikhs who have abandoned the Sikh way of life
Prasad
The holy food distributed at the end of a *diwan*, it is made of equal amounts of ground wheat, sugar and *ghi* (clarified butter)
Punjab (Panjab)
'Land of five rivers': this is the area of India where Sikhism originated
Rehat Maryada (Rahit Maryada)
A source of instruction in ethics and religious practice, it contains the *Khalsa* disciplinary code
Romalla
A silk cloth used to cover the scripture when not in use
Sac
Truth: one of the six concepts for the divine Self-Expression
Sach Khand
The last of the five stages towards liberation, this is when a person achieves Truth, when he/she sees what God sees and can enjoy the whole of Creation
Sadhsangat(Sangat)
Congregation or assembly of Sikhs
Sarowar
A bathing pool at the gurdwara

Sahaj

A state of oneness with God *Sangat* – a congregation of Sikhs espec. when gathered for public worship

Sahajdharis

Members of the Sikh community who have not been initiated

Saram Khand

The third of the five stages towards liberation, it is the stage of spiritual endeavour

SatGuru

A synonym for God

Sangrand

A minor festival held when the Sun moves from one zodiac sign for another

Sewa

Service directed to the *sangat* and *gurdwara*; also to humanity in general

Shabad (Sabad, shabd)

'Word'; a hymn from the Adi Granth; the divine word

Siddha

84 Legendary figures who achieved bliss through the practice of yoga, and who live in the wilderness of the Himalayas

Sikh

Punjabi word for 'disciple', a follower of Guru Nanak

Singh

Sanskrit word for 'lion'; name given to all male initiates of the *Khalsa*

Sodar

An evening prayer

Sohila (Sohilla)

A bedtime prayer

Takht

Throne

Tankhah

Reinstatement into the *Khalsa* of someone who has broken his vows or the rules

Vaisakhi (Baisakhi)

The name of a month, and a festival that celebrates the formation of the *Khalsa* in 1699 CE

Vak

A random reading taken for guidance from the *Adi Granth*

Waheguru

'Wonderful Lord'; a name for God

General questions

1. (a) Draw the symbol for **each** of the **two** religions you have studied   *(2 marks)*

   (b) In which country or region did **each** of these **two** religions begin?   *(2 marks)*

   (c) When did **each** of these **two** religions begin?   *(2 marks)*

   (d) What name is given to a religious leader, teacher or holy person in **each** of these **two** religions?   *(2 marks)*

   (e) (i)   Name **one** festival or fast from **each** of these **two** religions.   *(2 marks)*
      (ii) What does **each** celebrate or commemorate?   *(2 marks)*

   (f) (i)   Name **one** sacred writing from **each** of these **two** religions.   *(2 marks)*
      (ii) In which language was **each** of these originally written?   *(2 marks)*

   (g) Briefly describe the main beliefs about life after death in **each** of these **two** religions   *(4 marks)*

(Total 20 marks)

2. **Pilgrimage**

Buddhism	Kandy
Christianity	Lourdes
Hinduism	Varanasi (Banares)
Islam	Makkah (Mecca)
Judaism	Jerusalem
Sikhism	Amritsar

   (a) Choose the **two** places, from those listed above, which you have studied and explain why they are centres of pilgrimage.   *(10 marks)*

   (b) What religious activities are people likely to take part in whilst on pilgrimage to these places?   *(10 marks)*

   (c) Read what the people in the illustration below have to say about pilgrimage.

      Do you agree with them? Give reasons for your opinions.   *(10 marks)*

Pilgrimage is essential.

Pilgrimage changed my life.

A holiday would do people more good.

Why don't they stay at home and do something useful with their time?

(Total 30 marks)

3. Principal beliefs and teachings

Buddhism	*Anicca* (impermanence); *Anatta* (no self); *Dukkha* (suffering).
Christianity	Beliefs about Jesus in the Apostles' Creed.
Hinduism	*Brahman* (the supreme being); *Avatars* (gods in human or animal form).
Islam	*Tawhid* (the oneness of God); *Shahadah* (declaration of faith).
Judaism	The *Shema*; the Covenant.
Sikhism	The nature of God and the *Mool Mantar*.

(a) Explain the beliefs and teachings, from those listed above, of the **two** religions you have studied. *(10 marks)*

(b) How are these beliefs and teachings reflected in **either** worship (meditation) **or** festivals in these **two** religions? *(10 marks)*

(c) 'People who have a religious faith lead better lives than people who have no faith, because they see life differently.'

How far do you think this is true? Give examples and reasons for your opinions *(10 marks)*

(Total 30 marks)

General glossary

Agnosticism
Genuine doubt, open-mindedness about whether God or any supernatural domain really exists

Altar
An elevated surface prepared for the offering of sacrifices to deities; often the slaughtered animals were burned on the altar

Amulet
A protective charm, worn to ward off evil, misfortune, or illness, may be inscribed with magical formulae

Anima
Latin: 'soul': the non-bodily aspect of humans

Animatism
A pre-animistic stage in human development when the world was 'animated' by impersonal forces; there was no clear distinction of spiritual beings, and magic and religion were indistinguishable

Animism
'The deep lying doctrine of Spiritual Beings' (Tylor, 1871). These are thought to live in trees, mountains and other natural objects

Anthropomorphism
From two Greek words meaning 'human' and 'form': the attribution of human form and characteristics to gods

Apotropaic
see *magic*

Archetype
Primordial image or pattern that recurs in literature and dreams, for example, heroic rescue, seasonal decay and rebirth

Asceticism
Ascetic practice and discipline; the belief that the ascetic life releases the soul from bondage to the body and the earthly physical life, to permit union with the divine

Astrology
The calculation of the movement of the heavenly bodies in the belief that their relative positions influence a person's character and destiny

Atheism
The denial of the existence of God

Augury
Divination (foretelling the future) based on the flight and behaviour of birds

BCE
Before the Common/Christian Era

Belief
The acceptance as true/real of what goes beyond intellectual proof

CE
Common Era

Charismatic
A person or object possessing spiritual gifts: religious leaders or those who have received religious insight or inspiration

Cosmology
A comprehensive view of the world that finds structure and order (cosmos) in the universe

Divination
Interpretation of the past or insight into the future; also the discovering of the future by magic or supernatural means

Diviner
A person who attempts to predict or control the future by inspiration, intuition or magic

Dualism
The belief in the existence of two principles, Good and Evil, in the Universe

Eschatology
Beliefs concerned with 'last things', the end and purpose of existence

Ethics
The moral rules and principles that ought to govern human behaviour; these may be laid down by a religion or independently. Also, the study of moral beliefs and practices of different peoples and cultures

Evil
The force or power that gives rise to wickedness, the morally wrong, or wicked

Faith
A basic life stance associated with belief in God, it is the act of trust that holds a person in being, by relationship with God, gods or another person. Also, another word for a religion

Fast
Abstinence from usual activities such as food, drink, sex, work, play and so on; this is often in connection with a particular season or festival

Festival
A special day(s) celebrating some religious event; 'Holidays' were once 'holy days'

Fetishism
The worship of an object because it is believed to have magic powers, or because it is thought to have a spirit in it

Gnosticism
Greek: 'knowledge': systems of belief that impart special knowledge of God, of his relation to the world and humanity, and of redemption, only to those who are initiated in special ceremonies

God
The Supreme Being: most religions have a God or gods who are the source and purpose of the universe, and who are deeper, greater and higher than life itself

Haruspicy
Divination through the observation and interpretation of the entrails of an animal previously sacrificed

Henotheism
Belief in one God considered worthy of worship, while accepting that there may be other gods

Holy
That sense of 'otherness' and overpowering greatness before which humans may find themselves in awe

Humanism
Belief in the ability of human beings to understand, sympathise, be responsible and solve the problems of this world, it rejects the idea of any supernatural Power, Creator or after-life. Religious humanism believes that God uses the value of humanity and human thought, work and life

Ideology
A set of beliefs that provide a rationale for a way of life

Immortality
The doctrine that the soul survives the death of the body, and continues in an afterlife

Initiation
The induction of new members into a religion, community or organization, it also refers to rites of passage

Intercession
Prayer on behalf, of others; also, the use of an intermediary to reach God or gods – this person, living or dead, is seen as influential because of his/her sanctity

Judgement
The time when each person is judged for their thoughts, words and deeds

Laity
The people in a religious tradition, in contrast to its leaders and specialists

Libation
An offering of drink as part of a sacrifice to God

Life stance
The style and beliefs of a person's or community's relationship with that which is most important in their lives, it includes the consequences that come from it

Magic
There are four main headings for this:

(1) **Apotropaic**: The use of occult (hidden) powers to turn away evil, for example knocking on wood

(2) **Black**: The use of occult powers involving the powers of darkness and Satan and so on

(3) **Contagious**: The passing on of occult power through contact, for example rubbing a weapon with a similar weapon that has already killed an enemy

(4) **Sympathetic**: The use of occult powers in one sphere to produce similar results in another, for example acting out the killing of an animal before going out to hunt

Mana
An impersonal power that takes possession of an object which is then revered and worshipped

Mandala
A symbolic diagram surrounded by a circle representing wholeness and perfection: also, it can represent the Cosmos and its inhabitants, superhuman, human and sub-human

Meditation
Deep thinking, often in the light of an ultimate reference point and prayerful reflection, it can also be the concentration of the mind with the exclusion of all thoughts

Monism
Greek. 'One': the belief that only one Being exists; also, that reality consists of one basic substance

Monotheism
Belief in one Divine Being or God; Belief in a Creator God

Mysteries
Forms of religion where doctrines are closed secrets revealed only to the initiated

Mysticism
The attainment through contemplation or self-surrender, of truths inaccessible to understanding; direct intuitive experience of God; sense of unity with the divine or transcendent realm

Myth
A traditional story containing basic insights into life, death and the universe, ancient religious and supernatural ideas; it is not a fictitious story

Necromancy
Predicting the future by communicating with the dead

Numen
Lit: 'nodding': spiritual power that is inherent in a particular object; some of these godlings became gods and godesses, but most were not personified

Numinous
A sense of awe-inspiring mystery: Rudolf Otto introduced the concept in his book, *The Idea of the Holy* to describe human feelings when faced with the Holy or 'the wholly other'

Oracle
A shrine for the consultation of spiritual powers or deities for advice or prophecy; the medium of response or the response given

Panentheism
Greek: 'Everything exists in God': the concept of God being immanent in the Universe, but also transcendent; differs from *pantheism* which holds that everything is divine

Pantheism
The doctrine that God is all and all is God, merging all things in the divine and denying personality to God

Paradise
Iranian: 'Walled garden': the condition beyond death where justice, truth and beauty are given to all

Phenomenology
A method which selects and compares universal or common manifestations of religion, rather than dealing with religious traditions one by one

Pilgrimage
A journey to a sacred site, sometimes to achieve religious merit

Polytheism
Belief in more than one god; also refers to different forms of divine being: supernatural powers, gods and demons who are worshipped or warded off

Religion
Originates from a Latin word meaning scrupulousness or superstitious awe; later came to mean religious scruples or conscientiousness, religious feeling and worship of the gods, leading to the cult of sacred things or persons, and then to a religion

Sacrifice
The offering to God of oneself or of something or someone precious; this is to express thanksgiving, or to seek blessings or favours. It often involves the killing of an animal or person to give back life, represented by blood to the deity. The animal may be totally burned as a total offering; or part may be retained to be eaten, symbolizing a meal shared with God. There may be other gifts of food such as fruit and cereals

Salvation
Saving the soul by deliverance from sin, and, admission to a state of blessedness expressed as heaven, eternal life, paradise and so on

Scripture
Revered texts seen by a religion as the authoritative basis of its faith; they are often attributed as revelations from God to humans

Sect
A group who share particular interests with a strong binding community ethos/belief within a wider religious tradition; they are often sharply divided from general society

Secular
Excluding and rejecting religion; also, to put all religions and alternative life stances on an equal footing

Secularization
The decline in the influence of religion and religious affairs and institutions in human thought and affairs

Soteriology
A branch of theology which deals with human salvation

Soul
The non-material aspect of humans; the Greeks distinguished between the soul and the body. Plato said that a human being is a soul (*psyche*) trapped in a body. Hebrew theology says that the body is vitalized by the soul

Spiritual
What relates specifically to God; the highest expression and activity of the human person

Theism
Belief in God or gods, supported by appeal to rational experience

Theodicy
An account of the Universe and the ordering of it, vindicating the justice of divine government; the search for religious meaning in the face of inequalities and the unending problems of human existence

Theology
The systematic setting out of religious belief, the science of the study of religion or God

Theosophy
Various cults that seek direct knowledge of God by intuition of the divine essence

Totem
A natural object, usually an animal, taken as the symbol of a tribe or individual
Tradition
The customs, beliefs and practices that shape the views of societies and religions; a reference point for defining what is essential in a given religion
Ultimate questions
Concerning the meaning of life and death
Worship
The humble adoration and appreciation of the faithful to God or gods, in appreciation of their dependence on him/them

Appendix

1. Questions (a)–(d) can be answered in a single word, phrase or sentence. Question (e) requires a longer answer.

    (a) What is *Kashrut*?   *(1 mark)*

    (b) What is a covenant?   *(1 mark)*

    (c) Who received the Ten Commandments from God on Mount Sinai?   *(1 mark)*

    (d) Write out the first sentence of the *Shema*.   *(2 marks)*

    (e) Explain the meaning and importance of Shabbat for Jews.   *(5 marks)*

                                                                              (Total 10 marks)

2. Questions (a)–(d) can be answered in a single word, phrase or sentence. Question (e) requires a longer answer.

    (a) Give **one** other name for the eucharist.   *(1 mark)*

    (b) Name **one** of the four gospels.   *(1 mark)*

    (c) What is the word for the Christian belief that God is three persons in one?   *(1 mark)*

    (d) Name **two** people who visit Jesus' tomb and find it empty according to Luke chapter 24.   *(2 marks)*

    (e) 'Any set pattern for worship will always end up being lifeless and boring.'

         How far do you agree with this statement? Give reasons to support your answer and show that you have thought about different points of view.   *(5 marks)*

                                                                              (Total 20 marks)

3. Questions (a)–(d) can be answered in a single word, phrase or sentence. Question (e) requires a longer answer.

    (a) During which month should Muslims obey the command to fast?   *(1 mark)*

    (b) What is *Tawhid*?   *(1 mark)*

    (c) What does the word *Qur'an* mean?   *(1 mark)*

    (d) Name **two** groups of people who are excused from making the pilgrimage to Makkah.   *(2 marks)*

    (e) Explain the importance of prayer in Islam.   *(5 marks)*

                                                                              (Total 10 marks)

4. Questions (a)–(d) can be answered in a single word, phrase or sentence.
   Question (e) requires a longer answer.

   (a) What name is given to the Ultimate Reality (Supreme Being) worshipped
       by all Hindus?   *(1 mark)*

   (b) Which is the earliest of the Vedas?   *(1 mark)*

   (c) What special name is given to the 'eternal self' by Hindus?   *(1 mark)*

   (d) Name **two** avatars of Vishnu.   *(2 marks)*

   (e) Explain, using examples, the importance of symbols in Hindu worship.   *(5 marks)*

                                                                    (Total 10 marks)

5. Questions (a)–(d) can be answered in a single word, phrase or sentence.
   Question (e) requires a longer answer.

   (a) What does the title *Buddha* mean?   *(1 mark)*

   (b) What is *Anicca*?   *(1 mark)*

   (c) Which section of the *Tripitaka* gives rules for monks?   *(1 mark)*

   (d) List two of the Three Jewels in which a Buddhist promises to take refuge.   *(2 marks)*

   (e) Explain the main features of **one** method of meditation.   *(5 marks)*

                                                                    (Total 10 marks)

6. Questions (a)–(d) can be answered in a single word, phrase or sentence.
   Question (e) requires a longer answer.

   (a) Who is the founder of Sikhism?   *(1 mark)*

   (b) Which guru set up the Khalsa?   *(1 mark)*

   (c) Give **one** belief contained in the Mool Mantar.   *(1 mark)*

   (d) Name **one** of the 5 Ks **and** explain its symbolic meaning   *(2 marks)*

   (e) Explain how and why the Guru Granth Sahib is given respect during
       worship.   *(5 marks)*

                                                                    (Total 10 marks)

Index

Puri   184
Purim   17, 26
Purim rabbi   27

Q
Qadhf   123
qadi   138, 139
Qatl   123
qiblah   126, 128, 129
Quakers   87
Qur'an   115, 119, 122

R
rabbis   10
Rabbi Amran of Susa   18
Rachel   4
Ragjir   215
Rahula   210
Rajagaha   215
Rama   155
Rama Krishna Movement   157
Ramadan   130–1
Rameshwaram   184
Rebekah   4
Reform Jews   14
Reformation   58, 59
Rehat Maryada   273
Resurrection   56, 57, 101
revelation   53
riba   123
Rig Veda   173
rishis   174
romalla   272
Roman Catholic Church   58
Roman Empire   54
Romans, the   9
Rosh Hashanah   25
ruku   126
Rule of Faith   62
rupa   227
Ruth   17

S
Sabbath   20
Sacred Heart of Jesus   80
Sahih   121
Sailendra Dynasty   220
saints' days   81
Sakyamuni   209
salat   124
salvation   73
Salvation Army   87
Samaria   7
samina   228
samsara   158, 160–1
samskara   228
sanatan dharma   156

sanctuary   90
sandek   35
Sangha   231
Sangrand   278
Sangharakshita   220
sannyasin   158, 163
Saqim   121
Sarasvati   172
Sarvastivadins   214
Sat Guru   264
Satan   122
sati   192
saum   124
scripture   16
Second Vatican Council   59, 84
seder   27
Sefer Torah   36
seikbadi   236
Seleucids   8
sendah   36
shabbat   25, 36
shahadah   124
Shakti   155
Shavuot   29
Shaytan   122
Shingon   219
Shehina   12
Shema   12, 20, 22
sheol (hell)   15
Shevat   25
Shfarot   25
Shi'ah   121
Shinto   219
shirk   123
Shiva (Siva)   155, 159, 167
shiva   40
shofar   25, 26
Shpeel   27
Shrove tuesday   76
Shwe Dagon   236
Siddur   18
Simhat Torah   29
sihr   123
Sikh   257
Sivan   24
skandhas   227
Society of Friends   see Quakers
Sodar Rahiras   273
Soga clan   219
Sohilla   273
Soka Gakkai   219
Solomon   7
Song of Songs   17
Spy Wednesday   78
Sri Lanka   219
St Alban   58
St Augustine   58

St Patrick 58
Sthavira 214
stupas 236
Sudra 164
sujud 126
sukkah 29
Sukkot 17, 28, 29
Sunnah 120
Sunni 121
surah 115, 119, 120
Susah 8
Sutta Pitaka 216
Suttee 192
Swami Nariyan movement 157
synagogue 10
Synoptics 56
Syria 8

T
Tabernacles 6, 28
Tacitus 53
tallit(h) 20, 29, 36
Talmud 10, 17, 18
Tammuz 24
tantras 217
tanzil 119
Taryag 6
tashlikh ceremony 25
tathagata 230
tefillin 21, 22, 36
Temple, the 8, 9, 17, 29, 31, 32
Ten Commandments 6, 14
Tendai 219
Terah 3
Tevet 25
Theravada 214
Theravadin 241
Thessalonians 71
Thirteen Principles 19
Three Baskets 214
T'ien T'ai sect 218
Timothy 72
Tishri 25, 28
Titus 72
Torah 6, 10, 15, 29, 57
transcendental complex 158
Transfiguration (of Christ) 80
transmigration 160
Trimurti 168
Trinity 60, 62
Trinity Sunday 80
Tripitaka 214, 216

U
Ummah 137
United Reform Church 87
upajjhaya 234
Upanayana 189
Upanishads 173
Uposatha 217

V
Vaishya 164
vanaprasth 163
vedana 227
Vedas 173–4
vijnana 228
vinaya 214
Vinaya Pitaka 216–17
Virgin Mary 60, 80
Vishnu 155, 159, 168
Vrindavan 184

W
Wailing Wall 32
Wahaeguru 264
Wesak 239
Wesley, John 87
Western Wall 32
Whitsun
World Council of Churches 59, 88
wudu 126

Y
Yad Vashem 32
Yajur Veda 173
yamulkah 20
Yasodharo 210
yatra 157
Yom Kippur 26

Z
Zakat 124
Zam Zam 139
Zealots 9, 34
Zechariah 31
zemirot 31
Zeroa 27
Zikhronot 25
Zionism 34
Zionists 12

304   *INDEX*